Readings In
CITIZEN
POLITICS

Readings In CITIZEN POLITICS

studies of political behavior

edited by

James David Barber

YALE UNIVERSITY

MARKHAM PUBLISHING COMPANY
Chicago

MARKHAM POLITICAL SCIENCE SERIES
AARON WILDAVSKY, Editor

BARBER, *Citizen Politics: An Introduction to Political Behavior*
BARBER, ed., *Readings in Citizen Politics: Studies of Political Behavior*
CNUDDE and NEUBAUER, eds., *Empirical Democratic Theory*
COPLIN, ed., *Simulation in the Study of Politics*
LYDEN and MILLER, eds., *Planning-Programming-Budgeting: A Systems Approach to Management*
RANNEY, ed., *Political Science and Public Policy*
RUSSETT, ed., *Economic Theories of International Politics*
STRICKLAND, WADE, and JOHNSTON, *A Primer of Political Analysis*

For Sarah Couch Barber *and*
Nell Graham Sale, *public servants*

INTRODUCTORY NOTE

THESE READINGS are meant to be used, not simply accepted. They are not holy writ but raw material, drawn from a much larger store of political behavior research. They are short enough to enable the busiest of students to grasp the author's argument and technique and then to think through an independent approach of his own.

That active exploration is the more important because these materials bear closely on key issues of contemporary politics, including foreign policy, the crisis of the cities, students in politics, race relations North and South, poverty in America, and the rightward drift of political sentiment. No attentive citizen comes to such topics with a wide-open mind. What is necessary for effective use of this book is the ability—and the industry—to get the facts, to make the material part of your intellectual equipment, and to use it to gain a clearer awareness of your political thinking. The behavioral approach to politics does not require a devotion to precision about the trivial. It *does* mean systematic attention to relations between theories and evidence, especially with respect to the politics of the present.

The chapters come in pairs. The first two are on participation. They illustrate how quantitative data can be arranged to reveal patterns of political activity, regularities underlying contrasts, and changes in participation rates. Chapters Three and Four are about political thinking, offering the opportunity to see how abstract models which are much simpler than the realities can nevertheless help one order real evidence. Chapters Five and Six, two studies of political feelings, illustrate a functional approach to the study of opinions, an approach which asks: "Of what use to a man are his opinions?" Chapters Seven and Eight take up political persuasion. This material concerns the power dimensions of politics, particularly the ways persuasive communications are filtered through the social structure and the dependence of powerful leaders on their followers. Chapters Nine and Ten concern political change, a topic of great significance and great uncertainty. These final two chapters lend themselves to the student's creative analysis of how and why political change occurs when and where it does.

I would welcome your comments about these readings, particularly how they could be improved to encourage the active interest and the analytic abilities of students in the future.

J.D.B.

CONTENTS

CHAPTER ONE

TAKING PART

POLITICAL PARTICIPATION is an abstract phrase too gross to catch the lively and varied ways citizens act their political parts. Voting is the base line, but talking, writing, petitioning, demonstrating, and a wide range of other organized and individual activities are significant forms of participation. The identification and measurement of these activities—when possible in quantitative terms—is a beginning point in understanding citizen political behavior. Quantitative measures acquire scientific meaning, however, only in the context of theories. The simplest form is the hypothesis linking two variables. For example, it is clear that in almost every culture the more education one has the more active one is *likely* to be in politics. (Likely, not certain: very many uneducated people take part and very many educated people do nothing.)

In the following selection, Sidney Verba moves beyond the simple hypothesis to explore mixtures of variables entering into different kinds of participation. Using data from five nations, he is specially concerned to show the *relative* importance of the elements in the mixture. How important is the special political culture in which the citizen operates? How important are cross-national variables like education? By the use of controls (roughly, holding one variable constant and seeing how that affects the relationship among two others), he produces surprises for the analyst who would rely on some simple, one-factor explanation.

POLITICAL PARTICIPATION AND STRATEGIES OF INFLUENCE: A COMPARATIVE STUDY*

SIDNEY VERBA

Democracy refers in some rough way to the degree to which power and influence over significant decisions for a society is diffused throughout that society. Political participation, therefore, will increase the extent to which a nation is democratic only insofar as such participation involves at some point influence by the participant over governmental decisions. Participatory acts whose main function is to express support for the government are important, but not as crucial to democracy as are acts that involve influence.

The influence of a group or individual over a governmental decision may be defined as equal to the degree to which governmental officials act to benefit that group or individual because the officials believe that they will risk some deprivation (they will risk their jobs, be criticized, lose votes) if they do not so act. Thus influence involves both the outcome of the decision (it will, to some extent, be more advantageous to the influential groups or individual than it would have been if that group or individual has not been influential), and the motives of the decision-makers (they act to benefit the group because they believe they will otherwise

Reprinted from *Acta Sociologica*, Vol. 6 (1962), pp. 22–42, by permission of the publisher and author.

* This paper is part of a larger comparative study of attitudes toward politics and citizenship in Germany, Italy, Mexico, Great Britain, and the United States being carried on under the direction of Gabriel A. Almond and the author. Further material on the study will be reported in a forthcoming publication by the study directors. The study is sponsored by the Center of International Studies of Princeton University, and is supported by a grant from the Carnegie Corporation of New York.

The material reported is based on approximately 1000 interviews carried on in each nation using a national, multi-stage probability sample.

suffer some deprivation). The latter criterion is important. Officials may act to benefit a particular group for a variety of reasons—out of a feeling of paternalism, for instance. But it is only when officials act because they fear the consequences of not so acting, that a group may be considered to be influential and a participant in the decision.

Influence, and consequently democracy, are defined in terms of the way in which governmental elites make decisions. But the problem of studying the way in which such decisions are made is enormous, especially when one is dealing with an entire nation, or as in this paper, with five nations at once. No such attempt is made here. Rather, this paper concentrates not upon the perceptions and behaviors of governmental elites but upon the perceptions and behaviors of the ordinary citizen. It will report some preliminary results to a series of survey questions on the amount of influence individuals believe they can exert over the government, and the ways in which they would go about it. The paper will concentrate on differences among the five nations surveyed—the United States, Britain, Germany, Italy, and Mexico. In subsequent publications, attempts will be made to explore and explain these differences further.

We are interested in the perception of the ordinary man as to how much influence he has over the decisions of his government. Thinking that one can influence the government or even attempting to influence government is not the same as actually influencing it. An individual may think he has influence over decisions or he may attempt to exert influence over decisions, and the government official may be unmoved. Conversely, he may believe that all government decisions are made without any consideration of his needs and desires and of the needs and desires of his fellow citizens, when, in fact, government officials constantly try to calculate the reactions of groups to their acts. In the latter case, an individual will exert influence without being aware he is doing so.

If the degree to which individuals believe they can influence the course of governmental decisions is not necessarily related to their actual level of influence, why study their subjective views as to their competence? There are several reasons. The perception that one can participate furthers such participation: if an individual believes he has influence, he is more likely to attempt to influence the government. A subjectively competent citizen, therefore, is more likely to be an active citizen. And if government officials do not necessarily respond to active influence attempts, they are more likely to respond to such attempts to influence than to a passive citizenry that makes no demands. If the ordinary citizen, on the other hand, perceives government policy as being far outside of his sphere of influence, he is unlikely to attempt to influence that policy and government officials are unlikely to worry about the potential pressure that can be brought to bear on them. Thus the extent to which citizens in a nation perceive themselves as competent to influence the government should be closely related to the extent of democracy in that country.

A good deal of the influence that individuals and groups exert over their government may not involve any conscious attempt on their part to influence. As our concept of influence specifies, governmental officials are being influenced if they respond to what they consider a possible deprivation. This implies that the citizen or group of citizens from whom they fear some deprivation may, at the time the government officials are acting, neither have attempted to influence these officials nor intend so to attempt. The government officials act in anticipation of certain consequences if they do not so act. They believe that if they do not act to benefit a group, that group will at some point in the future withdraw its support or its vote. In many respects a good deal of the influence that the ordinary citizen has over the decisions of the government officials may be of this anticipatory type.

But if one is interested in the extent of the perception that one can influence the government, one will have to concentrate on more overt and conscious attempts to affect actions of the government. Several questions may be asked about conscious attempts to influence the government:

1. Under what circumstances will an individual make some conscious effort to influence the government? Direct political influence attempts are rare. For the ordinary citizen, the activities of government—even local government—may seem quite distant. At the time that a decision is being made, the citizen will not be aware that it is being made or of what its consequences for him are likely to be. It is likely then, that only in situations of some stress in which a government activity is perceived to have a direct and serious impact upon the individual will a direct influence attempt be triggered off.

2. What method will be used in the influence attempt? Some major dimensions along which the method used can vary include: whether or not the attempt is made through legitimate channels; whether the attempt is violent or non-violent; whether the individ-

ual attempts to influence the government alone or attempts to enlist the support of others; and, if he seeks support, whose support does he seek.

3. What is the effect of the influence attempt? The problem of the extent to which the government official changes his behavior in response to some influence attempt on the part of a citizen is beyond the scope of this study. However, since it concentrates on the perspectives of the citizen, we shall consider his view as to the likelihood that an attempt made by him to influence the government would have any effect. That, after all, is a key question.

THE DISTRIBUTION OF SUBJECTIVE COMPETENCE

Does an individual feel he can influence his government? How would he go about it? Would it make any difference? Respondents were asked questions that attempted to place them in hypothetical stress situations. Each respondent was asked to suppose that a law were being considered by the national legislature that he considered very unjust and harmful. Could he do anything about it and, if so, what? He was then asked how much effect he thought any action he took would have, and how likely it was that he actually would do something. A similar set of questions was asked about an unjust and harmful regulation being considered by the most local governmental unit.[1] These questions attempted to get some notion of the respondent's views as to the extent of his political competence and, more important, of the strategy of influence open to him.

The question as to the amount of influence the ordinary man has is a fundamental political one and the response to it reflects an

---

[1] The exact question wording on the national government was:
—Suppose a law were being considered by (Appropriate national legislature specified for each nation) which you considered to be unjust or harmful, what do you think you could do?
—If you made an effort to change this law, how likely is it that you would succeed?
—If such a case arose, how likely is it you *would actually* try to do something about it?

The exact question wording on the local government was:
—Suppose a regulation were being considered by (Most local governmental unit: Town? Village? etc., specified) which you considered very unjust or harmful, what do you think you could do?
—If you made an effort to change this regulation how likely is it that you would succeed?
—If such a case arose, how likely is it that you *would actually* do something about it?

individual's perception of the nature of his government and of his own role as a citizen. Let us look at responses as to how amenable to influence is a local government. This is a good place to start because the impact of local government tends to be more immediate. And, for obvious reasons, people in all countries tend to think that one can do more about a local regulation than about a law considered by the national legislature. But what is striking are the sharp differences among nations in the number who think they can do something and in what these people think they can do. In response to the question on whether one can do anything about a local law that is unjust American and British respondents most frequently say that there is something they can do. More than three-quarters of the people interviewed in each of these two countries express the opinion that they have some recourse if they believe the local government is planning a law they consider unjust. (The data on what individuals say they can do about a local regulation is reported in Table 1. The figures we are considering here are near the bottom of the table.) In each country, only 17% say that there is nothing they can do. In the other three countries over 30% of those interviewed report that there is nothing they can do in such a situation. In Germany more people (62%) say they can do something than in Mexico and Italy (52% and 51%). In the latter two countries, respondents are more likely to say they do not know what they can do. Clearly then the images that citizens have of their roles and potentials differ from nation to nation. Britons and Americans are more likely to think of themselves as competent to influence their local government than are people in the other three countries.

That an individual believes there is something he can do if the government is planning an unjust or unfair act does not mean that he will in fact try to do something. This was a hypothetical situation and, of course, one does not really know what respondents would do if they ever were in fact faced with such a challenging situation. But they were asked for their opinions on whether or not they actually would act. In all countries many who say they can do something about an unjust regulation report that in fact they probably would do nothing. But the number who report that there is at least some likelihood that they would make an effort, reflects the same national pattern reported above. Fifty-eight percent of the American respondents and 60% of those in Britain say that there is some likelihood that they would actually make an effort to influence an unjust regulation. In Germany 44% made some such affir-

TABLE 1

WHAT CITIZENS WOULD DO TO TRY TO INFLUENCE THEIR LOCAL
GOVERNMENT, BY NATION

	U.S.	U.K.	Germany	Italy	Mexico
Some citizens would try to enlist the support of others by:					
Organizing some informal group; arousing their friends and neighbors, getting them to write letters of protest or to sign a petition	56%	34%	13%	7%	26%
Working through a political party	1	1	3	1	—
Working through some other formal group of which they are a member: union, church, professional group	4	3	5	1	2
TOTAL WHO WOULD ENLIST SUPPORT OF OTHERS*	59%	36%	22%	8%	28%
Other citizens would, as individuals:					
Directly contact political leaders (elected officials) or the press. Write a letter to, or visit a local political leader	20%	45%	15%	12%	15%
Directly contact administrative officials (non-elected officials)	1	3	31	12	18
Consult a lawyer; appeal through courts	2	1	3	2	2
Vote against offending officials at next election	14	4	1	1	—
Take some violent action	1	1	1	1	1
Just protest	—	—	—	12	—
Other	1	2	—	3	5
TOTAL WHO WOULD ACT AS INDIVIDUALS**	18%	42%	40%	43%	25%
TOTAL WHO WOULD DO SOMETHING WITH OTHERS OR AS INDIVIDUALS*	77%	77%	62%	51%	52%

TABLE 1 (continued)

	U.S.	U.K.	Germany	Italy	Mexico
Other respondents say they can do nothing	17%	17%	31%	31%	32%
Others say they do not know if they can do anything	6%	5%	7%	18%	15%
TOTAL (respondents)	100%	100%	100%	100%	100%
TOTAL (responses)	123%	115%	111%	101%	118%
Number of cases	970	963	955	995	1295

* The total percentage is less than the total of the individual cells since some respondents gave more than one answer.

** This row includes only the respondents who replied that they could do something, but did not mention working with others. Hence, the total is less than some of the individual categories which contain respondents who may have mentioned both group activity and an individual activity.

mation, while in Italy 41% of the respondents say that they might act in these circumstances. (The question was, unfortunately, not asked in a comparable form in Mexico.) The American and British respondents express a willingness to act much more frequently than do the respondents in Germany and Italy.

Lastly, there is some evidence that the subjective estimate of one's propensity to act in such a challenging political situation is not completely unrelated to actual attempts to influence the government. In all five nations a substantially larger proportion of those respondents who say there is something they can do about a local unjust regulation (let us, for convenience, call them "local competents") report some experience in attempting to influence the local government than is reported among those who say there is nothing they can do. These data are reported in Table 2.

At this point we are merely describing differences among nations in the political attitudes of respondents. In this connection it is clear that the frequency with which individuals report that they could have some effect upon a law contemplated by the local government differs from nation to nation. The explanation of these differences is more difficult. At least part of the explanation of the differences in the degree to which individuals believe they are politically competent rests upon the differing structures of government. The individual who says he can do nothing to oppose the local government may be making a quite realistic appraisal of his potentialities. Thus the lower frequency of subjective political competence in Italy, for instance, may be largely a reaction to a politi-

TABLE 2
Proportion of Those Respondents Who Say They Have Attempted
to Influence the Local Government among Local Competents
and Local Non-competents

	Proportion of respondents who have attempted to influence the government	
	Among local competents	Among local non-competents
U.S.	33% (745)*	10% (225)
U.K.	18% (748)	3% (217)
Germany	21% (590)	2% (355)
Italy	13% (508)	4% (487)
Mexico	9% (677)	2% (618)

* Numbers in parentheses refer to the base upon which percentage was calculated.

cal structure—the Italian prefecture system—that does not allow the individual to be politically competent. It is not that individuals choose to be uninfluential. It may be that they have no choice.

The frequency with which individuals say they could exert some influence over the local government is clearly a case in which attitudes are affected significantly by governmental structure (although there is evidence that they are not completely determined by these structures). Let us turn to a more significant aspect of political competence than the extent to which individuals believe themselves competent; an aspect of competence that is not as clearly affected by the structure of the local government. This is the strategy an individual would use in attempting to influence the government. The way in which those individuals who report that they *could* influence the government report they *could go about* exerting this influence is, of course, important. It makes a difference whether an individual has, on the one hand, only the vaguest notion as to what he can do in such a situation or on the other, a clear and explicit view of the channels open to him for expressing his point of view. It also makes a difference what resources he believes he has available to use in such a situation. Furthermore, the strategy that an individual would use will naturally have an effect on the extent to which his subjective view of his ability to influence will represent real influence potential—that is, represent the sort of activity that has some chance of changing the behaviors of the government officials. Lastly, by concentrating on how those who think they can have influence would go about exerting that influence, we can partially eliminate (but only partially) the effect of the differing degrees to which local governments are amenable to influence. We shall deal primarily with those who think they have influence, the "local competents," and ask how they would exert that influence.

THE STRATEGY OF INFLUENCE

The strategies of influence that individuals report they would use are summarized in Table 1. Consider first the question of what social resources the individual feels he has available to him in attempting to influence the local government. When one looks at the individual and his government, one is tempted to see him as lonely, powerless, and somewhat frightened by the immensity of the powers he faces. Whatever the validity of this view may be in terms of the actual amount of power the average man has and the social resources available to him, our data suggest that a large number of our respondents think of themselves neither as powerless nor, what is more important, as alone, in their relationship to the government.

This fact is reflected in the data reported in Table 1. A number of respondents believe that they can enlist the support of others in their attempts to influence the government. What is most striking is the variation from country to country in the numbers who feel they can call on others to aid them. In the United States, 59% of the respondents indicate that they would attempt to enlist the support of others if they wish to change a regulation they consider unjust. At the other extreme, only 8% of the Italian sample mention the use of this social resource. In the other countries, the percentages reporting that they would try to enlist the support of others varies from 36% in Britain, to 28% in Mexico, to 22% in Germany.[2]

Who is it that citizens would enlist to support them? Individuals as we know are members of a large number of social structures. They are not merely citizens of their nations; they are members of families, communities, churches, voluntary associations, trade unions and a myriad of other groups and organizations. Much has

---

[2] Since question wording can seriously affect responses, it is important to note here that the notion that one can enlist the support of others was in no way suggested by the question or by the interviewer's probing of the question. Interviewers were carefully instructed not to ask such questions as: "Is there anyone you could get to help you?" or "Would you attempt to do this alone or with other people?"

been written about the important role of formal organizations in the political process—in particular, the role of political parties and formal associational interest groups. But what the data show most strikingly is that when it comes to the support that individuals believe they could enlist in a challenging political situation, they think much more often of enlisting the support of the informal face-to-face groups of which they are members than they think of enlisting the support of the formal organizations with which they are affiliated.

In all countries, the numbers are few who say that they would work through their political party if they were attempting to counteract some unjust regulation being considered by the local government. Less than 1% of the respondents—with the exception of Germany, where the figure is about 3%—mention that they would work through their political party. Clearly, no matter how important the role of political parties may be in democratic societies, relatively few citizens think of them first as the place where support may be enlisted for attempts to influence the government.[3]

In all countries, more individuals report that they would attempt to work through other formal organized groups than would attempt to work through political parties. But even when one considers the entire range of formal organizations to which people may belong, the numbers who report they would enlist the support of these organizations is small, in no country going above 5% of all the respondents (as seen on Table 1) or 9% of the local competents.[4] Of course, not all respondents have some formal organization at their disposal. Such organizations are more frequent in

---

[3] To some extent the infrequent mention of a political party in this context probably understates the role of parties in this influence process. Many more respondents mentioned contacting government officials. If they explicitly mentioned that the partisan affiliation of the official was relevant in giving them access to him, they would be coded as working through a party. But many may have considered this affiliation relevant, even if it was not mentioned.

[4] The percentage of respondents mentioning a particular strategy of influence can be computed either as a percentage of the entire population or as a percentage of the local competents—in this latter case, that is, as a percentage of those who feel there is something they can do. Both figures are important. The first figure reflects frequency of certain types of political behavior in a nation. But if we are interested in how nations differ in the strategies their citizens will use, we must use the second figure—the percentage of local competents who would use a particular strategy—for, otherwise, differences between nations in the percentage choosing a particular strategy might be merely a reflection of the fact that there are more in one country than another who report that there is "nothing" they could do.

some nations than in others. And the percentage who report membership differs substantially from country to country. Furthermore, not all formal organizations are equally politically relevant. But even if one considers only those respondents who belong to some formal organization that they report is involved in politics, the percentage invoking such membership in a stress situation is much smaller than the percentage who are members. In the United States where such memberships are most frequent, 228 respondents report membership in some organization that they consider to be involved in some way with government or politics, but only 35 Americans report that they would work through such an organization if they were trying to influence a local regulation. In Italy where such memberships are least frequent, we find the same pattern. Fifty-six Italians belong to some organization they believe is involved in political affairs, but only 13 Italians would work through a formal organization if they were trying to influence a local regulation. The greatest frequency of mention of formal organization is found in Germany, but it is still only half as frequent as the frequency of membership in a politically relevant organization.

That formal organizations are rarely invoked as the resource that individuals would use if they were trying to enlist some support for their attempt to influence the government does not mean that these organizations are unimportant politically. They still operate on what we have called the passive level—that is, the citizen has influence over government officials by being a member of such a group, but he does not necessarily make any overt attempt to influence the government. And this sort of influence is of a great significance, perhaps of greater overall significance than the overt influence attempts that citizens from time to time will make. Furthermore though individuals would not use their formal organizations as the means to influence the government directly, such formal membership enhances the prospects that an individual will believe himself capable of influencing the government and will in fact make some such attempt. Thus, even though he does not directly use his group membership in attempting to influence the local government, an individual may, for a variety of reasons, develop greater self-confidence in his own political competence through organization membership.[5]

---

[5] The relationship between organization membership and political attitudes will be discussed in a forthcoming publication.

COOPERATIVE POLITICAL BEHAVIOR

If one is interested in who it is that citizens believe they can enlist to support them if they are trying directly and consciously to influence an act of their local government, one must turn to the informal face-to-face groups to which they belong. In all countries, respondents more frequently mention enlisting the support of such groups—arousing their neighbors, getting friends and acquaintances to support their position, circulating a petition—than they mention using some formal organization. This is seen in the top row of Table 1. The differences among nations are quite sharp here. These differences are highlighted if one considers the proportion of local competents (i.e., those who believe they can influence the local government) who say they would cooperate with their fellow citizens in attempting to influence the government: 73% of American local competents would use informal groups, whereas only 13% of Italian local competents and 22% of the German would do so. In Mexico, though the proportion of local competents is relatively low, the proportion of these local competents who would work through informal groups is quite high—50%. And in Britain, the proportion of local competents who say they would seek the cooperation of others is about as great—43%.

The belief that cooperation with one's fellow citizens is both a possible political action and an effective one, it may be suggested, represents a highly significant orientation from the point of view of a democratic political system. The diffusion of influence over political decisions by which we define democracy implies some cooperative ability among the citizenry. This cooperation would appear to be necessary in terms both of the amount of influence the ordinary man could otherwise expect to have and the results of the influence of the ordinary man on governmental decisions. By definition, the "average" man's influence over the government must be small. Compared with the forces of the government and the state he is a frail creature indeed, and this would apply to local as well as national government. If the ordinary man is to have any influence vis-à-vis the government, it must be in concert with his fellows. Secondly, uncooperative and completely individualistic influence attempts could only lead to dysfunctional results from the point of view of the output of a democratic government. Every individual demand cannot be met or the result will be chaos. If the government is to be responsive to the demands of the ordinary man, those demands must be aggregated, and the aggregation of interests implies cooperation among men. The aggregation of interests involved in the cooperation of groups of like-minded individuals is aggregation on a rather low level, but it does suggest a propensity to work together with one's fellows that is relevant for larger political structures as well. In any case, one may suggest that the citizen who believes that he can work cooperatively with others in his environment if he wants to engage in political activity has a quite different perspective on politics from the individual who thinks of himself as a lone political actor.

Furthermore, the notion that one can affect a government decision by bringing one's peers into the dispute is a highly political notion. It represents a fairly clear attempt to use political influence in one's relations with government officials. The invocation of others in the dispute indicates that in this way the individual hopes to bring pressure on the officials, to threaten them with some deprivation if they do not accede to his demands. The threat that many make—whether it be the threatened loss of votes or of support, or the threat of public criticism—is, other things being equal, greater than the threat that one can make. Thus the individual who mentions getting others to join him in his dispute with the government is more likely to be an individual who sees himself as able to influence his government. And the variation among the five nations in the frequencies with which such groups are mentioned reflects a varying distribution of such citizen competence.

Lastly, the importance of this propensity toward cooperation with one's fellow political actors is stressed not merely because such behavior has significant consequences for a political system, but because it is a type of behavior which cannot be understood and explained solely in terms of differences in the structure of local government. The difference between the individual who responds that he would write a letter to the local council and the individual who responds that he would write a letter to the local council *and try to induce his friends to do likewise* cannot be explained by differences among nations in the structure and powers of their respective local councils.[6] Furthermore, as we shall see shortly, the

---

[6] This is not completely true. Governmental structure may be more amenable to group influence in some countries than in others. But this is more likely to be the case because of experience in the past with such groups, rather than formal structure. On the other hand, there is no doubt that certain structures of government foster such "banding together" protests more than others. Structures where power is diffused among a large number of autono-

propensity to cooperate politically can not be explained in terms of differing levels of social and economic development in the five nations. The origin of this propensity toward political cooperation must be sought elsewhere.[7]

Though the use of primary groups as a resource for influence is most common in the United States, Britain, and Mexico, several interesting differences between the United States and Britain on the one hand and Mexico on the other in this respect much be mentioned. The notion that one can mobilize an informal group to aid one in the process of attempting to influence the government, appears to be of greater significance for the actual exercise of influence in the former two countries. Earlier it was pointed out that those who report they can do something about an unjust local law (the local competents) are much more likely also to report some experience in attempting to influence the government. If we look only at the local competents and ask how those who would work through groups and those who would attempt to influence the government alone differ in terms of the extent of their experience

---

mous or semi-autonomous boards and councils and the like (especially elected boards and councils) are more likely to foster such protest than structures dominated by a centrally appointed official whose domain includes a larger area (as with the Italian prefect system). But this is an example of the general proposition that there will be an interaction between political orientation and political structure. In this case, however, the explanation of the origins of this group-forming attitude in terms of formal structure alone would be quite hard. One has to look beyond the structure of the local government.

[7] The relationship between social and economic groupings and the propensity to form groups will be discussed at the end of the chapter. The explanation of this group-forming propensity in terms of social values and partisan fragmentation will be attempted in a forthcoming publication.

That one can show the relationship between social grouping and the propensity to form groups as well as attempt an explanation for this propensity in terms of other attitudes illustrates the advantage of "discovering" this group-forming propensity in a study based on a systematic survey rather than "discovering" this group-forming propensity through the sort of keen but unsystematic observation of a writer like Tocqueville—who certainly noticed and was impressed by the way in which political groups could be easily formed when needed in the United States.

In the first place, one now knows about the relative propensities to form groups in a new way. Those of us who work on studies of this sort like to think that the data are more reliable when systematically gathered. Secondly, the knowledge is more precise. One can not only distinguish among nations more finely, one can specify who it is within the nation who is likely to think of forming groups of this sort. And lastly, one can explore the roots of this group-forming propensity by seeing the ways in which those individuals who think of forming such groups differ from other respondents who do not. Thus, not only is the knowledge more precise, it is more useful since it can lead to further knowledge.

in attempted influence, we find that in the United States and Britain those who would work through groups are more likely to be those who have had experience in attempting to influence their local government. In the United States 36% of those who report they would work through informal groups (n: 547) report experience in influence attempts, whereas only 25% of those local competents who would use some other strategy (n: 198) report such experience. In Britain the parallel figures are 23% for those who mention informal groups (n: 315) and 15% for other local competents (n: 414). On the other hand, in Mexico, those who mention informal groups are a bit less likely to be the experienced respondents—7% report experience of those who mention informal groups (n: 339) as against 10% of the other local competents (n: 344).[8]

Furthermore, in the former two countries, the use of informal groups as a means of influencing the government is seen not only as a means to protest but as the key to effective protest. In order to test the extent to which individuals felt they could influence their local government, respondents were asked another question: "If you made an effort to change this regulation, how likely is it that you would succeed?" Of interest to us here is that a large number of American and British local competents volunteered the statement that their protest would have some likelihood of success only if others joined with them. (The percentages were 30% in the United States and 20% in Britain.) In Mexico, though a good percentage felt that there was some likelihood that they would succeed if they attempted to influence their local government, fewer than 10% of the Mexican respondents suggested that this would only be the case if they had the support of others. Thus, though the use of informal groups is perceived as a means of influence in Mexico, it is not yet perceived as the key to effective influence.[9]

One further difference deserves mention. In the United States and Britain, the use of informal groups as a means of influencing a governmental decision is considered much more appropriate on the local level than on the national level. In the United States 73% of

---

[8] In Germany, those local competents who mention informal groups are somewhat less likely to be experienced. Seventeen percent of those who mention informal groups (n: 126) report experience as against 23% of local competents who do not mention such groups (n: 460). In Italy, those local competents who mention groups are slightly more likely to be experienced: 16% (n: 67) as against 13% (n: 438) of those who do not mention groups.

[9] In Germany the percentage of local competents who mentioned that they would succeed only if others joined them was 12%; in Italy it was 5%.

the local competents report that they would work through informal groups in attempting to influence the local government, whereas only 38% of the national competents (i. e., those who believe they could do something if the national government were considering a law they thought unjust) would work through such groups. In Britain, similarly, 43% of the local competents would work through informal groups, while only 28% of the national competents would do so. On the other hand, in Mexico, the proportion of local and national competents who would use informal groups is about the same—50% of local competents mention informal groups as the means they would use to influence the local government and 46% of national competents say that this is the means they would use to influence the national government. The fact that the use of such groups is more closely related both to experience and to expectations of success in Britain and the United States than in Mexico, coupled with the fact that such strategy is considered more appropriate in connection with the local government in the former two countries suggests that such informal group strategy is based on a more realistic appraisal of the potentialities of such a strategy—a realistic appraisal deriving from actual experience with such groups on the local level. In Mexico, this influence strategy is less well grounded in actual local experience.

INDIVIDUAL ACTIVITIES

Among those respondents who spoke of themselves as acting as individuals in an attempt to influence the government there is some variation, as Table 1 indicates, in the strategies they mention. In the United States and Britain respondents are more likely to say that they would approach an elected government official rather than an appointed official of the bureaucracy. In Mexico and Italy, respondents are as likely to say they would direct their protest toward one type of official as toward the other. In Germany, in contrast, more respondents mention appointed officials than mention elected officials as the target of their protest. It is tempting to consider these results to be a reflection of a more highly developed political competence in the United States and Britain. A protest to an elected official would appear to be inherently more of a political protest in the sense of involving an implied threat of deprivation to the official if he does not comply—since the loss of the vote is the most usual deprivation with which the individual can threaten an offending official. To some extent this may be an explanation of the differences among the nations in the chosen targets of influence attempts, but it is more likely that these differences merely reflect differences in the relative position and importance of elected and appointed officials within the structures of local governments in the respective nations.

Lastly, in considering the strategies that local competents say they would use, it is important to note that not all those who say they could do something about a local regulation they consider unjust have any clear strategy in mind. As Table 1 indicates, 12% of the Italian respondents say that they can "protest" if faced with a regulation they consider unjust, but when asked how or to whom they can protest, give no more specific reply. The 12% who would "protest" represent about one-fourth of all Italian local competents. While this answer shows a higher level of subjective competence than the answer that one could do nothing (the right to gripe and complain being perhaps one of the last and most basic of democratic rights), it certainly reflects little awareness of the political channels through which one might effectively approach the government.[10]

Distribution Patterns of Influence and Influence Strategies

The data presented so far indicate some rather sharp differences among the nations. But the data are rather crude, representing, as they do, national totals. One would want to go further and seek some explanation for these differences. This will not be attempted in this paper, but the question will be considered of the extent to which such differences are explicable in terms of differences in the social class compositions of the samples for the various nations (and, since these were national samples, in the social class compositions of the nations). We shall consider three questions: the extent to which the attitudes reported in the previous section are related in similar ways to social groups in the five nations (does, for instance, perceived influence increase with social class in all five nations?); the extent to which differences among nations diminish when one compares similar social groups; and the extent to which differences among differing social groups

---

[10] The data on the response to the question about the national government cannot be discussed here. In general, there is less competence expressed in connection with an unjust act of the national government, but the patterns of differences among the nations are about the same.

within a single nation are greater or less than differences among similar social groups across the nations. The answer to the last question, of course, depends on the first two. If, when one controls for some social class variable, one finds that the frequency of a political attitude varies sharply and in a similar manner with that variable from nation to nation and that the differences among nations tend to disappear, one will then find that differences among groups within a nation are greater than differences among similar groups across the nations.

The answers to these three questions will help us decide if the differences in political attitudes discussed in the earlier part of the paper are, in some sense, "real" differences in political style among the nations, or if they are explicable in terms of differing levels of social and economic development in the various nations—in terms, for instance, of the fact that there are many more respondents with no education in our Italian and Mexican samples than in the other nations. If a political attitude varies sharply with a social attribute in all the nations, if the differences among the nations tend to diminish when one controls for the social attribute, and if those of a particular social group are more like others of a similar social group in other nations than they are like their fellow citizens of a different social group one probably has a political attitude less intrinsic to the political style in a particular nation and more dependent on the level of social and economic development in the nation. On the other hand, if the attitude is not closely related to social grouping, if all groups in a nation are likely to respond the same way, and in ways that differ from similar groups in other nations; if therefore, an Italian from the upper class is more likely to respond like an Italian of the lower class than like a German of the upper class, one is probably dealing with an aspect of political style more intrinsic to a particular nation.

As an indicator of social group, we shall use the respondent's educational attainment. This is selected because it is a social attribute that is closely related to political attitudes and that differs sharply in its distribution from nation to nation. (For instance, 35% of the sample in the United States did not go beyond primary school education, in contrast with 69% of the Italian sample.) It will not be possible to report data for other social attributes, but suffice it to say that the pattern of attitudes one would find if one considered such characteristics as occupation or income would be almost identical.

As Figure 1 clearly points out, in all countries the more educa-

FIGURE 1

PERCENTAGE OF RESPONDENTS WHO SAY THEY CAN DO SOMETHING
ABOUT A LOCAL REGULATION THEY CONSIDER UNJUST,
BY NATION AND EDUCATION

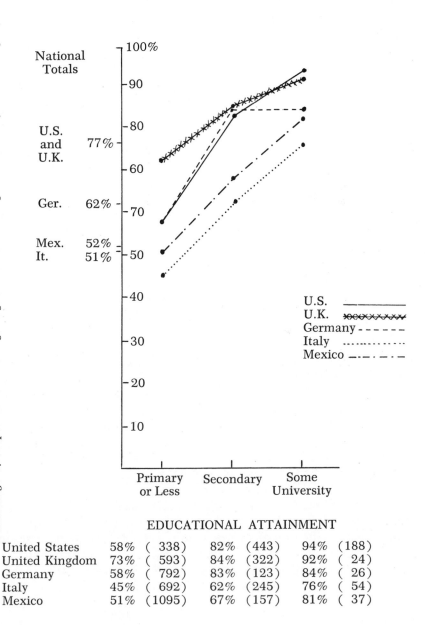

EDUCATIONAL ATTAINMENT

	Primary or Less		Secondary		Some University	
United States	58%	(338)	82%	(443)	94%	(188)
United Kingdom	73%	(593)	84%	(322)	92%	(24)
Germany	58%	(792)	83%	(123)	84%	(26)
Italy	45%	(692)	62%	(245)	76%	(54)
Mexico	51%	(1095)	67%	(157)	81%	(37)

tion an individual has, the more likely is he to consider himself capable of influencing the local government; that is, to be what we have called a local competent. (The percentage of individuals who say they could affect a local law is measured on the vertical axis; the level of education on the horizontal.) Fifty-eight percent of those who did not get beyond primary school are local competents in the United States; 94% of those with some college education are. And the pattern repeats itself in each country. This then is a clear uniformity across national lines. No matter what the frequency in a nation of local competence, the incidence of this competence is greater among those with higher education.

What about the question of the differences among and within nations? The question is a bit harder to answer for differences exist both among educational groups within the same country (as the slopes of the lines indicate) and within similar educational groups among nations (as the different lengths of the lines indicate). Some differences among nations diminish significantly within matched educational groups. For instance, though the national totals for local competents are quite different as between the United States and Germany, the differences between the two countries almost disappear when similar educational groups are compared. On the other hand, the two pairs of nations that are most similar in terms of the national totals, the United States and Britain, on the one hand, and Mexico and Italy on the other, differ somewhat more from each other within matched educational groups than they do on the national level. This is the case among those with primary school education in the case of the United States and Britain, where Britons show a higher rate of citizen competence, and in all educational groups for Italy and Mexico, with the Mexicans showing somewhat higher competence on the lower two levels and somewhat lower competence on the higher level.

What about the problem of which are greater, national differences or educational differences? The measure of this is rough, but if one compares the range between the highest and lowest nation within each educational group with the range between the highest and lowest educational group within each nation, the results suggest that there is certainly as much if not, on the average, more variation among educational groups within a single nation than among those with similar educational attainment in different nations. The range between the nation with the greatest frequency of local competents and the nation with the smallest frequency is 28 percentage points (between Britain and Italy) on the elementary school level, 22 percentage points (again between Britain and Italy) on the secondary school level, and 18 percentage points (between the United States and Italy) on the university level. Within each nation, on the other hand, there is about as much if not more difference among the differing educational levels in the frequency with which respondents believe themselves competent to influence the government. The ranges between the educational group that most frequently reports itself competent to influence the government (those with some university education in each nation) and the group that least frequently reports such competence (those with only primary education or no education in each country) are: United States, 36 percentage points; Britain, 19 percentage points; Germany, 26 percentage points; Italy, 31 percentage points; and Mexico, 30 percentage points. These figures compare extremes in terms of education and in terms of nation. But they do suggest that in terms of overall local competence, similar educational groups compared cross-nationally are at least as similar and perhaps more similar than are different educational groups within a nation.

So far we have considered the extent to which individuals believe they can influence a local unjust regulation. But the strategy an individual would use may be more important than the simple distinction of whether or not he thinks he can do anything. In particular the belief that one can cooperate with one's fellow citizen as a means of influencing the government appears to be important. Does this particular political strategy depend to as large an extent upon educational attainments as does the existence of local competence? The data in Figure 2 suggest that this is not the case. The percentage of local competents who would work through informal groups varies sharply from country to country even within each educational group, but varies very little among educational groups within the individual countries.[11] Only in the United States does the frequency with which such activity is mentioned vary directly with educational attainment, and even in this case the relationship is not as strong as that between education levels in terms of local competence in general. Consider again the contrast between the United States and Germany. When we consider similar

---

[11] The data are calculated as a percentage of local competents not of the total population. This is to isolate the political strategy that competents would use from the fact that the frequency of competents differs from country to country.

FIGURE 2

PERCENTAGE OF LOCAL COMPETENTS WHO WOULD ENLIST THE
SUPPORT OF AN INFORMAL GROUP IN ORDER TO INFLUENCE A
LOCAL REGULATION THEY CONSIDER UNJUST, BY NATION
AND EDUCATION

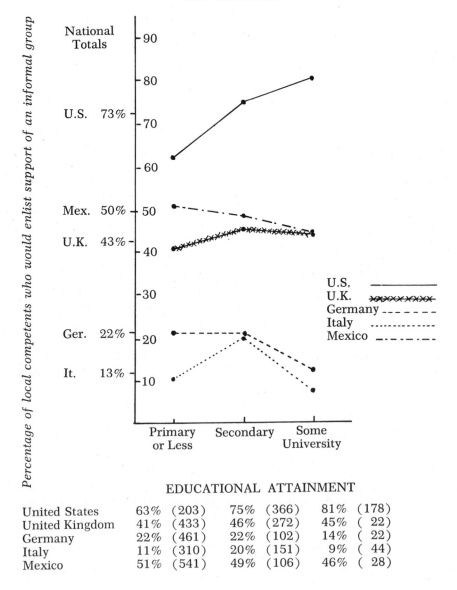

	Primary or Less		Secondary		Some University	
United States	63%	(203)	75%	(366)	81%	(178)
United Kingdom	41%	(433)	46%	(272)	45%	(22)
Germany	22%	(461)	22%	(102)	14%	(22)
Italy	11%	(310)	20%	(151)	9%	(44)
Mexico	51%	(541)	49%	(106)	46%	(28)

educational groups, German and American respondents hardly differ in the frequency with which they say that there is something they can do about a local unjust regulation. But if we compare the percentage of the local competents who would cooperate with their fellow citizens, we see that on each educational level, German respondents are much less likely to mention such activity. Furthermore, more highly educated German respondents are no more likely to talk of such activity than are less highly educated ones. In general, unlike the situation in relation to overall local competence where the range of difference among nations was no greater and perhaps a little less than the range of variation among educational groups, the variation among nations in the frequency with which political cooperation is mentioned is much greater on all educational levels than in the variation among educational groups within a nation.[12] Here, then, may be a pattern of political behavior whose existence is independent of the educational level in a nation. Education, the data suggest, may lead individuals to believe that they can influence their government, no matter what country they live in (providing, of course, that there is at least some institutional structure to support this). The data also suggest that as the overall educational levels of nations rise, they will become more similar in this respect. But education does not necessarily increase the potentiality that individuals will create groups to support them. The ability to create political structures through cooperation with one's fellow citizens in time of stress seems to be typical of some nations and not of others. It is an element of political style, not a result of educational attainment.

The data on differences among social groups in citizen competence suggest that it makes a great deal of difference who you are within your own country whether or not you believe yourself able to influence a local regulation. If you have more education, a higher status or are male, you are clearly more likely to consider yourself competent. In this sense, one's self-perceptions of one's role as a citizen vary greatly with one's social position within a nation. But whether or not the local competent believes that his friends and neighbors are available to help him in a situation of this sort depends relatively little on his social position within a nation, but depends heavily on what nation he happens to be in.

---

[12] The difference between the pattern in relation to the extent to which individuals think they have influence and that in relation to their strategy of influence is quite striking if one compares Figures 1 and 2.

Political competence, thus, grows with higher education or occupational status, but the style of political competence seems to be rooted more in general political culture.[13]

---

[13] As mentioned earlier, a similar pattern would appear if one controlled for other indicators of social group. The intriguing question is, of course, how does one explain the differences in propensity to form groups if such social variables do not explain it. In a forthcoming publication by the author and Gabriel A. Almond, an answer will be suggested.

CHAPTER TWO

POLITICAL ACTION
SITUATIONS

Historically new citizens—the propertyless, women, Negroes—have had to battle their way into the political system. Victory in getting the laws changed to *permit* their participation came hard. But in each case this was only the beginning. To establish participation in fact as well as in law has required political mobilization, the complex, difficult process of opening up practical opportunities for taking part, building resources to enable citizens to take part, and motivating people to want to take part.

In their careful and imaginative study of *Negroes and the New Southern Politics*, Donald R. Matthews and James W. Prothro focus on the contemporary South and more intensively on four southern communities (given mythical names), to show how these basic factors are being combined by active organizational efforts. In the selection below, the interactions among political motives, opportunities, and resources are developed. Matthews and Prothro draw together data on the environments in which activation is attempted, the internal organizational character of Negro activist groups, and the effects of organized efforts on voting. They show how each factor bears on each other factor to produce a political synthesis. Their findings are generated in a particular social context—they are talking about real combinations—but much of what they say has applications beyond Bright Leaf, Piedmont, Crayfish, and Camellia Counties.

PRECONDITIONS FOR AND EFFECTS OF NEGRO POLITICAL ORGANIZATION IN THE SOUTH

DONALD R. MATTHEWS
JAMES W. PROTHRO

The four southern communities we studied in detail differ greatly in the development of Negro political organization. Good reasons can be found for this variation. In some communities, social, economic, and political factors tend to encourage—or at least not to inhibit—the growth of effective political organization. In others, these factors impose severe limits on the extent and effectiveness of Negro organization. These variables fall into two classes—those that are "external" to the Negro community and those that grow out of the Negro community itself. Let us look first at the "external" or situational variables.

THE RACIAL ATTITUDES OF LOCAL WHITES

White attitudes about the proper "place" of the Negro help determine the success or failure of Negro efforts to organize. In Crayfish County, for example, the white community is solidly opposed to any relaxation of rigid segregation. Given a choice between "strict segregation, integration, or something in between," every white Crayfish respondent except one said that he favored strict segregation. The exception was a young lady who had grown up in Los Angeles and who was living in Crayfish temporarily because her husband was driving a truck for a construction com-

Reprinted from Donald R. Matthews and James W. Prothro, *Negroes and the New Southern Politics* (New York: Harcourt, Brace & World, 1966), pp. 218–35. Copyright © 1966 by Harcourt, Brace & World, Inc., and reprinted with their permission.

pany.[1] Whites in the other counties are not unanimous in their dedication to rigid segregation: the proportion drops to 87 percent in Bright Leaf, 65 percent in Camellia, and 58 percent in Piedmont. When we add Negro views to those of the whites, we find that a small majority of the total population of Piedmont rejects strict segregation.

More important, whites in Piedmont believe that Negro opinions *ought* to count in the community. On the proposition that "colored people ought to be allowed to vote," a majority of whites in Piedmont (69 percent) and in Camellia (68 percent) agree "quite a bit." Almost half the whites in Bright Leaf (49 percent) but only 4 percent of the Crayfish whites similarly endorse the principle of suffrage for Negroes. If we add those who agree "a little," white acceptance of the proposition becomes overwhelming in three of the counties: 90 percent in Piedmont, 93 percent in Camellia, and 82 percent in Bright Leaf. But it reaches only 16 percent in Crayfish! In the face of such determined opposition from those who control all the political and economic power, efforts to organize politically must assume the form of conspiracies.

White attitudes—either in themselves or as an index of other community factors—are not the only constraints on Negro efforts to organize. If they were, we would expect Camellia County to follow closely behind Piedmont in the scope and effectiveness of Negro political organization. Other situational factors, of varying importance and specificity, are suggested by a close examination of the four communities: the political style of white leaders, locally and statewide, in dealing with racial questions; the factional system peculiar to the community; the local electoral system; the relative homogeneity or heterogeneity of the community in nonracial terms; and the Civil War and Reconstruction experiences of the community. Added to public opinion on racial questions, these overlapping situational variables pretty much determine whether or not the Negro community can organize for political ends. And, taken together, they provide a reasonably clear and specific meaning to the ordinarily vague concept of "political culture."

THE POLITICAL STYLE OF WHITE LEADERS

The white leaders in Crayfish openly espouse white supremacy. Only there can the leaders pretend that they have no "race

---

[1] The resident white interviewer, recognizing the heretical nature of this respondent's views, commented that "she wouldn't last long in Crayfish County."

problem." Crayfish Negroes are so browbeaten that the whites can sing the old refrain about having "good, happy niggers," and can repeat the old joke about the local Negro who finds life so miserable in the North that he wires his old "boss man" for money to return to the happy life on the farm. One of the leaders commented: "We have the best colored people in the world . . . our colored people are not giving us any trouble." And if they do give trouble, it is not reported. Merely from reading the *Breedville Weekly* one might conclude that no Negroes lived in Crayfish.

In Bright Leaf, the white leaders express paternalistic attitudes sometimes mixed with genuine benevolence. The response of the superintendent of schools to a question about relations with "the colored community" is illuminating:

Rather good, I think. There are some hotheads but a group of us are working to establish communication. I do what I can to show my love for them—get scholarships. Nigrahs come in the back door and stand—I tell them to have a seat, and suggest that they go out the front door—it's nearer. I call janitors in the schools "custodians." This is more than words and acts; they know I'll fight for them, for instance, give them money. The point is: treat them as humans, call them "Mister" and "Miss"; nothing special, just what human beings deserve.

The superintendent of schools is not typical of Bright Leaf's white leaders, most of whom hold more clearly anti-Negro stereotypes. But it is remarkable that we can find such a leader, who says that his prime objective is to prepare teachers for integration, in this community. This is not a transient, but an old and widely admired leader. The new high school in Farmington bears his name, and generations of graduates remember him with affection and respect.

Camellia County is more cosmopolitan and liberal than Bright Leaf, mainly because it is more urban and is the home of the state capitol and the state university. Although some Camellia whites, mostly from the university, have actively championed integration, the officials of Capital City have been virulently anti-Negro. Officeholders talk about the fine relations that existed with old-style Negro leaders before the bus boycott confronted them with the undeniable fact of mass Negro dissatisfaction. The chief of police, under whose direction the local police force has ruthlessly broken up demonstrations, says, "They want to be good, but the NAACP has caused friction—whites and colored are farther apart than in years. The college people and Negro preachers start things—they prey on younger niggers." The municipal judge, who has handed down stiff sentences to demonstrators, observes: "CORE is a Communist front, I'm convinced." Most Camellia leaders recognize that the two colleges in Capital City are the source of much racial agitation and regard them almost as alien institutions. They value the colleges as a source of entertainment (in the form of athletic events) and as a source of income, but they look on them with great suspicion. Crayfish's governing authorities can indulge themselves in the myth that neither Negroes nor whites in the community disapprove of the established system; Camellia's leaders are fighting against change, embittered by Negro defiance of segregation and infuriated by some white support of that defiance.

In Piedmont County the white leaders do not regard Negro demands as unreasonable in themselves. Although hard bargaining occurs and ill will exists, the right of the Negroes to work through the Urbania League for Negro Activities (ULNA and other organizations is unquestioned. "The top leadership of Negroes is good, just top flight," was the comment of the city manager.

LOCAL FACTIONAL AND ELECTORAL SYSTEMS

In a study of Negro leadership in northern cities, James Q. Wilson found that the structure and style of Negro politics reflected the general politics of the city in which the Negroes lived.[2] We may similarly expect the factional systems and the electoral systems of southern communities to help determine the nature and extent of Negro political organization.

Crayfish County has a purely personalized politics, with no identifiable factional structure. The Negro community has no factional structure and no politics of concern to the general community. Public officials are elected on a district basis. Normally this system tends to give Negroes a good chance of winning public office, because segregated housing concentrates the Negro population in a few districts where they may constitute a majority. With Negroes excluded from politics, however, Crayfish whites can keep an electoral system that results in heavy representation of the county's numerous hamlets. The emerging Negro political organization of Bright Leaf County is facilitated by the loose bifactionalism of the county, which provides a limited number of factions with which the Negroes can deal. Like Crayfish, Bright Leaf once

---

[2] James Q. Wilson, *Negro Politics: The Search for Leadership* (Glencoe, Ill.: The Free Press, 1960), pp. 52ff.

elected public officials on a district basis, but this arrangement was dropped as soon as the Negroes organized to take advantage of it.

Camellia County's politics are conducted through white factions at least as recognizable as those in Bright Leaf. But the Negro factions are semi-atomistic and personalized. Accordingly, we must explain the rivalry among Negro leaders and their inability to create any enduring political organization with mass support in some other way than to say that they are simply a reflection of white factionalism. Camellia officials are elected at large, an arrangement that has denied recent Negro candidates any real chance of success. Piedmont has the most clear-cut system of factional competition, and the Negro community there has organized to win recognition and commitments from the enduring white factions. Many public officers are elected by district in Piedmont, and the system was not changed when Negroes began to win office: too many white politicians were indebted to the organized Negro vote.

DIVERSITY OF INTERESTS

The white population of Crayfish is extremely homogeneous. Almost the entire population depends, in one way or another, on the farming, cattle, and dairy interests of the county. The only industry of any consequence is absentee-owned and serves simply to supplement the incomes of poorer whites by giving work to the white women in the county. In Bright Leaf, which is almost as homogeneous, farming interests dominate the county and a chamber of commerce viewpoint dominates Farmington. Competing interests have arisen in Farmington, however, as "newer elements" jostle "older elements" for advantage. Should this factionalism crystallize, the incipient Negro organization may be stimulated to greater activity. Camellia County is similarly dominated by business interests and "old families" that have grown rich with Capital City's growth. The general provincialism is mitigated by the presence of professionals in the colleges and the state government, but they are an ill-organized and "alien" interest.

Only Piedmont has enough industries and unions to furnish economic as well as social heterogeneity. Union leaders, for example, negotiate with Negro leaders in seeking common candidates to support; in the other communities white laborers generally oppose candidates who are known to have Negro support.

LOCAL HISTORY

The history of each community is the final situational variable affecting political organizations. For example, a community that was the scene of long and bitter violence between labor and management as far back as the 1920's or 1930's might be expected to be organized politically along class lines to an unusual degree. In the South, the common experiences most important for a community's response to Negro political organizations are the Civil War and Reconstruction—or, more accurately, secondhand memories of "The War" and Reconstruction. These events have shaped all southern politics.

In Crayfish and Camellia counties, memories of that cataclysmic period are particularly bitter. The leading lawyer in Breedville (the only other lawyer is a drunk) delights in explaining how an outside land company exploited the corrupt legal system during Reconstruction by grabbing much of the land away from the people who had settled the Crayfish area. His delight appears to be enhanced by the violence used to drive the land company out and by the fact that he still gets an occasional fee from cases based on that period of confusion.

At the site of the state government, Camellia residents witnessed Negro and "carpetbag" control of the state government at first hand. A minor skirmish was fought near Capital City during the Civil War, and the townspeople stir up old memories every year in a formal celebration of the rout of the Yankees by a few old men and the brave young boys who were left in the university. At the turn of the century Camellia was still strictly a plantation county, with 80 percent of its population made up of Negroes. Many "old family" leaders still act as if they were living in Crayfish rather than in a metropolitan area.

Bright Leaf residents have few exaggerated notions about an aristocratic past. The school superintendent explained:

> I call this a new town and a new community. Some nearby counties have pre-Civil War aristocracy; this county developed *after* the Civil War, and new leaders are recognized. Bright Leaf is a plebian county. It has no old aristocracy to fight.

He suggested that this lack of an ante-bellum history explains why Bright Leaf has better race relations than neighboring counties. Piedmont residents have favorable recollections of the Reconstruction. Before the Civil War the county was populated by poor farmers with few slaves, so the war itself produced no violent change in the way of life. Moreover, the end of the war and the presence of Union troops in the area triggered a local industrial revolution in textiles and tobacco. The development of successful industry rather than concern about the new status of Negroes thus dominated the Reconstruction period in Piedmont.

PRECONDITIONS FOR EFFECTIVE NEGRO POLITICAL ORGANIZATION: THE NEGRO COMMUNITY

Favorable circumstances do not ensure effective Negro political organization, but they make it possible. The characteristics of the Negro community itself determine how well circumstances are exploited for political purposes. All the factors that we found in the preceding chapter to be conducive to high-quality leadership also tend to produce effective Negro organizations. More specifically, three factors seem to be particularly important for organizational effectiveness in the Negro communities examined: close ties between leaders and followers, organizational continuity, and organizational cohesion.

Most of the leaders of the Urbania League for Negro Activities won their positions through successful business, professional, or union activity *within* the Negro community. A few of the business leaders have Negro customers in a number of states. This economic relationship frees the ULNA leaders from dependence on whites; equally important, it demands that the leaders stay in close touch with the needs of ULNA members and nonmembers alike. In Camellia County the gap between leaders and followers is not so neatly bridged by economic ties; the largest pool of potential Negro leaders are employed by the college, and there is no economic incentive for them to remain in communication with the Negro masses. The "town-gown" division within the Negro community also tends to encourage leadership rivalry.

The continuity of the ULNA in Piedmont has resulted in experienced leaders and organizational prestige. The Inter-Civic Committee in Camellia was created to take over the direction of a single great effort—the bus boycott—and it has been unable to take on new functions. The Progressive Voters League in Bright Leaf grew out of the rivalry between two older organizations in the heat of an election campaign. This organization may be able to persist, but there are some indications that it may not survive for many other campaigns.

A high level of cohesion is necessary if political ambition and self-interest are to work for, rather than against, the racial cause. Southern whites traditionally assume that they can exploit individual Negroes, and it is easy for them to extend this assumption to politics. Moreover, many Negroes are highly vulnerable to economic inducements and threats. Urbania Negroes once competed for the largesse of white politicians seeking small blocs of Negro votes. Today such efforts are channeled through the ULNA, and Negro votes are "sold" for policy commitments, not for pre-election payoffs. Two Negro leaders in the Bright Leaf Civic Association, irritated because their candidate had been rejected by the Benevolent Brothers, were bribed to defect in a recent election. In Camellia County organizational rivalries produce competing slates of candidates endorsed by Negroes, with the result that white candidates refuse to place confidence in any Negro organization. One white politician explained that he was forced to rely on his personal organization:

> Three Negro groups were hauling to the polls on election day . . . and it was questionable as to whether they were getting them to vote correctly because they were handing out different lists even though CORE had distributed a list to the voters. I sent my own car with my name on the side and hauled Negro voters to the polls myself.

NEGRO ORGANIZATION AND THE "BLOC VOTE": THE SOUTHWIDE PICTURE

So far we have concentrated on the preconditions for effective political organization among the Negroes of the four communities we studied in detail. Now we want to shift our attention to the *effects* of political organization on the Negro vote *for the region as a whole*.

EFFECTS ON VOTER REGISTRATION

We analyzed data from all southern counties and discovered that extensive Negro organization is associated with a substantial (7-percentage-point) excess of registered Negro voters over what we would have predicted from the social and economic characteristics of southern counties. In a survey of the general population it is difficult to spot the organizational activity that produces this increment. Nevertheless, aggregate data from the 21 counties in our sample strongly support our earlier findings on the importance of Negro political organization.

Our interviewers came up with more accurate and detailed information on political and racial organizations in the survey counties than we could possibly obtain for all counties in the South.[3] We have used this information to classify the survey counties as low, medium, or high in Negro political organization. Again holding social and economic characteristics constant (through residual analysis), we find that the counties with low Negro political organization have an average (mean) residual of −5.2. This means that Negro registration in the counties with no Negro political organizations falls, on the average, some 5 percentage points below what we would expect from the generally depressed social and economic characteristics of those counties. The counties with a medium amount of Negro political organization have an average residual of −0.2, almost exactly what we would expect from their social and economic attributes alone. The counties with a high degree of Negro political organization, on the other hand, have an average residual of +16.7.

The relationship between Negro registration and organiza-

---

[3] Data were secured from each county in our sample on the presence or absence of these Negro political organizations: a biracial Human Relations Council; Negro religious, fraternal, or occupational groups active in politics; a county chapter of the NAACP; a Negro Voters League. Counties with no such organizations are classified as low, those with some but not all types of organization are classified as medium, those with all four types of organization are classified as high in political organization.

This factual information on each county in the sample was secured by the interviewing staff through the procedure described in these instructions: "The following information is needed for *each county* in which interviews are conducted. . . . If you are interviewing in your home county, you may be able to fill it in yourself. If so, fill in the information but contact one of the five people in the county named below and go over it with him to see if he has anything to add: (1) any Negro in elective public office, (2) the editor of the Negro newspaper, if there is one, (3) the minister of the largest Negro church, (4) the Negro mortician with the largest business, (5) the principal of the largest Negro high school. For counties other than your residence, contact *two* of the persons named and get each of them to fill in the information on a separate form." This use of interviewers to secure factual information permits the combination of survey data with aggregate data of a sort that cannot be found in the census or other published sources. The potentialities of using interviewers to secure political facts on communities in addition to the opinions of individuals have not, to our knowledge, been exploited previously.

tional activity thus shows up more clearly when we confine our analysis to counties on which we have detailed information. When we were considering all southern counties, we found a difference of 9 percentage points that could be attributed to differences in organization. Now, from more refined data on a smaller number of counties, we find a difference of 22 percentage points.[4] The farther we pursue political factors, the more important they appear to be as an influence on Negro voter registration.

We can only expect to tease out faint residues of organizational activity from the southwide survey data. If Negro organizations are more active in politics than are white organizations, for example, we would expect more Negro voters to have registered initially as a result of outside encouragement rather than simply on their own initiative. Slight differences in the predicted direction do appear. When white voters are asked if there was "any special reason" why they first registered to vote, most say that there was no special reason or that they had simply come of age. Only 1 percent say that they were urged to register by a candidate, organization, or leader. Among Negroes, this trace of organizational activity is slightly more visible: 7 percent of the Negro voters and 25 percent of the Negroes who tried unsuccessfully to register say that they made the effort at the prompting of a candidate, organization, or leader.

EFFECTS ON VOTER TURNOUT

Any successful political organization must be able to deliver the vote. Typically, the organization tries to increase turnout and crystallize sentiment in favor of a candidate most supporters of the organization would tend to vote for anyway. In view of the other indications of organizational effectiveness we turned up in the survey counties, we would expect to find greater turnout in counties with Negro political organizations. The findings reported in Table 1 completely confound this expectation. The percentages in the table are based on voters only, and the small proportion of registered Negro voters in counties with no Negro organization are as regular in their turnout as the larger proportion in counties with a full range of Negro organizations. The success of Negro organiza-

---

[4] In the case of the southwide analysis, the difference is that found between counties with no Negro political organization and those with an NAACP chapter plus a local organization. For the survey counties, it is the difference in residuals between counties with no Negro political organization and those with the four types of organization mentioned above.

TABLE 1

PERCENTAGE OF NEGRO VOTERS PARTICIPATING IN ALL OR MOST
ELECTIONS, BY EXTENT OF NEGRO POLITICAL ORGANIZATION

Type of electoral contest	No Negro organization	Some Negro organization	Four types of Negro organization
Presidential elections	54%	44%	59%
Gubernatorial primary elections*	46	28	44
Gubernatorial general elections	34	24	43
Local or county elections	46	35	39
School board elections	29	12	32
N	24	61	170

* Democratic primaries only.
NOTE: See footnote 3 for a description of the four types of Negro organization.

tions in the South appears to lie in their getting greater numbers of Negroes registered, not in maximizing the turnout of those who are registered.

On closer inspection, the relationships reported in Table 1 appear to be curvilinear: regularity of turnout is relatively high among voters in counties with no organization and in those with high organization; it is low in the middle group of counties with incomplete organization. So we can say that the figures reflect two different phenomena—one motivational, the other organizational. In counties where Negroes have, through their own initiative, overcome barriers to voting, the voting lists include people with relatively high motivation. In counties with organizational support for Negro voting, people with only a mild commitment may be led to register and to vote. But a relatively strong organizational structure may be necessary to get these "extra" voters to the polls; such a structure is absent in the counties with an incomplete set of Negro organizations.

EFFECTS ON VOTER PREFERENCES

Anti-Negro whites in the South frequently complain about the Negro bloc vote—and, of course, they denounce the candidate who seems to enjoy Negro support. The term "bloc voting" implies that the Negro vote is organized, that Negro voters self-consciously stick together, that bloc voting is somehow conspiratorial. But most

TABLE 2
EFFECT ON RESPONDENT'S VOTE OF DISCOVERY THAT MOST NEGROES
SUPPORT A CANDIDATE IN A CAMPAIGN IN WHICH RESPONDENT IS
UNCERTAIN OF HIS PREFERENCE

	White	Negro		
	South-wide	South-wide	Counties with no organization	Counties with some organization	Counties with four types of organization
Vote for	1%	31%	22%	23%	40%
No difference, make up own mind	78	63	71	72	55
Not vote for	18	0	0	0	0
Other, don't know	3	6	7	5	5
TOTAL	100%	100%	100%	100%	100%
N	690	618	149	155	314

Negroes may vote for the same candidate simply because the candidate ignores the race issue while his opponent devotes his campaign to denouncing Negroes and civil rights. No leadership, organization, or even communication between Negro voters would be necessary; a "bloc vote" might emerge as a result of similar but independent responses to the same stimuli. Basically, southern Negroes may tend to vote the same way because they all hurt in the same place. How much is the unity of the Negro vote in the South *self-conscious* "bloc voting"? How much is it merely the result of independent action by individuals with similar goals?

Indirect evidence on this question may be gained by examining the proportions of Negroes who admit that their votes would be influenced by the discovery that "most of the Negroes" or "the strongest white segregation leaders" in the area favor a particular candidate in an election.[5] As Tables 2 and 3 show, 63 percent of

---

[5] Respondents were not asked directly whom they would vote for in such a situation but were asked to "suppose that you . . . hadn't yet made up your mind who you would vote for." Then the discovery of Negro or segregationist support for a candidate occurs. "What difference would it make to you?" The open-ended form of this question and its highly permissive wording make it easy for respondents to say that such a discovery would make no difference or that "I'd make up my own mind." Given the widespread disapproval of bloc voting, we would expect Negroes to be reluctant to admit that it exists.

TABLE 3

EFFECT ON RESPONDENT'S VOTE OF DISCOVERY THAT WHITE SEGRE-
GATIONISTS SUPPORT A CANDIDATE IN A CAMPAIGN IN WHICH
RESPONDENT IS UNCERTAIN OF HIS PREFERENCE

	White	Negro		
	South-wide	South-wide	Counties with no organization	Counties with some organization	Counties with four types of organization
Vote for	23%	2%	2%	3%	1%
No difference, make up own mind	61	47	62	56	35
Not vote for	7	39	24	31	51
Other, don't know	9	12	12	10	13
TOTAL	100%	100%	100%	100%	100%
N	688	618	149	155	314

southern Negroes say they would make up their own minds when
Negro support for a candidate is suggested, but only 47 percent say
the same thing when segregationist support for a candidate is
suggested.

Few people like to admit that they simply go along with the
crowd; this may help account for the larger proportion of Negroes
who say their vote would be influenced by a candidate's segregationist support than by his support from Negroes. But, among
those who say they would be influenced, the direction of influence
is unanimously toward the Negro-supported candidate and almost
as solidly against the segregationist-supported candidate.

The response of whites to the same questions is less clear-cut:
78 percent deny that they would be influenced by the discovery that
most Negroes supported a particular candidate, 18 percent say they
would vote against such a candidate, and 1 percent say they would
join the Negroes in voting for him. Support of a candidate by the
strongest white segregation leaders would be enough to induce
support from 23 percent of the whites and opposition from 7
percent. Although the bloc vote by whites in campaigns involving
racial issues is no doubt understated in these findings—and involves, even as stated, greater absolute numbers than the Negro
bloc vote—the proportion of whites who deny being directly influ-

enced by such issues is greater than the proportion of Negroes who deny it. And whereas almost all whites who admit to being influenced by Negro support say they would oppose the Negro-backed candidate, a fourth of those who would react to strong segregationist support would *oppose* the candidate so identified. As anticipated, then, Negroes are particularly sensitive to the "race issue" in politics, and they are virtually unanimous in their reactions to it.

Negro political organizations thus have a fertile field in which to work. Tables 2 and 3 suggest that they are already cultivating it. The proportion of Negroes who say they would vote for a candidate if he had the support of most other Negroes is almost twice as large in counties with all four kinds of Negro political organization as it is in counties with none or only some of these organizations. The proportion who say they would oppose a candidate supported by strong segregationists goes up from 24 percent in counties with no Negro political organization, to 31 percent where some such organizations exist, to 51 percent where all four types of organization are found. Without attempting to unravel the causal factors in these strong relationships, we can conclude that a rational vote in terms of Negro interests is much more likely in counties that have a rich structure of Negro organizations.

Occasional comments suggest that political organization is directly responsible for at least some of these differences. A young wife employed as a cashier in Houston, which has a full assortment of Negro organizations, responded negatively when asked if Negro support for a candidate would influence her decision. But then she contradicted herself by saying, "The Harris Council of [Negro] Organizations endorse a candidate, and usually me and other people vote for him." Here the existence of a trusted organization helps individual voters to make up their minds. In a Columbia, South Carolina, slum, on the other hand, an elderly Negro lady spoke for a different generation. "I'm 105 years old," she claimed, "and have never voted and am not going to vote." [But just suppose you were voting?] "No, I wouldn't go along with no colored people." Negro organization may be necessary to a high level of Negro cohesion at the polls, but it is not sufficient in itself.

Negro political organizations must, if they are to survive, have an effect that is discernible at the polls. Aggregate county data demonstrate that Negro oragnizations achieve relatively high rates of voter registration in their counties. The data in Tables 2 and 3 also suggest that Negroes are more attuned to racial cues in counties with a wide range of Negro organizations. How much of this response is attributable to the work of these organizations is difficult to say.

Despite our fear that Negroes would be reluctant to talk about bloc voting, respondents were told, "In some places, you hear that Negroes get together and all vote for the same candidate." Then they were asked, "Have you ever heard about that happening here?" In the counties with no formal Negro organization, 3 percent said yes; affirmative responses went up to 27 percent in counties with an incomplete set of organizations and to 32 percent in counties with a full array of organizations. Of course, not all Negroes are equally familiar with the organizational effort behind this cohesion in voting. An Arkansas maid who belongs to an organization but cannot remember its name describes the process vaguely, "Some person with influence calls a meeting and they all decide on the candidate they think is best." Piedmont residents are more aware of the organization behind the effort. One voter simply said, "Yes. The Urbania League for Negro Activities sponsors this." Another explained how, again naming the organization, "Well, this League for Negro Activities pass out leaflets."

White residents are not so well-informed about these activities. Even when the analysis is confined to those who say that Negroes vote in their locality, white images of Negro bloc voting do not appear very realistic. In counties with a full set of Negro organizations, 38 percent of the whites have heard that local Negroes vote together. But in counties with an incomplete array of organizations, only 16 percent have heard of such activity, and the proportion goes up to 29 percent in the counties with no Negro organization at all. The greater perception of bloc voting in areas with no organization to promote it than in counties with some such organizations suggests that, at least in the more repressive counties, this question triggered expressions of white fears rather than the facts of the situation.

But white candidates for public office cannot afford to be unrealistic. Their efforts to win Negro votes differ greatly with the extent of Negro political organization. As Table 4 indicates, only 11 percent of the Negroes in counties with no Negro political organization report that white candidates do anything to get Negro votes, compared with 40 percent where some Negro organizations are found and 52 percent where a more complete set of organizations exists. Success in commanding the attention of candidates, a prerequisite for political influence, thus appears to be greatly increased by the presence of Negro political organizations.

TABLE 4

NEGRO RESPONDENTS' PERCEPTIONS OF EFFORTS OF WHITE CANDIDATES
TO WIN NEGRO VOTES, BY EXTENT OF NEGRO POLITICAL ORGANIZATION

White candidates' relation to Negro voters	No Negro organi- zation	Some Negro organi- zation	Four types of Negro organization	Negro southwide
Try to win support	11%	40%	52%	39%
Uncertain ("don't know")	11	34	28	25
Do not try to win support	78	26	20	36
TOTAL	100%	100%	100%	100%
N	149	155	313	617

The extent of bloc voting probably can be most clearly dis-
cerned from the voting preference of Negroes in gubernatorial
primary elections. Even in a state like Alabama or Mississippi—
where candidates often vie with each other to prove that they are
the most extreme segregationists—some marginal differentiation
can generally be detected. The 1964 inaugural address of Governor
Paul Johnson of Mississippi, for example, revealed some uneasiness about that state's reputation as a "closed society."[6] In every
state in our survey, a majority of the Negro voters reported that
they voted for the gubernatorial candidate who would be judged
least anti-Negro by outside observers. But the size of the majorities
varied markedly with the extent of Negro political organization. In
counties with no such organization, 60 percent of the Negro voters
supported the "pro-Negro" candidate, compared with 84 percent in
the middle group of counties and 88 percent in those most organized.

In view of the common interest of Negroes in the race issue,
majorities as great as 60 percent may be expected without any
organized bloc voting at all. Where organizations reinforce these
common tendencies, cohesion in voting approaches the 90 percent
level. We cannot attribute all this increase in solidarity to organizational effort. To some extent, the differences we are discussing are
differences between rural and urban counties. Although an urban
environment may be a necessary condition to a rich Negro organi-

---

[6] James W. Silver, *Mississippi: The Closed Society* (New York: Harcourt,
Brace, 1966), p. xx.

zational structure, urban life in itself does not appear sufficient to explain differences of the magnitude that we found. Solidarity as great as that reported seems to represent the payoff that comes from organizational efforts.

An illustration of this payoff is provided by the performance of the ULNA in a recent gubernatorial primary. In order to nullify charges of Negro bloc voting between the first and second primary, the ULNA leaders decided to support a candidate in the first primary who was not the most liberal on either racial or economic policy. This stratagem left the ULNA free, of course, to throw its entire strength behind the liberal in the runoff. As Table 5 demon-

TABLE 5

THE ABILITY TO DELIVER THE NEGRO VOTE IN AN "UNNATURAL" DIRECTION: THE VOTE IN PREDOMINANTLY NEGRO PRECINCTS IN A FIRST GUBERNATORIAL PRIMARY IN FOUR PIEDMONT STATE URBAN AREAS

Racial stands of gubernatorial candidates	Predominantly Negro Precincts			
	Urbania	City X	City Y	City Z
Most pro-Negro	207	4,209	2,352	2,209
Moderate	2,623	93	158	63
Moderate	79	103	66	44
Most anti-Negro	32	31	74	20

strates, the ULNA was able to deliver in the first primary an overwhelming majority of the vote in predominantly Negro precincts to a candidate who was not the "natural" choice of Negroes. While Negroes in other cities of the state were turning in solid votes for the liberal candidate, Urbania Negroes were equally solid for the choice of their organization. This is one of those rare cases in social science when an imputation of causal relations can be made without reservation. Where efficient leadership capitalizes on favorable conditions for Negro organization, the results may be so dramatically effective that we must attribute them directly to organizational effort.

THE NEGRO CHURCH AND POLITICS

Negroes must create their own organizations before they can become a significant force in southern politics. But these organizations do not have to be *explicitly political*. All kinds of "nonpolitical" groups and organizations play an important part in the politics of the larger white community.[7] Why not in the Negro community, too?

The church—an almost totally segregated institution in the South—is the most likely "nonpolitical" agency to organize and direct Negro political activity in the region. Southern Negroes are a God-fearing, churchgoing people; 77 percent of them report that they attend church with considerable regularity. Marx felt that capitalism contained "the seeds of its own destruction" because it brought workers physically together in factories and cities where they could be easily organized into a class-conscious, revolutionary

TABLE 6

DISCUSSION OF ELECTIONS AT CHURCH, AS PERCEIVED BY THOSE WHO ATTEND

	Negro	White
Elections discussed	35%	18%
Elections not discussed	54	63
Don't know	10	18
No answer	1	1
TOTAL	100%	100%
N	597	622

proletariat. Southern whites, by teaching Negro slaves their religious practices but insisting that Sunday morning be segregated, may similarly have planted the seeds for the destruction of segregation. The church provided Negroes a common meeting ground, a corps of verbally skilled leaders who are economically independent of whites, and supernatural support for the overthrow of segregation. The fact that the most common occupation of Negro "leaders" in the South (as nominated by the Negro masses) was that of minister lends additional credence to this line of reasoning.

In order to examine this possibility, all our respondents who attended church were asked if election campaigns were ever discussed there. The most common response of both Negroes and whites was negative (see Table 6). But the minority who reported campaign discussions at church was twice as great among Negroes as among whites. And, despite the higher average education of

---

[7] D. B. Truman, *The Governmental Process* (New York: Alfred A. Knopf, 1962).

whites, they were more likely than Negroes to say they did not know whether campaigns were discussed or not. Carrying the question of the church as a political organization a step farther, 5 percent of the whites[8] and 18 percent of the Negroes who attend say that their minister has said something about which candidate the members of the church ought to support. Almost a fifth of the Negroes who go to church thus receive direct clues as to how they should vote, and over a third hear some kind of discussion of elections.

The political nature of the Negro church in the South may be a result of compensatory activity by people who are excluded from open political participation. Or does it result from the high salience of politics for southern Negroes? If the former is the case, we would expect discussions of politics to be more frequently reported from counties where relatively few Negroes are registered to vote. Seventeen counties in our sample included enough Negro church-goers to permit a test of this expectation. Among these seventeen, five rank extremely low in Negro voter registration (with 10 percent or less of their eligible Negroes registered). All five of these counties also rank low (24 percent or less) in the proportions of churchgoers who report discussions of politics at church. A reasonable amount of Negro political participation thus appears a necessary condition to a politicized church.

Discussions of elections at church seem to serve as an additional form of participation in areas where Negroes vote. Nor is the church a covert substitute for manifestly political organizations. In five counties with no Negro political organization, the average proportion of Negro church attenders who report election discussions at church is 11 percent. In five counties with some but not all four kinds of Negro political organization, the proportion reporting church discussions of elections goes up to 26 percent. Finally, in seven counties with a high level of Negro political organization, the proportion reporting church discussions of elections reaches 50 percent. When the Negro church gets into electoral politics, then, it

---

[8] Our interviews were conducted shortly after the 1960 presidential election, during which John F. Kennedy's Roman Catholicism was a matter of great concern in the overwhelmingly Protestant South and had a major impact on white voting in the region. See Philip E. Converse, *et al.*, "Stability and Change in 1960: A Reinstating Election," *American Political Science Review*, Vol. 55 (1961), p. 269; and Donald M. Freeman, "Religion and Southern Politics: A Study of the Political Behavior of Southern White Protestants" (Ph.D. dissertation, University of North Carolina, 1963).

is supplementing rather than substituting for more explicitly political organizations.

CONCLUSIONS: ORGANIZATION, BLOC VOTING, AND POLITICAL PAYOFFS

We have argued that southern Negroes must *create* their *own* political organizations before they can become a significant force in southern politics. Their greatest political asset is the vote; they are very poor in other political resources. And, in order to maximize the impact of their votes on political decision-making, they must organize those votes. This can be denounced as "bloc voting" by white southerners, and it generally is. But all political organizations seek a "bloc vote," and many white groups—the local chamber of commerce, the KKK, the country-club set, southern congressmen and senators, for example—often achieve a degree of unity in voting that rivals or surpasses that of Negroes. "You can talk all you want to about bloc voting," the political brains of the ULNA said, "but we learned it from you."

The opportunity of Negro communities to develop effective political organizations in the South depends, to a very large degree, on factors outside Negro control. Our survey of the development of Negro political organizations in Crayfish, Bright Leaf, Camellia, and Piedmont counties demonstrated this quite well. Favorable white attitudes and styles of political leadership; an electoral system in which the votes of Negroes are not submerged by those of whites; a white factional system that gives local politics enough structure so that Negroes have someone to bargain with; social heterogeneity and a community ethos that does not glorify the (largely mythical[9]) ante-bellum days—all these factors facilitate the development of Negro organization. The characteristics of the Negro community itself also shape organizational opportunities, primarily by facilitating or inhibiting close ties between Negro leaders and the masses and by facilitating or inhibiting organizational continuity and cohesion.

The effects of Negro political organization are difficult to judge, because the apparently more effective organizations tend to

---

[9] W. J. Cash, *The Mind of the South* (New York: Alfred A. Knopf, 1941).

be found in areas where Negroes probably would be active and influential anyway. Nonetheless, our analysis suggests that Negro organizations do have a substantial *independent* impact on the number of Negroes registered to vote and a smaller influence on the turnout of those Negroes who already are registered. And although, as Douglas Price has written, "Negro leaders have generally been unable to deliver the Negro vote except in the direction toward which Negroes were already inclined . . . ,"[10] we did detect some traces of influence beyond this point.

Most Negroes tend to vote the same way in most elections even when no organizational effort is made—after all, they all hurt in the same place. But the existence of an efficient and respected Negro political organization can increase the number of these votes, and it can also concentrate them in support of friends. This last gain is incremental—from perhaps 60 percent of the Negroes voting the same way to a maximum of about 90 percent—but it is a sizable increment. Thus although effective Negro political organizations require conditions that are not present in many—probably most—southern communities today, those that do exist stimulate a larger, more rational, and more concentrated Negro vote than would exist if there were no such organizations.

But a large and disciplined vote is not an end in itself. It is only a means of influencing government decisions and, through those decisions, of opening up an avenue to a better life for southern Negroes. A substantial organized vote is powerfully attractive to all politicians—be they northern or southern, white or black— but the governmental response to a sizable Negro bloc vote is not automatic. Indeed, the Negro vote appears to operate at a considerable discount. Negroes are a minority in almost all southern communities where organized voting is possible. They are highly visible. Where whites are so fearful and hostile toward Negroes that politicians run the risk of losing two white votes for every Negro vote gained, candidates are not likely to be *overtly* responsive to Negro wants and needs. Where the white vote is less predictably and less overwhelmingly anti-Negro, some ambitious politicians will try to build a biracial coalition of supporters. Even when this strategy works—as it has in Piedmont County, for example—the Negroes in the coalition are likely to receive a smaller "payoff" than

---

[10] H. Douglas Price, *The Negro and Southern Politics* (New York: New York University Press, 1957), p. 86.

their numbers merit. And such a coalition is very fragile—the white segment of the coalition may desert the first time someone cries "nigger." Because the Negroes can rarely win without white allies, especially in races in large geographical districts, they have to settle for considerably less than half a loaf or give up eating bread altogether. . . .

CHAPTER THREE

POLITICAL THINKING

O NLY A SMALL fraction of the American citizenry can be called really well-informed about politics. Not only does the great majority not know many facts about politics, but most citizens do not see the facts they have as part of an overall philosophical framework, an ideology. The strongest mental organizer of political thinking discovered so far is party identification—a rather indefinite sense of continuing allegiance to a rather indefinite organization.

There is a good deal of evidence on ways citizens do *not* think: in the main, they do not do systematic research, they do not build abstract models, they do not philosophize delicately about the issues facing the nation. Yet the very volume of political talking in our society—on the street-corner and in the kitchen as well as in print and television—makes it obvious that a good deal of political thinking goes on. How does it go on? How do individuals use their brains to develop and modify their opinions? Public-opinion polls normally turn up about three-fourths of the respondents with opinions on most anything asked. What is the thought content of these expressions on war abroad, riots at home, candidates for President, race relations, educational policy, or what have you?

In the next selection, Robert E. Lane draws upon evidence from his intensive study of fifteen working-class men to show how the bits and pieces of citizen opinions represent certain patterns or practices of thought. These add up to a style of political thinking, a way of approaching political questions. Politicians who want to persuade voters to a new point of view—and those who want to keep things as they are—will need to know how the American mind makes a certain kind of sense out of the fluctuating pictures of politics.

CONCEPTUALIZING IN POLITICAL DISCOURSE

ROBERT E. LANE

> The typical citizen drops down to a lower level of mental perform-
> ance as soon as he enters the political field. He argues and analyzes in a
> way he would readily recognize as infantile within the sphere of his
> real interests. He becomes a primitive again.
> —JOSEPH SCHUMPETER, *Capitalism, Socialism and Democracy*
> (1950), p. 262

At least three times in Western history a society has developed a
brilliant civilization characterized by self-knowledge and a groping
comprehension of the forces ruling its destiny—indeed, with something of a mastery of these forces and then has fallen back into a
condition of irrationality and mystification. In each of these societies, science as well as art was a flourishing branch of knowledge;
the spirit of rational inquiry was abroad, the desire to perceive
reality clearly, without the aid of myths and demons and divine
forces. "In the ancient world ruled by the irrational, by dreadful
unknown powers, where a man was utterly at the mercy of what he
must not try to understand, the Greeks arose and the rule of reason
began."[1] But the rationalism of the third- and fourth-century Greeks
began to run into stronger opposition in the second century when
men like Archimedes were confronted by the rising cult of astrol-
ogy; and, says Dodds, by the first century "the tide of rationalism,
which for the past hundred years had flowed ever more sluggishly,
has finally expended its force and begins to retreat."[2] For whatever
reason, the failure to develop an experimental method, the impor-

---

Reprinted from Robert E. Lane, *Political Ideology: Why the American
Common Man Believes What He Does* (New York: The Free Press of Glencoe,
1962), Chapter 22, pp. 346–63, by permission of the Macmillan Company.
Copyright © 1962 by The Free Press, a Corporation.

[1] Edith Hamilton, *The Greek Way to Western Civilization* (New York:
New American Library, 1948), p. 19.

[2] E. R. Dodds, *The Greeks and the Irrational* (Boston: Beacon, 1957),
p. 247.

tation of new religious and mystical doctrines from the East, "the unconscious flight from the heavy burden of individual choice which an open society lays upon its members,"[3] a turning away from science and reason in human affairs as well as in the study of nature, laid waste a great civilization.

Prompted by a revived humanistic interest in ancient Greece, the restless rise of trade, and the curious ancillary products of petty wars as well as great crusades, the Italian Renaissance once again lifted the spirit of rational inquiry into prominence.[4] Although it was under the influence of a capricious church and challenged by the pseudosciences of the stars, nevertheless Italy at the close of the fifteenth century offered the world a forum where Palo Toscanelli, Luca Pacioli, and Leonardo da Vinci might speak. Later, Galileo was to crown these Italian efforts. This spirit was not the exclusive possession of a narrow elite. Burckhardt says that it is "unquestionable" that in the Italy of the Renaissance, "a whole people takes a natural delight in the study and investigation of nature, at a time when other nations are indifferent, that is to say . . . the discoverer is not threatened or wholly ignored, but can count on the friendly support of congenial spirits."[5] But the Counter Reformation, the Inquisition, the astrologers sometimes working with the church, and "a stupid fatalism" in human affairs robbed this new beginning of its momentum. A second flowering of the rational spirit of inquiry, a capacity to look nature and man in the face, was lost, if only temporarily.

A third—but much more modest—instance of the triumph of the irrational in human affairs, the escape from freedom of mind and, in this case, body too, is too recent to need citation. It is not, of course, that the Second Reich represents a flowering of the rational spirit, but the broader German culture, particularly when combined with the Austrian culture, nourished in the late nineteenth and early twentieth centuries a coterie of remarkable scientific talent, natural and social, including Weber, Simmel, Sombart, and

---

[3] *Ibid.*, p. 252.

[4] Etienne Gilson places "the primacy of reason," as opposed to revelation, earlier, linking it to the work of Averroës in the twelfth century. Averroës' work is a species of scholastic reasoning, however, which, as Gilson says, "is wholly unrelated to scientific discovery." This should caution us on the various meanings of the word; by "rational" and "reason" I mean Man's reason, not God's, a secular orientation with a penchant for evidence and a tropism toward verification procedures. See Etienne Gilson, *Reason and Revelation in the Middle Ages* (New York: Scribner, 1948), pp. 37–66.

[5] Jacob Burckhardt, *The Civilization of the Renaissance in Italy* (London: Phaidon Press, 1944), p. 174.

Freud, with, in the last instance, many associates and disciples in Vienna and a few in Berlin. The destruction of this cultural effort by the myths of race and blood and the cult of nationalism impresses the modern mind with the power of the irrational and the capacity of the common man to borrow and use explanations for his plight that may easily set the world in flames. This is no more than a backdrop for an inquiry into the nature of the thinking the men of Eastport devote to public events, great and small, of the day —their day. But it will serve to remind us of the fragile thread of reason that has snapped in several other periods, one of them not so long ago.

PRINCIPLES AND PRAGMATISM

Tocqueville thought that "the Americans are much more addicted to the use of general ideas than the English and entertain a much greater relish for them." The English, he says, were concerned only with "particular facts" and "only generalize in spite of themselves." On the other hand "Among the French . . . the taste for general ideas would seem to grow to so ardent a passion that it must be satisfied on every occasion."[6] André Siegfried says of the French, "Principles and ideals are the very heart and soul of our politics."[7] But of the Americans no one has repeated Tocqueville's observation; on the contrary they are said to be as pragmatic and as addicted to facts as Tocqueville says the English were some 120 years ago.

The discussion of this issue is loose; it is complicated by the fact that every explanation of an event requires, implicitly or explicitly, a set of generalizations. Thus one interpretation of these alleged differences is that some people tend to *describe* situations rather than to explain them. If this were the allegation with respect to the American pragmatism—that it is a discourse based on description—the evidence from Eastport would tend to refute it. In the discussion of "major problems," of the causes of war and poverty, of the functioning of government, and elsewhere, there is a marked tendency to explain, a focus on why things happen the way they do.

But a causal explanation has two main ingredients. Popper

---

[6] Alexis de Tocqueville, *Democracy in America*, Phillips Bradley, ed. (New York: Knopf, 1945), II, 14.

[7] André Siegfried, *America Comes of Age: A French Analysis* (New York: Plenum Publishers, 2nd ed., 1968), p. 293.

says, "To give a *causal explanation* of an event means to deduce a statement which describes it, using as premises of the deductions one or more *universal laws,* together with certain singular statements, the *initial conditions.*"[8] When the French, with their alleged emphasis upon principles, explain an event, they may elaborate the universal laws, generalizing about the nature of men and society, and they may slight the statement of particulars, the facts, or, in Popper's phrase, the initial conditions. When Americans explain an event—and certainly this is true in Eastport—they may assume the universal laws and focus upon the initial conditions, the facts that characterize the situation. It is, indeed, true, that the man of Eastport tends to explain matters in terms of latent principles and manifest facts, and when he argues the argument more often turns on the characteristics of the situation, not on the rules that govern the universe. But, of course, he has ideas about these rules, ideas that remain part of his somewhat inarticulate and often unconscious assumptions of the nature of things.

The latency of the principles employed in social explanations tends to be supported by two other features of the American ideology. In the first place there stands the belief that most men are more or less the same; thus the rules governing human behavior are intuitively known through introspection. They are assumed, not discussed. Second, the common unchallenged assumptions about government derive from the almost universal acceptance of the same Lockean model, as Louis Hartz has pointed out.[9] One consequence of this latency is that the American finds it difficult to argue about political principles, and there is little doubt that one reason why Americans become so furious over the arguments of the Communists is that their own political principles are hard to tear from their native bed in the unconscious.

MORSELIZING AND CONTEXTUALIZING

"Our way," said Edith Hamilton of contemporary civilization, "is to consider each separate thing alone by itself." On the other hand, she says, "the Greeks always saw things as parts of a whole, and this habit of mind is stamped upon everything they did. It is the underlying cause of the difference between their art and ours."[10]

---

[8] Karl R. Popper, *The Logic of Scientific Discovery,* 2nd ed. (New York: Basic Books, 1958), p. 58, his emphasis.

[9] Louis Hartz, *The Liberal Tradition in America* (New York: Harcourt, Brace and World, 1955).

[10] Edith Hamilton, *The Greek Way,* p. 169.

Others, too, have spoken of the fragmentation of the world in modern times. Yet one of the features of what is sometimes called "understanding" is to grasp the context of an event, that is, temporally to know what went before and what is likely to follow, spatially to know the terrain, in human terms to see the play of the many motives involved. To understand an event in this way is to *contextualize* it; not to do this is to *morselize* it, to see it isolated from the surrounding features that give it additional "meanings." What education does for a man is to help him to contextualize events, particularly public events, but the unusual man, as we shall see, can capture some of this context without formal education.

In Eastport, as elsewhere, some men morselize the political world and some contextualize it. We can see how this works by stripping their discourse bare of the "I don't knows," the repetition, the false starts, and giving a summary outline of the ideas presented by three men as they discuss Soviet-American relationships. DeAngelo, who left school in the seventh grade but who is now shop steward of his plant and a hard-working factory operator, sets forth the following ideas on this subject: "It doesn't seem like you can negotiate with them [because] they've just got their minds set." "We're trying to do things with 'em peacefully." "We are keeping them surrounded with air bases, kind of keeping them in check." "They'll start trouble somewhere." "It's not our fault." "It's just like Germany—they want to conquer the world." "There's no religion . . . if a man doesn't believe in anything, you can't bargain with him." "I don't know who's behind the Russians." "We must protect ourselves." "The whole world today is all fouled up." There is no dearth of ideas here; DeAngelo, with his tongue getting in the way of his speech, is a rough, untrained observer, but not unintelligent.

McNamara finished high school and went to night school to learn bookkeeping. He says: "Inflation and defense policy are related." "Russia's come a long way in twenty years." "No one knows what the Russians have accomplished." "It appears they are ahead of us in the science field." "You've got to be careful." "They're probably now as powerful as Germany was, and Germany stirred up a lot of trouble." "Our policy is pretty well-set: go along carefully and every once in a while pass out a few threats; a display of power here and there doesn't hurt." "We are now in a scientific race." "Barriers between nations don't help; perhaps we should open up more trade." "We're making the same mistakes with them we made with Germany." "War may not be inevitable."

Flynn, who did finish high school but never had any training beyond that, except what he picked up as a young assistant on a water-company survey, says: "The trade problem and the defense problem are related." "Mutual scaring of each other by us and the Russians is risky." "The philosophy of disarmament runs into the difficulty that the Russians won't compromise." "A firmer foreign policy ten years ago would have prevented some of this." "While we have been building up other countries, the Russians have been building up their military strength." "You will never get disarmament until each side is certain of armament parity." "Full-scale disarmament is too idealistic." "We believe that you can't trust the Russians, and they believe they can't trust us." "Agreement is difficult because of the many nations involved." "War is probably inevitable, but the horror of nuclear war may prevent it." "Agreements are worthless in preventing atomic warfare." "We set the precedent for dropping the bomb."

What do we learn from this? It is a pretty fair sampling of the way these men wrestle with a policy problem somewhat more remote from their experience than the problems they like to deal with. In the first place, there is a wonderful "off the cuff" quality to it; judgments are made with an abandon that terrifies and paralyzes the analytic mind. (How would you, the reader, analyze and meet the proposition: "It's just like Germany—they want to conquer the world"?) There is not in any of the three a real argument, a building up of a case. Instead their statements represent a series of impressions. Third, there is a marked difference among them that reflects something we have said about the scope of the concepts involved; for DeAngelo, these are somewhat narrow and tied to the specific instances involved (a defense policy defined by bases, negotiation as a function of religious faith). McNamara seems to broaden out this straitened view somewhat so that the instances of the present case fall into a larger context. For one thing the idea of Russia is not limited to Russia *now;* it is a part of the larger notion of historical and developing Russia; then too, an important link between domestic and foreign policy is forged, and the concept of a broader fiscal-defense unit of thought is created. Still, the thinking is fairly instance-specific; the conceptual setting is rather meager. With Flynn, however, it broadens again. Like McNamara he links several problems together, for example, defense and trade, and our foreign aid and Russia's rapid advance. His conceptualization includes the Russian side—when he speaks of how we see them he adds how they must see us; it is a conceptualization that embraces one more step then, a feedback concept. He refers not simply to disarmament, but to "the philosophy of disarmament," including by reference, then, a much broader con-cept of an idea, one to which he is opposed at this time. Like McNamara, his conceptualization includes a time perspective— American foreign policy over the past ten years. He broadens the conceptualization to include other nations: negotiations, he under-stands, cannot be only bipartite anymore. His concept of a problem and a policy, then, is topically broader, spatially more inclusive, and has historical depth. But more of the men are like DeAngelo than like Flynn, or even McNamara.

If one does not see the instance in its context, the man in his setting, the event in a pattern of events, he misses the significance of what he sees, and missing this, he has no adequate means of dealing with the relevant social or political problems. Sokolsky tells of juvenile delinquency where the delicious details are the focus of his attention and the limit of his observation; Woodside, a railroad guard, sees it in a broader framework; he sees it as falling within a class of minor crimes likely to happen in two or three familiar parts of the city and to be committed by youth with certain charac-teristics; Farrel, the educated man who slipped into our panel by the processes of randomization, sees it as a part of a social pattern with a broad metropolitan distribution, certain family and psycho-logical correlates, and consequences affecting educational programs and school-leaving age requirements. This treatment of an instance in isolation happens time and again and on matters close to home: a union demand is a single incident, not part of a more general labor-management conflict; a purchase on the installment plan is a specific debt, not part of a budgetary pattern—either one's own or society's. The items and fragments of life remain itemized and fragmented—at least at the conscious level.

Contextual political thinking, then, is not just pigeonholing, not labeling, not in any necessary way associated with the "ismatic" terminology of today (Fascism, Communism, Federalism). It re-flects a configurative and relational turn of mind—in several ways. One way is to picture an event as part of a stream of events; that is, it is historical. Another is to compare and contrast events so as to group them in some way that sheds light on their common charac-teristics. Still another is to bring the event into contact with a conceptual framework such that it may be seen to illustrate or modify or rebut some part of that framework. Yet it is true that any one of these ways of placing "figure against ground," "contextual-izing" an event or an idea, often reaches beyond the experience of the individual in time or place; they are not encouraged by a quality of thought that is characteristic of Eastport workingmen: the tendency to keep concepts narrow and close to personal experience. For while this intellectual sobriety may ensure that the men know the evidential basis for their observations, it deprives them of some of the sources of interpretation that make an event meaningful. And in a curious sense this itemization may then mean that they derive their interpretation of an event from a free associative fantasy process rather than through the social and historical context to which the isolated events may be said to "belong."

CONTEXTUALIZING AND IDEOLOGIZING

Now, the very morselizing tendency that prevents these men from discovering the pattern and significance of an event also prevents them from ideologizing. While they do not place events in the context of a pattern of history or policy, neither do they place them in the context of some more or less rigid and exclusive interpretation of world affairs, a forensic ideology. They do not make events illustrate a predetermined theory of the way the world lies for the simple reason that they do not have such a theory; rather, they have several conflicting theories with vague referents.

Only in one or two instances did it seem to me that these men of Eastport attempted consciously to increase their understanding of an event by explicitly placing it in the context of a forensic ideology, though of course the individual, private, latent ideology of each man served as a constant sentinel at the gate of his mind. Sokolsky, arriving in an angry mood because of his brush with the supervisor on his part-time janitorial job, argues against equal income for everyone regardless of occupation on several personal and pragmatic grounds ("I look with horror on everybody exactly the same"), but he finds room for one more argument of an ideological sort: "I think that would be swinging a little toward your Communists, wouldn't it?" This is more window dressing than anything else, but it illustrates what it is that, on a larger scale and with more emotional force, and with greater elaboration, might be the central characteristic of a political debate. (The fact that we must use this slender example for illustration is significant in itself.)

Consider the difficult case of Sullivan, an over-the-road truck driver, with a laconic but penetrating style of discourse. His argument must be read with the understanding that four out of five of the Eastportians hold that Communists should have no right to free speech in the United States. He does not suffer fools gladly, and while in the Army nearly beat a man to death because he talked after "all quiet" (and brought down punishment on the barracks). Turning to the question of whether or not Communists should be allowed to speak, he says: "Well, [pause] it's a hard thing to say 'no' to, because—I mean I'm not too happy about it, but [pause] you can't very well have a democracy, and freedom of speech, if you don't let them, even though it's [pause] it's not something you agree on or particularly like. There's not too much you can do without changing the policy or the foundation of the country. [pause] I wish there was, but I guess there just isn't something." The logic is clear. This son of a former Jesuitical student argues: freedom of speech for Communists is a necessary part of the general class of things included in the concept "democracy." Since democracy is established by law, and not subject to change, freedom of speech for Communists is not subject to change—and probably shouldn't be. Substitute the right of an employer to contract individually with each of his employees for the rights of free speech for Communists, and substitute "due process" for "democracy," and you have the reasoning of the Court in *Hammer* v. *Dagenhart* and other child-labor cases.

When is a person contextualizing and when is he ideologizing? In each case he adds to his understanding by bringing additional material to bear upon a single event; in each case he must select which material to use; in each case he is guided either explicitly or implicitly by a theoretical construct. The difference centers on the need to confirm the pattern of ideas employed in this process; if the event is used and needed to support an emotionally involved theory or interpretation, the tendency is toward ideologizing. Moreover this frame of mind protects the sacred theory by admitting ideas only from approved sources. The ideologue takes his cue on the interpretation of information from its source; the contextualist is more open to information from all sources. Furthermore, the ideologue keeps the things he believes quite separate from those he doesn't believe so that their colors, their whiteness and blackness, do not mingle; the contextualist permits a shading in his pictures of the world. For the contextualist information is a positively useful tool, an enjoyment; for the ideologue information is a threat, and therefore suspect, unless it can be made familiar by attaching it to a known system of ideas.[11]

---

[11] Some of these distinctions derive from the excellent discussion in Milton Rokeach, *The Open and Closed Mind* (New York: Basic Books, 1960), pp. 54–82.

Judged by these standards, Sullivan's wrestling with the problem of civil liberties for Communists by placing the problem in the context of democratic principles could not be said to be ideologizing, for instead of forcing an event into a preferred interpretation he is reluctantly yielding a preferred position to the logic of an overall pattern of ideas. But Sullivan is exceptional only in the explicitness of the conflict; the others not infrequently confront an event with a cherished principle and tolerate the conflict. Those who believe that unions advance working-class interests accept evidence of their abuse; lifelong Democrats admit that it is unfair to blame the recession on Republicans; 100 percent American "working-class capitalists" admit that the Russian people are better off these days. Theories of the advantages of unions, Democratic administrations, capitalist economies make room for contrary evidence. Thus in two senses we must say that Eastport tends not to ideologize: first, the use of forensic ideologies, of theoretical constructs with well-defined referents, is minimal; second, the smaller and vaguer theories, the segments of ideologies employed, are used more as guides to interpretation than as defenses against the real world.

RIGIDITY AND COMPROMISE

Closely allied to the concept of ideologizing is that of rigidity, the inflexible mind, whether because it is doctrinaire (ideologized) or merely stubborn, willful, unyielding. Perhaps these men are, in this sense, rigid; that is, they may tend to uncompromising assertion in the face of contrary evidence and argument. Uncertainty of the kind modern men face sometimes produces rigidity. There is good psychoanalytic evidence for this, and some further evidence that it is exactly when their faith seems most at odds with the evidence that religious sectarians become most assertive about their beliefs.[12] I cannot say that I found the men of Eastport rigid, for, of course, I did not argue with them, but rather supported and rewarded the views they brought out themselves to create the most permissive atmosphere possible. But my associate James D. Barber did arrange for some debate among them in a room where a recording apparatus had been set in motion (with the knowledge of the men) and where the men were then left alone to thrash out a

---

[12] Leon Festinger, Henry Reicken, and Stanley Schacter, *When Prophecy Fails* (Minneapolis: University of Minnesota Press, 1956).

problem by themselves. There were two groups of three; one group was selected because of the prickly personalities of the men, and another group for their rather more easygoing dispositions. They argued a half-hour each on four topics. I have taken the last topic discussed, on the grounds that by then the men were most heated and free; as it turns out this is also the most controversial topic: "Are unions doing a good job?" The angry, prickly group (whose members I shall not identify, since they have met each other) includes one who recently knocked down a man for a slighting remark, another who nearly beat a man to death in the Army, and a third, who not long ago punched someone in the face for an alleged slur on his mother. At the end of the fourth half-hour argument, Number One, a member of a strong trade union, has been defending the union; Number Two has just been telling of how unions caused his brother-in-law to go backrupt by "stalling along on the jobs." Number Three finds abuses everywhere but generally thinks unions are a good thing. Here are their summary statements:

NUMBER ONE: Well, I'd say that [pause] the unions are good. You have to have them—the workingman has to have them, and well, I think they're a little too strong, some of them, now. And some of them are a little bit too lax, too. But on the whole, they're good, and on the whole I think [pause] any man that's a union member is getting paid what he's worth. And every union man's got a right to make a little bit more than a nonunion man. . . . A nonunion man just sits back, and when the unions get raises for other members he just falls right in.

NUMBER TWO: Well, I think that unions are a necessity. We've got to have them. But then, again, I think they're getting out of hand. I think they should be controlled, for one thing. I think they're lax—the union itself is lax, as they do allow certain undesirable elements into the union that shouldn't be there, and as a whole I don't think they're doing a good job. I think they're taking advantage of this organization, and just running hog-wild, right now.

NUMBER THREE: [after some critical comments about unions and a statement of agreement with number one—"where they do need unions"]: Yes and no—I think it's just about fifty-fifty.

During the course of the prior discussion, which revealed some real differences of opinion and some strong feeling, there was a tendency to accept part of the opponent's argument, just as there is in the summing up just quoted.

The theme that these three men are working out in these

passages, not quite rising above their passions, might be stated as "there is good and bad in unions." Indeed, this general theme could be emblazoned on Eastport's crest: "There is good and bad in everything." When a man speaks evil of something, he will retract it a little later on by saying something good. In Anna Freud's phrase, we are always "undoing" the evil that we do. On the other hand, there is little glorification, either. The exposed evaluative position is rarely rigidly defended—there is, instead, a search for neutral ground.

There are several routes to the "neutral ground" they seek.[13] One is to *deny that there are real differences* of interest among men, and this often follows from their position on the reality of a true public interest. Another is to stress the reconciliation of apparent differences by *bringing the conflicting partisans together*. Johnson discloses this penchant in his belief that the "race problem" might be solved by bringing the parties together. Discrimination in certain areas is "not the American way of doing it," he says, and, in a pleading and rather desperate tone, he adds, "But I should think there should be some way of bringing it out between them." It is his vain hope that the Negroes could be persuaded to accept a segregated arrangement, and thus relieve him of what is really a rather bad conscience. DeAngelo gives the idea of bringing labor and management together a classic expression. He has just said that he believes union pressure is partly responsible for the high cost of living, and continues: "Well, I don't know; the union—they won't press for wages unless, y'know, things keep goin' up. I mean, [pause] I think the government, big business, unions—they gotta get together and straighten the thing out, as best they could. Y'know what I mean? Talk it over; see what the hell they can do about it. [pause] I mean, I don't know, it's gotta be settled some way —if—I think the only way they can settle it, they gotta get together and settle it."

But for these men in their difficult tasks of suggesting policy, the main device is to pursue a kind of *centralist* tendency, something like the one described by Alfred Jones in Akron, Ohio, some twenty-five years ago.[14] Given three policy choices the men will choose the "middle" one; given two choices they will yield a little on each, borrow something from the other, obscure the differences.

---

[13] For a discussion of basic roots as well as routes of this flexible non-doctrinaire theme in America, see Erik Erikson, *Childhood and Society* (New York: Norton, 1950), pp. 275–277.

[14] Alfred W. Jones, *Life, Liberty, and Property* (Philadelphia: Lippincott, 1941).

You see this in the concluding statements of the three men on the unions; it is true of many other situations as well. This holds for "feeling strongly," too. On tests where they are given an option to state how strongly they agree or disagree with a proposition, they tend to squash their feelings down into a middle range. Inevitably this produces a certain uniformity of opinion, roughs off the edges and idiosyncrasies, factors that may have caused Bryce to remark how "Americans appear to vary less, in fundamentals, from what may be called the dominant American type, than Englishmen, Germans, Frenchmen, Spaniards, or Italians do from any types which could be taken as the dominant type in any of those nations."[15]

Something might be said here of how this search for neutral ground, this tendency to try to adjust between apparently disparate positions, produces, in the end, that minimal speculation and originality characteristic of Eastport's common man. If everyone is trying to be a broker of opinion and to bring other people's opinions into harmony, none will range far in the pursuit of new ideas. In a way, this represents the substitution of "goodwill," a quality Laski says Americans believe will solve all problems,[16] for hard thinking. For the functioning of a political system, of course, both are required, but in Eastport, at least, the balance is in favor of goodwill; the common man there is likely to be only a middle man.

Perhaps this is a condition of any successful democracy; perhaps it is more specially American. A hundred and twenty years ago, Tocqueville argued that "the great privilege of the Americans does not consist in being more enlightened than other nations, but in being able to repair the faults they may commit."[17] We are able to acknowledge our mistakes and to correct our errors—something incompatible with rigid thinking. If, as Riesman says, there are penalties to the loss of inner-direction and the conscientious knowledge of what is right, flexibility and the lack of rigidity are the contrasting benefits.

DIFFERENTIATION

There is an economy in stereotypes, says Walter Lippmann. "For the attempt to see things freshly and in detail, rather than as

---

[15] James Bryce, *The American Commonwealth* (4th ed.; New York: Macmillan, 1910), II, 886.

[16] Harold Laski, *The American Democracy* (New York: Viking, 1948), p. 708.

[17] Alexis de Tocqueville, *op. cit.*, I, 231.

types and generalities, is exhausting, and among busy affairs practically out of the question."[18] Stereotypes are the mind's shorthand for dealing with complexities. They have two aspects: they are much blunter than reality; they are shaped to fit a man's preferences and prejudgments. Thus two principles are involved: differentiation or its lack, and biased preferential perception. "An attitude toward Russia may be focused upon a highly amorphous subjective impression of that country or upon a highly differentiated one. . . . The object of an attitude varies in its differentiation. . . ."[19] This is our problem for the moment.

There are many reasons for a blunted differentiation, of which we distinguish three: insufficient information (cognitive bluntness), blockage by strong emotion, especially anger (emotional bluntness), and remoteness from one's own beliefs and values (ideological bluntness). Dempsey, who never advanced beyond the sixth grade, illustrates the first of these. He says the word "government" suggests to him, "Well, someone to govern, to rule over, probably [pause] to guide people in the right way." While interesting for many reasons, not the least of which is the passive and dependent tone of this response, it is certainly a blunt and undifferentiated idea of government. The next "witness," a week later, said: "To me it means organization. [pause] It brings to mind, at least, a society which is regulated, that is, it's governed by a set of rules and a governing body." This is our friend Flynn speaking, a white-collar worker who has completed high school. Dempsey's comment has the bluntness of tautology, with the "guidance" feature added; Flynn breaks down the idea into three, still large but more explicit ideas: organization, the rules of law, an organ through which government acts. Flynn goes on later to develop these ideas, while Dempsey has little more to say. (I ask him what kinds of things the government ought to do, and he responds, "That I couldn't say; I'm not up on that.") This is what we call a cognitive difference in differentiation based upon information, but there are others.

Rapuano, a volcanic man with the burden of his Americanism lying heavily across his broad but stooping shoulders, answers the same question, after a pause and some heavy breathing, as follows, "Government? What do I think of?" He pauses again. "Politics, for

---

[18] Walter Lippmann, *Public Opinion* (New York: Penguin, 1946), p. 66.
[19] M. Brewster Smith, Jerome S. Bruner, and Robert W. White, *Opinions and Personality* (New York: Wiley, 1956), pp. 34–35.

one thing. Oh, yes, [pause] politics is about all I could think of. [pause] There ain't anything that's unpolitical that's not—that's government. Everything that seems to be government is politics." I ask him what kind of things the government ought to do, and he answers after another short pause: "Well, that's hard to say. I mean, I'm not that smart. Let's see what the hell they should do." But he can find things for them to do; he almost finished high school, has an active mind, and is interested in political affairs. What accounts for the bluntness in this case, of course, is the emotional reverberations that echo so loudly in his mind that, so to speak, "he cannot hear himself think." This, then, is a case of emotional bluntness.

This pattern is marked in the cases of four men (Rapuano, Ferrera, Sokolsky, and Kuchinsky) and observable in others. But as we said above, in Eastport the level of indignation is generally low; the flow of affect is moderate; the responses to "things in the news that made me mad" are not very "mad"; the tendency to avoid blaming keeps emotion at a modest level; the adjustive strategies make the nursing of anger dysfunctional, and all in all emotional bluntness is kept at a minimum. As a system, the American low-keyed political style keeps open the windows of perception and differentiation to a remarkable degree.

The third type of failure to differentiate, ideological bluntness, is based on the principle that the further away from a person's beliefs and values a group of objects lies, the less significant do the differences between those objects appear. Rokeach illustrates this with the difficulty a follower of Senator McCarthy had in distinguishing between Communists, Socialists, and advanced liberals.[20] In the same way, in 1961 liberals found the distinction between positions held by the *National Review*, the John Birch Society, and Barry Goldwater hard to discern, although conservatives saw important differences. Now, it is significant that a search through the discussion of "subversives in America," "big business," "Russia," "the causes of war and poverty," and other areas of discourse where rejected groups or conspiracies or evil systems have their abode does not discover much blunting of perception. The measure for blunted differentiation includes: (1) an increased use of derogatory labels instead of descriptive terms, such as "a crazy bunch," "madmen," "bloodsuckers," and so forth; (2) a substitute of programs of quick violent action prior to, or probably instead of,

---

[20] Milton Rokeach, *op. cit.*, pp. 38–39.

description and analysis; (3) dismissal of a problem or group with a phrase, refusal to treat it seriously, contemptuous withdrawal. Only in the case of the domestic Communists was there much evidence of undifferentiated perception and quick prescription— and not by any means in all such cases. Here, for example, is the way Costa begins his discussion of subversive elements in America. Costa is a frequent and militant defender of "the American way." He says:

Well, I think there are too many. Too many leaks, too much of our secret information gets out. I don't know whether that's because we're a democracy or whether there's just people—I mean, I can think of several things, like the Rosenbergs, for one, like that Dr. Fuchs over in England. . . . Are you asking me does Russia have an organized [group]? I think they do.

In the context of Costa's usual level of differentiation there is no loss of differentiated thinking here, no ideological bluntness. Thus the over-all impression (the reactions of about half of the men to domestic Communism excepted) is one of continuity of perception, differentiation, conceptualization—each at his own level—as one moves from areas of belief and support to areas of disbelief and opposition.

Differentiation, as the anthropologists tell us with respect to language, is a measure of social focus, a clue to what the society cares about. Speaking loosely, and about this stratum of lower-middle- and upper-working-class men, I would say the American political mind is differentiated more in terms of rights than duties —almost all men mention and illustrate the various rights that Americans enjoy; they had more trouble in explaining the nature of citizenly or patriotic duties—here the terms were more global and more derivative. Secondly, their capacities to distinguish and deal intellectually with the problems of race relations were greater than those of interclass relations—they had thought more about the one than about the other. Third, their concepts of appropriate means of social adjustment, of how to behave in different situations, are elaborate and clear in their minds—much more elaborate and clear than their pictures of themselves. If one may be elliptical to make the point: each person knows more about *what* he should do than about *who* he is. The American tendency to objectify, rather than subjectify the world is reflected here. They have differentiated and easily articulated concepts about work, money, and consumption, but their conceptualization of their religious beliefs, the duties of the church, and the purposes of life are blunt and unsophisticated. It is as though they put forth a special effort to homogenize all religious and moral thought. When it came to commentaries on the dogmatic beliefs of their churches, the products were indeed a meager gleaning; and, as we noted before, their time perspectives are differentiated by short-range matters, which may account, in a way, for the optimism of the American outlook. It is only in a perspective that encompasses the period of death that a profound sense of tragedy is likely to develop.

We have said that the political mind of Eastport tends to emphasize one of the ingredients of an explanation, the initial conditions, at the expense of the other, the universal laws. Eastportians tend to morselize their knowledge rather than to contextualize it, thus losing much of the significance or meaning of an event. On some intercultural ideologizing scale, I would guess that they would be "low"; they use events to confirm or defend a world view less frequently than others. They avoid exposed positions, yield quickly in an argument, seek middle ground, and compromise where they can. And while they often use stereotypes and blunted perceptions of events, these tend to flow from lack of information rather than from disagreement or anger.

There are other characteristics of their thought with consequences for the political system: they rarely *organize* their views. Kuchinsky begins his interview as follows: "We have a lot of problems today, and, um, in this country concerning the other side, [Europe] uh, which I think, uh, this country's really gone overboard on a lot of things—I mean throwing a lot of money away." About four sentences later he is speaking of the rent increase in Hilltop—it is a kind of stream of consciousness. On the other hand Flynn begins his interview: "The major problems? Of course that means defining, Number One, what the major problems are. They're in two areas, I guess, foreign and domestic." He turns to the domestic first and discusses this before he moves on for a fuller treatment of the foreign problems. The group mode is closer to Kuchinsky than it is to Flynn; there is an almost complete lack of an effort to think through a question before attempting to answer it; it is a rare moment when a man speaks of the "areas," "levels," "stages," or "phases" of a problem, or uses the apparatus of analysis of component elements of a complex affair, treating them one by one.

These men rarely acknowledge a difference between the speculative and the known, making a point of the *differences in certainty* or familiarity. One blends into the other without a break. There is no *strategy* to their discourse, no attempt to persuade through such a logical development that if one admits one point, the next must follow. In short, their discussion is not self-conscious, not planned; it has a kind of "free form" associative quality. In this sense they are open to new information, open to experience. Without the blockages of strong emotion, or the walls of ideological defensiveness, their minds, like the society itself, seem pluralistic, with both liberal and conservative roots to which new ideas can attach themselves and grow.

CHAPTER FOUR

THE DEBATING MODEL

S HOULD THE UNITED STATES enter into agreements with the Soviet Union and others to stop the spread of nuclear weapons? Should there be an end to the military draft? Should federal funds for education be withheld from schools showing no desegregation progress? These were a few of the issues in the 1968 presidential election. They were also issues in the 1956 election. In the following selection, Stanley Kelley, Jr., analyzes how issues get "debated" in a national presidential campaign, using the second Eisenhower–Stevenson contest as an illustration.

Formal debating situations in which the candidates confront one another before an audience and argue over a proposition are rare in politics. In 1968 negotiations among the candidates for television debates like the Kennedy–Nixon ones in 1960 broke down, primarily because Nixon did not want to risk his large lead in the public opinion polls. Possibly we will see formal debates in future campaigns, but in a larger sense every campaign is a kind of debate. Ideally, campaigns highlight the differences between candidates so as to enable voters to make a rational choice between them. In this way the citizen's mental task is vastly simplified: he can concentrate his attention on the relatively few topics which divide the contenders. Thus the debating model points toward one social technique for adapting the tasks of political choice to the capacities of citizens for political thinking.

POLICY DISCUSSION IN POLITICAL CAMPAIGNING

STANLEY KELLEY, JR.

If it is obvious that rational electoral decisions presuppose the ability of rival parties and candidates to make their views known, it should be equally obvious that what voters hear is at least as important as whether they hear. Discussion—as anyone who has participated in it well knows—may obscure as well as illuminate the grounds for rational choice, may favor nonrational as well as rational behavior. No assessment of the value of discussion in campaigns, therefore, can fail to take into account the way in which politicians shape and mold its content.

This conclusion is apt to be somewhat disturbing to the reformer, for if the content of campaign discussion is weighed and found wanting, no remedial action readily suggests itself. Given the constitutional protection of free speech and publication, it is clear that no authority exists for enforcing any particular pattern of communication on campaigners; one that contributes to rational electoral decisions must somehow develop naturally out of the competition of parties and candidates for electoral support. The democrat and civil libertarian is tempted, therefore, to dismiss any further consideration of what is a potentially serious flaw in his political philosophy by assuming campaign discussion to be valuable, whatever form it may take. Not to do so would be an apparent capitulation to those who have argued that free discussion of public issues can in practice be either an evil or worthless.

In fact, however, he is faced with a problem, not a dilemma. Anyone who examines the course of discussion in campaigns can hardly fail to conclude that it is often as well-designed to subvert as

Reprinted from Stanley Kelley, Jr., *Political Campaigning: Problems in Creating an Informed Electorate* (Washington, D.C.: The Brookings Institution, 1960) pp. 50–84, by permission of the publisher and author.

to facilitate rational voting behavior. What candidates say frequently lacks relevance to any decision voters face, exposes differences in the views of candidates imperfectly, and is filled with evasions, ambiguities, and distortions. But campaign communication is not all of a piece. Its content varies with the form campaigning takes, a fact that has important implications for those who would like to see a change in its character. It is the purpose of the present chapter, therefore, to analyze in detail this relationship between form and content in campaigning, particularly as it affects the discussion of policy issues.

POLICY ISSUES IN CAMPAIGN SPEECHES, 1956

This analysis can appropriately begin by examining the way policy questions were treated in the candidates' speeches in the presidential campaign of 1956. Of all the policy pronouncements made in the course of campaigning, those made by the candidates are given the most serious attention by the electorate and are regarded as most responsible. Where political parties show as little discipline in policy matters as they do in the United States, it could hardly be otherwise. The policy statements made by the candidates in 1956 cannot, of course, necessarily be taken as representative of those in all campaigns, but their choice for the purpose of illustrating the way candidates deal with issues is at least a defensible one. There was little that was bitter and almost nothing that could be called scurrilous in the second Eisenhower–Stevenson race for the Presidency. On the contrary, it was at the time remarked upon as unusually "high level." An analysis of the quality of campaign discussion based on it, therefore, is unlikely to lead to unnecessarily pessimistic or alarmist conclusions.

Nonetheless, to measure policy discussion as it was carried on in the Eisenhower–Stevenson speeches against an ideal standard is not reassuring. Much of the time, both candidates described their policy positions in terms so general that their statements lacked any clear relation to issues on which voters had to make decisions. Both were for peace, social welfare, full justice for farmers, honest government, a strong national defense, the expansion of civil liberties, full employment, the development of individual talents, a vigorous economy, a flourishing world trade, and a large number of other objectives of similarly general appeal. They voiced their allegiance to these ideals again and again. Sometimes they did so in slightly different words, and sometimes one mentioned goals that were not mentioned by the other, but at no time did either candidate declare himself to be opposed to any statement of fundamental belief that his opponent had advanced. This kind of expression by candidates of their basic policy objectives has a place in campaign discussion, for voters need to know if they differ in this respect. At the point it becomes clear that they do not, however—and this point was reached rather early in the 1956 campaign—such discussion of fundamentals ceases to have relevance to the voter's choice.

Indeed, the two candidates enunciated clearly-defined pro and con positions on only a few policy issues in the course of the entire campaign. Farm policy was one of these. Governor Stevenson advocated government support for basic farm commodities at 90 percent of parity. President Eisenhower opposed guaranteed price supports at that level. Policy on H-bomb testing was another. Stevenson said that the American government should initiate action to bring an end to hydrogen bomb tests. Eisenhower said that it should not. The latter issue was perhaps the best discussed of the campaign. While the statements of the two candidates on farm policy had a more or less static character—they simply stated and repeated what they apparently believed to be their best arguments—their discussion of H-bomb testing showed a kind of progression. As it continued, they defined their positions more and more carefully, clarified their differences, and began to subject each other's reasoning to criticism.

Governor Stevenson, who had previously spoken on the subject of H-bomb testing, introduced it into the 1956 campaign in his address to the American Legion Convention in Los Angeles. He regretted the fact, he told Legion members on that occasion, that his proposal to "halt further testing of large nuclear devices . . . conditioned upon adherence to a similar policy by other atomic powers,"[1] had been so casually dismissed by the administration. He left the matter stand at this, however, until the President termed his statement, some time later, a "theatrical gesture." Then the press reported in mid-October that Stevenson had decided to give the issue major emphasis.

This decision taken, Stevenson defined his proposal with more precision. He now said that he favored a halt on all further tests by any nation of larger-sized nuclear weapons and advocated that the United States take the lead in establishing this world policy. He

---

[1] *New York Times,* Sept. 7, 1956.

would not go further than this. His proposal implied no halt in the production of nuclear weapons and no reduction of nuclear weapon stockpiles. It did not mean that the United States should abandon tests of smaller nuclear weapons. It did not mean that the United States should halt preparation for H-bomb tests.

Having stated his position, Stevenson began also to state the reasons that, in his view, favored its adoption. He contended that a moratorium on further testing would: (1) leave the United States superior to the Russians in atomic technology; (2) prevent the spread of H-bomb technology to nations other than Russia, Great Britain, and the United States; (3) win the respect of neutralist or uncommitted nations; (4) break the United States–Soviet Union stalemate in negotiations on disarmament; and (5) diminish air pollution from radioactive fallout and the dangers fallout involved for health and heredity. The proposal was a practical one, said Stevenson, because an agreement to stop tests would be self-enforcing. H-bomb explosions violating the agreement would be detectable without inspection.

President Eisenhower at first appeared intent on avoiding involvement in controversy. On September 19 he told a campaign audience that: "We cannot prove wise and strong by any such simple device as suspending, unilaterally, our H-bomb tests."[2] In his press conference on October 12, he advised reporters that he had said his last words on the matter.

But this decision did not stand. In later statements the President gave reasons for rejecting Stevenson's proposal. In the first place, he argued, stopping the tests was less important than stopping the use of nuclear weapons in a war, and this latter objective could be accomplished only as a part of a general disarmament agreement. Secondly, the Soviet superiority in manpower meant that the United States must at all costs preserve its superiority in nuclear weapons. Since tests require long preparation, the United States could fall far behind the Russians in nuclear research by the time an explosion was detected, if it should halt its tests and test preparations. Thirdly, the danger to health from radioactive fallout attending the tests was not serious. He cited a report of the National Academy of Science in support of this contention. Fourthly, further tests would allow progress toward a "clean" bomb, that is, one creating less fallout. Finally, the assumption that all tests could be detected by monitoring was unverified.

---

[2] *Public Papers of the Presidents of the United States, Dwight D. Eisenhower, 1956,* p. 786.

This analysis of the course the argument took could be carried further, for each of the candidates suggested new evidence for his contentions as these were subjected to criticism by his opponent. It has been carried far enough, however, to show that policy issues can sometimes be discussed in campaigns with reasonable clarity. Stevenson's introduction of the issue of H-bomb testing into the campaign may have been—probably was—politically inexpedient, since the matter had been given little public attention beforehand. It is the form the discussion took that is under consideration here, however, and it should be evident that, in this instance, discussion both defined a choice for voters and gave them a great deal of information useful in choosing.

This last judgment must be qualified somewhat, because the H-bomb issue was in reality discussed on two quite different levels. The arguments summarized above are drawn from a few of Stevenson's speeches, a memorandum he prepared, a memorandum released by the White House, and some of President Eisenhower's statements in press conferences. In many of their campaign addresses, however, both candidates presented their cases in a quite different fashion—the speeches of one candidate seemed often not so much to reflect the content of his rival's as to refract it. In answer to Stevenson's statement that he wanted to suspend testing "conditioned upon adherence by other atomic powers," President Eisenhower derided the idea of stopping our testing program unilaterally. Both candidates relied heavily on unsupported assertion in their treatment of the subject, and frequently ignored opposition reasoning.

It has already been noted that discussion defining issues as clearly as that which centered on H-bomb testing was rare in the 1956 campaign. More often, points on which differences in the policy views of the two candidates might have been clarified never were, because one or the other failed to take any notice of what his opponent was saying. At different times Governor Stevenson criticized the Eisenhower foreign-aid program as putting too much emphasis on military aid, and too little emphasis on economic aid. He attacked the administration's handling of the security investigations of federal employees. He called the President's defense strategy an "all or nothing" policy, implying an improper balance of defense expenditures. He attacked the administration's information policy. There is no reason to believe that the policies he had questioned were not susceptible to discussion or that such discussion might not have contributed to public understanding of the reasons such policies had been undertaken. In none of these cases, however, did President Eisenhower acknowledge that there had been any questioning. Candidates act as people professing hardness-of-hearing sometimes do. They hear what they want to hear, whether it is shouted or whispered.

President Eisenhower's silence was not without advantage to his cause. By not answering these criticisms, he avoided giving them added publicity. The President's failure to answer was also in some ways helpful to Governor Stevenson. He could capitalize on dissatisfaction attending the governmental actions he criticized without having to specify what he would do, or would have done, differently. Failure to answer meant that both candidates, however, could leave their positions in these areas essentially ambiguous. And they did.

Nor is this the only way in which ambiguity enters policy discussion in campaigns. The draft controversy is one of the best examples that 1956 provides of an issue that, while hotly disputed by both sides, never drew any clear line of difference between them. Governor Stevenson initiated the dispute in his address to the American Legion. As he developed it subsequently, Stevenson's position on the draft can be fairly stated as follows: Military thinkers foresee a need for a preponderance of highly professional units in the defense forces of the future. While an immediate end to the draft may not be feasible, changes in military technology "may well mean that we will need and want in the foreseeable future to turn to a method other than the draft" to recruit military personnel.[3] Thus, there should be a "fresh look" at the military manpower situation, for it might well indicate that the burdens of the draft on the nation's youth could be avoided and American defenses strengthened at one and the same time.

Questioned in press conference, President Eisenhower said that he saw no chance to end the draft in the immediate future. In his view, an end to the draft "under world conditions of today" would weaken American defense forces, encourage neutralist sentiment abroad, and discourage allies whom the United States was trying to get to maintain their own draft armies. All this meant continuance of the draft for the immediate future, although "every family naturally hopes for the day when it might be possible" to end compulsory conscription.[4]

As the campaign drew to a close, talk about the draft became

[3] Address delivered October 18, 1956. See Adlai E. Stevenson, *The New America* (1957), p. 61.

[4] Address delivered September 19, 1956. See *Public Papers . . . , Dwight D. Eisenhower, 1956*, p. 786.

more and more compressed into two contrasting themes. Governor Stevenson appealed to a hope that the draft could be ended and accused his opponent of "negativism." President Eisenhower held it to be against common sense to think that a stronger defense and an end to the draft were compatible aims. The volume and intensity of the words that were poured into propagating these appeals should not obscure the fact that the issue was never really joined. The disagreement—if there really was one—would appear to have been about when and under what conditions the draft could be ended. Yet nothing was said by either candidate that would not have permitted him with consistency and political decorum to (1) ask for an end of the draft, or (2) not ask for an end to the draft, in the period 1956–1960. Some deductions about the motives and characters of the candidates, but little notion of their differences on draft policy, may be possible from an observation of their conduct during this dispute.

This kind of ambiguity in the policy views of the two candidates was frequently complicated further by distortion. A voter who had asked their help in piecing together an account of the nation's recent political history, as one would fit together a jigsaw puzzle, might easily have quit his task in frustration and hopeless confusion. Each would have offered him pieces apparently destined for the same place in the puzzle, yet of entirely different shapes and colors. When the voter asked for other pieces needed to fill quite obvious gaps, he would have found that neither had any suggestion regarding where he might find them.

The needs of the nation's schools were, for example, one of the subjects most thoroughly discussed by both candidates in 1956. Both advocated federal aid to education. President Eisenhower told voters that his program for school aid had been rejected by the opposition in Congress and promised to ask the new Congress for legislation that would make up for the lost time.[5] Governor Stevenson charged that the President had failed to take any decisive action to meet school problems in his first term of office and that "the Republicans in Congress defeated a bill for federal aid to education."[6]

Thus the Eisenhower and Stevenson speeches succeeded in giving conflicting accounts of the congressional battle over aid to education, while they left the voter largely ignorant about what had actually happened. The statements each made were technically true,

---

[5] Address delivered October 9, 1956, *ibid.*, p. 874.
[6] *New York Times*, Sept. 23, 1956.

but what they said was less important for a realistic understanding of the school issue than what they did not say. The school program proposed by the Eisenhower administration and the Democratic program that "the Republicans in Congress defeated" differed significantly in only one respect—the formula by which funds were to be distributed to the states. The speeches of neither candidate gave any hint of this, nor of the fact that this difference had been largely compromised by the time the school bill came up for a final vote. They said nothing, moreover, of the crucial role played in the whole controversy by the Powell amendment, which would have denied funds to states maintaining segregated school systems. President Eisenhower had opposed this amendment, as had Southern Democrats. Many Northern Democrats had supported it, although doing so meant almost certain defeat for the school aid bill, and ninety-six Republicans in the House of Representatives had voted for it, but against the school bill as amended. But none of this could have been learned from the Eisenhower–Stevenson discussion of the issue.

It would not be too extreme to say that distortion was so integral a part of the cases presented by the two candidates in the 1956 campaign, that the campaign was in large part repetitious assertion of fictitious "issues." Each of the candidates reserved some of his most biting phrases for attacks on positions his opponent had never taken. Governor Stevenson, for example, again and again characterized the Republicans as complacent, fatuously complacent, fatuously optimistic, negative, smug, and self-righteous, insensitive to human problems, and purveyors of Pollyana politics. On one occasion, he observed that "the political lines in this country are now sharply drawn between those who are satisfied with things exactly as they are and those who feel, on the other hand, that there is still a tremendous lot to be done in America and in the world."[7] Presumably he had not heard President Eisenhower say, as he did in one speech, "Our task is far from done. New problems, and critical ones, rise before us."[8] Nor that "There will never be room for boasting . . . until there is not a single needy person left in the United States, when distress and disease have been eliminated."[9]

This is not to say that Stevenson's views were represented

---

[7] Address delivered October 18, 1956. See Stevenson, *The New America*, p. 59.

[8] Address delivered September 19, 1956. See *Public Papers . . . , Dwight D. Eisenhower, 1956*, p. 784.

[9] Address delivered October 1, 1956, *ibid.*, p. 832.

with any greater accuracy. The Democratic candidate, as leader of the opposition, naturally pointed to unsolved problems, but he also said, "We are told that America is prosperous. And it is—in part. We are thankful and we are proud."[10] President Eisenhower, however, professed to have heard the Democrats tell voters "you are not prosperous, you are starving—you are poor—we are not working."[11] And he often characterized the men to whom he had gratuitously attributed these words as "wailing politicians" who were painting, for partisan purposes, a false picture of gloom and doom.

What happened in the Eisenhower–Stevenson discussion of policy issues may be summed up at this point. Each candidate defined his position in terms so general that it became almost impossible to distinguish it from that of his opponent. Moderate differences that in fact characterized the two candidates' policy orientations were misrepresented or ignored. Each of them instead argued the virtues of his self-defined moderate program versus an extreme and largely fictitious one that he attributed to his opponent. Campaign discussion of policy questions was not one in which issues and differences were mutually acknowledged and defined. Rather it involved the independent and systematic propagation of competing notions of what the differences and issues were.

Policy discussion may not assume this pattern in all campaign speeches, but it undoubtedly does so very often. Lazarsfeld, Berelson, and their colleagues found a similar one in comprehensive analyses of campaign propaganda in the presidential campaigns of 1940 and 1948. In those campaigns, each side attacked its opponent's record much more often than it defended its own. Both "tended to 'talk past each other,' almost as though they were participating in two different elections."[12] Both devoted a great deal of time to discussing vaguely phrased goals, and little to specifying the methods by which such goals were to be realized. But the pattern has been best described, perhaps, by James Bryce:

> The object of each party naturally is to put forward as many good political issues as it can, claiming for itself the merit of having always been on the popular side. Anyone who should read the campaign literature of the Republicans would fancy that they were opposed to the

---

[10] *New York Times*, Sept. 4, 1956.

[11] Address delivered October 29, 1956. See *Public Papers* . . . , *Dwight D. Eisenhower, 1956*, p. 1056.

[12] Bernard Berelson, Paul F. Lazarsfeld, and William N. McPhee, *Voting* (1954), p. 236.

Democrats on many important points. When he took up the Democratic speeches and pamphlets he would be again struck by the serious divergences between the parties, which however would seem to arise, not on the points raised by the Republicans, but on other points which the Republicans had not referred to. In other words, the aim of each party is to force on its antagonist certain issues which the antagonist rarely accepts, so that although there is a vast deal of discussion and declamation on political topics, there are few on which either party directly traverses the doctrines of the other. Each pummels, not his true enemy, but a stuffed figure set up to represent that enemy.[13]

CAMPAIGN DISCUSSION: FORM AND SUBSTANCE

Because the speeches of the candidates are so central to campaign discussion, they tend to set the tone for campaign discussion in its entirety, leaving as the dominant impression in the observer's mind a peculiar pattern of both avoidance and manufacture of issues. That impression can easily be misleading, for the pattern is not an all-pervading one. In the 1956 campaign, for example, the issue of H-bomb testing was discussed somewhat differently than were other policy questions, although not so differently in the speeches as in other forms of communication. This latter fact suggests, if but faintly, that there may be a general relation between the medium used to distribute campaign appeals and the nature of the appeal distributed—that form affects substance. This relationship was also suggested by the analysis of debates in an earlier chapter, and the more one examines the way in which policy discussion is carried on in different media and in different situations, the stronger the suggestion becomes.

Policy discussion through radio and television spot announcements, for example, reflects the same basic tendencies present in campaign speeches, but exaggerates them to a point bordering on the grotesque. A brief analysis of a one spot announcement used by the Republicans in 1952 will illustrate this fact. Its text was as follows:

Voice: Mr. Eisenhower, what about the high cost of living?
Eisenhower: My wife, Mamie, worries about the same thing. I tell her it's our job to change that on November 4.

The information contained in these two sentences can be quickly summarized: General Eisenhower and his wife are aware that

---

[13] James Bryce, *The American Commonwealth* (1890), Vol. II, p. 208.

prices are high. They are concerned about the fact. The General, if elected, proposes to do something about it.

Though the statements of policy intentions in candidates' speeches are often highly ambiguous, ambiguity could hardly be greater than it is here. The announcement gives no notion at all of what kind of action Mr. Eisenhower might take, what the advantages and disadvantages might be of any measures he had in mind, why he would favor these measures over others. The advertising agency that had prepared the spot meant it to show only the General's "complete comprehension" of a problem and "his determination to do something about it when elected." He would thus inspire loyalty "without prematurely committing himself to any strait-jacketing answer."[14]

Nor could any statement have disregarded opposition arguments more completely. Standing alone as it does, it suggests that General Eisenhower must make a point of his concern about high living costs because his opponent is not similarly concerned. To appreciate the fact that it does carry such an implication, one need only consider how greatly the persuasive impact of the announcement would have been reduced, had it given any indication that Governor Stevenson was also expressing his determination to do something about the evils of inflation. In spot announcements, the tendency of candidates to talk past each other reaches an extreme.

General statements about the treatment of policy issues in campaign literature are of more limited applicability than those about policy discussion either in campaign speeches or in spot announcements. Considering the body of literature that was distributed in 1956 as a whole, one would conclude that discussion of policy problems in it closely paralleled that in the candidate's speeches. Both sides pointed with pride to their past accomplishments without describing those accomplishments very accurately or in much detail. They pledged themselves to resolve problems but failed to say how they would do so. Issues were often greatly oversimplified, history frequently misread, and statistics misused. This conclusion, however, obscures some significant deviations from this pattern in particular items of the literature. Policy discussion in the booklets, pamphlets, memoranda, leaflets, and post cards of the two parties was presented on at least two different levels.

In many instances, the appeals made were similar in charac-

---

[14] Quoted in Stanley Kelley, Jr., *Professional Public Relations and Political Power* (1956), p. 188.

ter to those in spot announcements. A Republican comic book, for example, advised that, "More people are employed today than ever before! There are 4,000,000 more jobs now in PEACE TIME than the Democrats had with their WARS!"[15] Two Democratic "score cards" stated in an equally bald fashion that the Republicans had "failed to do anything about overcrowded schools"[16] and had "tried to prevent" a one dollar minimum wage.[17] If the first statement is not to be put down as simply untrue, then it must be construed in a way that would make it equally valid to say that the Democrats had "done nothing" about the school problem. The second statement also suggests a conclusion unwarranted by the facts of the minimum wage dispute. President Eisenhower had indeed opposed a one dollar minimum wage, but he had been for raising the minimum wage to ninety cents.

There were other cases, however, where the campaign literature distributed in 1956 went further than the speeches in clarifying policy issues and the problems out of which they arose. This could be said of a number of the memoranda on policy questions prepared by Adlai Stevenson, and, on the Republican side, of Secretary Ezra T. Benson's pamphlet article, "Farmers at the Crossroads." The authors of these pieces attempted to show in detail the causes of the problems they discussed, to suggest remedies for them, to contrast these remedies with those advocated by the other side, and to justify the policy positions they advanced.

Campaign discussion as it occurred in the press conferences of the candidates followed a course still less like that which developed in the speeches. Under questioning by members of the press, Eisenhower and Stevenson modified considerably some of the themes on which they played in other propaganda. They found it more difficult to evade particular subjects and less easy to state their positions ambiguously. They found it necessary to address themselves to arguments made by the opposition and to accept or reject responsibility for what their supporters were saying.

The so-called "tight money" policy of the Eisenhower administration, for example, was subjected to continued and vigorous attack throughout the 1956 campaign by Adlai Stevenson, who said it meant higher interest rates for farmers, small businessmen, and home builders. The strength of his attack seemed to indicate that

---

[15] Republican National, Congressional, and Senatorial Committees, *Forward with Eisenhower-Nixon.*

[16] *What the G.O.P. Has Done to Joe Smith.*

[17] *Pocket Score Card, What the GOPs Did to You!*

he meant to do something about tight money if elected, and therefore raised questions about the relationship he meant to establish with the Federal Reserve System. The answers to these questions cannot be found in his speeches, but in a press conference he made it clear that he would ask for no change in the formal position of independence of the System. "Would you, if elected," a reporter of the Buffalo *Evening News* asked the Governor, "support and continue an independent Federal Reserve System and, particularly, the independence of the Federal Reserve System's Open Market Committee?" Stevenson's answer was " . . . on the basis of what information I have with respect to the working of the Federal Reserve System, I would suggest no legislation to alter the present position of the Federal Reserve System with respect to the Treasury Department and also with respect to its Open Market Committee."[18]

President Eisenhower's responses to questions from the press also qualified the meaning of statements he had made in campaign addresses. In one speech the President posed this question to his audience: "What do we want this country to be like as the next four years unfold?"[19] Part of the picture of America he himself constantly kept before him, he said, was "An America where the greatest possible government efficiency allows the lowest possible government costs—and, hence, lower taxes."[20] When a reporter asked the President in his next press conference to specify how soon such tax cuts might be expected, however, his answer made the prospect for lower taxes seem considerably less hopeful than it might have appeared to the audience from his speech. The chances for tax reduction were not "bright or something right around the corner." Efficiency in government would open up "the avenue by which tax reductions will properly be someday accomplished," but the President did not mean, he said, that they would come "right away, not at all."[21]

It was in a press conference, too, that the President declined to endorse a line of argument that was being pursued by the Republican National, senatorial, and congressional committees. This was their comic book charge, already noted, that identified past wars with the Democratic party. Would the President, asked a reporter of the Louisville *Courier-Journal*, agree that there had been

[18] *New York Times,* Sept. 18, 1956.
[19] Address delivered October 1, 1956. See *Public Papers . . . , Dwight D. Eisenhower, 1956,* p. 840.
[20] *Ibid.,* p. 841.
[21] *Ibid.,* p. 858.

Democratic wars? President Eisenhower's slightly embarrassed answer was: "They may be thinking of something I don't know anything about, but I don't believe when America gets into war we can afford to call it anything but our war."[22]

These few examples of the way issues are treated in press conferences are not, of course, meant to show that press conferences at present have any substantial impact on the character of campaign discussion considered in its entirety. Their impact is relatively slight for at least two reasons. In the first place, although they allow questioning, they rarely involve cross-questioning. A subject of inquiry may be opened but often cannot be pursued very far. Secondly, candidates tend to grant few press conferences. In 1956 President Eisenhower did continue the regular presidential press conference into the campaign period, meeting the press six times, but Adlai Stevenson, after his nomination, held only two press conferences not limited as to subject matter. In the 1952 campaign, Stevenson held only one press conference, Eisenhower none. What is of interest here, however, is that an examination of the texts of candidate press conferences reveals a different kind of discussion than that found in the speeches.

Something happens also, as has already been argued, when policy discussion involves face-to-face debates between candidates. It is not possible to illustrate this fact by comparing the treatment of issues in the 1956 Eisenhower–Stevenson speeches, with their treatment in an Eisenhower–Stevenson debate, since, of course, none occurred. Comparing policy discussion in two debates of the 1956 New York, senatorial race with that in the Eisenhower–Stevenson speeches, however, may give some indication of the way such discussion is modified in the debating situation. Such a comparison, though not ideal for the purposes of the present analysis, provides a reasonably satisfactory basis for it. The New York senatorial candidates (Jacob Javits, then Attorney General of New York State, and Mayor Robert Wagner) held policy views substantially like those of their respective parties' presidential aspirants, particularly on the two issues they met to debate—civil rights and foreign policy.

There was a striking difference in the treatment of the civil rights question in the two cases. Eisenhower and Stevenson emphasized and re-emphasized their general concern with the problems of minorities and their general desire to see minorities win their full legal rights. They said little about any specific programs for dealing

---

[22] *Ibid.*, p. 811.

with civil rights problems. Wagner and Javits, though each affirmed his belief in equality, devoted the greater part of their opening speeches to stating in quite specific terms what they would do about civil rights questions when confronted with them in the Senate.

The records and policy stands of the two parties were less distorted in the Javits–Wagner debates than they were in the Eisenhower–Stevenson speeches. It could easily seem incredible to anyone not familiar with American campaigning to learn that neither Eisenhower nor Stevenson ever gave more than the barest hint that their respective parties were not completely united in their approaches to civil rights problems. But they did not; Stevenson constantly referred to the "Democratic" stand on civil rights, Eisenhower to the "Republican" stand. Javits and Wagner made no attempt to maintain the fiction of united parties. Their discussion proceeded, therefore, on a considerably more realistic basis.

Apparently, Javits and Wagner also found it more difficult to avoid taking positions on policy questions than did the two presidential candidates. In the foreign policy debate, for instance, Javits chided Wagner for maintaining silence on Stevenson's proposals for suspending H-bomb tests, and the Mayor felt obliged, after the debate, to issue a statement indicating his support of Mr. Stevenson. In the civil rights debate, Mayor Wagner took advantage of the debating situation to use a tactic that most probably would have fallen on deaf ears had it been used in other circumstances. In his opening speech, the Mayor made a promise and issued a challenge:

> I expect as a newly elected member of the Senate to be on the floor of the Senate on January 3rd to make the motion to change the rules so that civil rights legislation can be readily enacted. That will be a crucial motion. I make this challenge to my opponent. My opponent, even if elected to the Senate, cannot be there to take his oath and support the move against the filibuster. I now invite him to explain why he could not be in the Senate on January 3rd to help in this crucial fight, and why he has surrendered, in advance, his obligation to join in this struggle. If he doesn't answer this question I will give the answer later in the course of this debate.[23]

It is almost needless to add that Javits did attempt an explanation.[24]

---

[23] New York Times, Oct. 21, 1956.

[24] Javits' difficulties grew out of the following situation: When a vacancy occurs in the office of the Attorney General of New York, a successor is elected by the State Legislature if it is in session or appointed by the Governor

The effect of the debating situation on policy discussion in this instance, then, supports the general conclusions about those effects reached before: It led the candidates to state their positions with greater clarity and in more specific terms. It led each to acknowledge the other's position. It reduced distortion in accounts of party records and party policies.

As a final point in this analysis of form and substance in campaign communication, it should be noted that policy discussion may be variously transformed when it is presented as news. This is a fact of considerable significance in making any overall assessment of the character of campaign discussion, since much of it comes to the public only as it has been selected for, and reflected in, the news and editorial comment of newspapers, magazines, radio, and television. News presentation is not uniform for the press as a whole, but some of the ways it can shape communication between politicians and the electorate can be outlined here.

The press can, for example, help reduce distortion in campaign discussion. Editors can show half-truths for what they are by noting inaccuracies or supplying missing information in reporting a candidate's version of political history or of his opponent's views. If they follow such a policy consistently, they may not only lessen the consequences of distortion but the campaigner's temptation to distort as well. A selective presentation of facts is a useful tactic in persuasion only when those whom one is trying to persuade are not aware that there has been selection.

The press may also make it less difficult for voters to compare the policy positions taken by candidates. Reasonably full and equal coverage of campaign activities is one obvious method by which it can do so. Several tricks of display are another: shared headlines; boxes that refer the reader to opposition speeches or to other news bearing on some point made by a candidate; and, when one candidate refers to a statement of his opponent, the bracketing in of relevant material. Nor is this all. Campaign statements as they are issued by candidates do not lend themselves nicely to running

---

if it is not. Since the Republican-controlled Legislature, which could be expected to choose a Republican to succeed Javits, did not convene until after the opening session of Congress, Javits could not be sworn in as a senator at that session without allowing Democratic Governor Averell Harriman to fill his former office with a Democrat. Javits, in his reply to Wagner's question, explained his predicament to the debate audience and promised that if Harriman would pledge himself to make no appointment before the Legislature met, he, Javits, would resign his office and attend the opening session of Congress.

comparisons. At any one time, rival candidates are most often talking about quite different subjects. Such discontinuities are at least partially remedied by weekly summaries of the campaign and feature articles that give detailed accounts of what candidates have said or not said on particular issues of public policy.

Finally, the press can encourage campaigners to debate. Radio and television have done so by organizing face-to-face debates and forums, although usually these do not involve candidates. A device newspapers have used is the so-called "battle page," a page where rival candidates or party committees are given an opportunity to argue their cases in adjoining columns. These efforts have not been uniformly successful—newspaper editors in particular have mixed feelings about the value of the battle page feature. They complain that copy submitted to them is often vague, platitudinous, and dull; that party committees frequently miss the newspaper's deadline; and that the committees delegate the task of writing battle page copy to anonymous press agents. On occasion, however, the battle page has been a highly successful feature. Candidates have begun to issue and answer challenges, and, when such has been the case, reader interest has been high.

Why do candidates sometimes take and sometimes fail to take the opportunity to debate what the battle page affords them? Willingness to debate undoubtedly depends in part on the size of the audience the newspaper offers them. Moreover, the usual practice of allocating battle page space to party committees rather than directly to candidates probably discourages debate, for, given the present organization of our political parties, there are few such committees that can really presume to speak for the men on their parties' tickets. The editorial initiative taken by the newspaper is probably important also. The Sante Fe *New Mexican*, for example, decreased the number of deadlines missed by enlisting the support of the League of Women Voters for its battle page project. And the rules set up for the battle page may make a considerable difference. The Toledo *Blade* found that its battle page made better copy once the editor began to require partisan contributors to address themselves to the same general topic on the same day.

It may be useful at this point to summarize the foregoing analysis of variations in the content and character of campaign discussion. Examination of policy discussion in most campaign speeches, spot announcements, and campaign literature discloses most of the shortcomings that have led critics to conclude that campaign discussion can contribute little to the rationality of electoral decisions. When such discussion is examined as it occurs in other forms of electioneering, these shortcomings are not present to the same extent. The pattern that dominates most campaign discussion, then—a pattern in which campaigners avoid or distort differences in their views that are moderate but actual, and create fictitious issues to replace real ones—cannot be put down as an inevitable result of the campaign situation, and certain common explanations of this pattern must be regarded as less than satisfactory. The desire of campaigners to maximize votes cannot wholly account for it; presumably, campaigners are attempting to maximize political support in all forms of campaigning. The quality of the electorate cannot explain it adequately, for different forms of campaigning may be aimed at essentially the same electorate. The lack of any issues capable of discussion is not an explanation, for those that are drawn in one form of campaign discussion may be ignored in another.

How can variations in the treatment of issues through different media and in different situations be accounted for? The deliberate policy of those who manage the news media is obviously responsible for some of this variation. The technical capacities and limitations of particular media are also a factor. It is not possible to argue a complex issue in a spot announcement. Nor can a problem be so fully canvassed in a half-hour television speech as it can in a pamphlet or memorandum. An explanation of wider applicability than either of these, however, would be this: The content of campaign communication varies with changes in the relationship between campaigners and between campaigners and their audiences.

The character of discussion in campaign speeches is more understandable if one thinks of speeches as designed for an audience with a highly variable membership that tends to expose itself unequally to the propaganda of opposing sides. Candidates constantly repeat statements of general belief because the membership of their audience shifts and changes. They are in the same position a debater would be, if he were to find that the audience for his opening speech was not the same audience as that for his rebuttal. Each candidate also finds it easy to ignore what his opponent is saying, to avoid answering his opponent's challenges, and to give a distorted account of his opponent's views because he believes himself to be addressing a different audience than that reached by his opponent. To state it another way, candidates in their speeches act as if the audience for their attacks would not hear their opponents' replies, as if the audience for their opponents' criticisms would not hear their own replies, as if the attention of the campaign audience were too casual for it to discern areas of agreement and disagreement, contradictions, and inconsistencies. Thus the existence of a segmented audience and an audience of variable membership is not just an indication that competition in political communication is imperfect; it also changes the character of the communication aimed at voters.

The content of spot announcements would seem to be shaped by the same general considerations as are speeches. Spot announcements are aimed primarily at those whose interest and involvement in campaign discussion are low; that is, they are designed to capture the attention of voters who do not attend on their own initiative. They are also used in an effort to gain a differential access to this kind of audience. The so-called Republican "blitz" campaign in 1952 was, for example, timed to reach voters "at too late a date for effective Democratic rebuttal."[25] Repetition, ambiguity, distortion, and ignoring of opposition arguments, therefore, reach their height in the spot announcement, for it is meant to define the campaign for voters who, it is hoped, will have minimum exposure to alternative definitions.

The pattern discussion takes varies in different items of the campaign literature, and, once again, differences in the relationship of the campaigner to his audience would seem to account for much of this variation. In general, the shorter the piece and the wider its intended audience, the more ambiguous is its representation of the candidate's position and the more distorted is its version of records and policies. This kind of literature, which takes the form of handbills, cards, and comic books is distributed for the most part by canvassers, either at random or to their own partisans. The more reasoned statements appear in pieces of literature that are designed for opinion leaders or others who are likely to be familiar with the arguments of both sides. Another aspect of campaigner-audience relationship seems to have a bearing on the character of discussion in the campaign literature, namely, the degree of anonymity that surrounds its authorship.

If it is true that the content of discussion varies with the relationship of campaigners to their audience, one would expect discussion to show the greatest amount of deviation from its normal forms in press conferences and debates, for there the communicator-audience relationship differs radically from that

---

[25] Quoted in Kelley, *op. cit.*, p. 188.

which attends most campaigning. The greatest change in content does occur in these two situations. The pattern of discussion in the Javits–Wagner debates was not like that in most campaign speeches, and the few Eisenhower–Stevenson press conferences helped to clarify their stands on issues.

In the debate, candidates address identical audiences and each must therefore assume that what he says will be compared with what his opponent says. In the press conference, discussion becomes a dialogue between the candidate and his immediate audience. The candidate is asked to respond to his opponent's criticisms, stated in his opponent's words. He is confronted by his own past statements and is asked to explain their meaning. He is questioned regarding matters he has not seen fit to treat in his campaign speeches. He is asked to indicate agreement or disagreement with statements made by his supporters. These are tests that he normally does not face, because normally his audience cannot talk back. In most forms of campaigning, it is the campaigner who determines the subjects he will discuss and the times and places he will discuss them.

CHANGING THE CHARACTER OF POLICY DISCUSSION

The conclusions reached in the preceding section suggest some of the measures that might be taken to increase the contribution of campaign discussion to the rationality of electoral decisions. The broad strategy should be to channel campaigning into those kinds of discussion situations that support, or tend to support, rational discourse. In practice this would mean seeking to establish debates, press conferences, and forums as campaign institutions. It would also mean asking the press to report campaigns in a manner calculated to stimulate debate, reduce the temptation for politicans to resort to distortion and falsehood, and encourage the electorate to expose themselves to the arguments of both sides.

There would, of course, be obstacles to changes of this kind. Individual politicians cannot alone change, or afford to change, the forms of campaigning, because contemporary campaign techniques do serve partisan objectives, however poorly they may serve an educational function. Similarly, the press may hesitate to use its potential power to change the character of campaign discussion for reasons both political and ideological. In any case, there are economic and technical limits to that power.

The technical and economic limitations on what the press can do to shape campaign discussion are considerable. Only relatively large papers can readily afford to prepare comprehensive features on what candidates have said, issue by issue. Even these, when their editors want to do that kind of story, may find that the reporter who specializes on some suddenly important issue has already been assigned elsewhere. Not all publishers favor so-called depth reporting, but, even when they do, they may find this policy a difficult one to implement. Reporters following in the wake of rapidly moving candidates cannot easily put background material into their reports, and the compelling drive to meet deadlines may prevent editors from doing what the reporters have been unable to do.

Whether or not the press will report campaign statements in depth is an issue of considerable importance, since depth reporting is one of the most effective ways to combat distortion, evasion, and ambiguity. Yet depth reporting is not only technically difficult, it is also inconsistent with the operational definition many newsmen have given the notion of objectivity. As an ideal, objectivity implies divorcement of the press's editorial function from its news function, of its attempts to persuade from its recording of events. Those whom Wallace Carroll has called the fundamentalists of the press take this to mean, however, that reporters "should simply get the facts and present them with as much detachment as they can, but should not try to fill in background, interpret or analyze, especially when they are handling an explosive subject."[26] Obviously, commitment to objectivity defined in this manner would make campaign discussion in the press little more than a photographically exact reproduction of campaign discussion as it is shaped by campaigners.

Unfortunately, some publishers have shown little desire to make it anything else. Newspapers are themselves instruments used in the struggle for power; and some publishers are more intent on influencing the outcome of elections than in changing the character of campaign discussion. H. G. Nicholas, noting with concern the lack of debate in the 1952 presidential campaign, has argued that the press has now more than ever a heavy responsibility to "persuade and bully the rival candidates into acknowledging each other's existence" and to force them into "according each

---

[26] Wallace Carroll, "The Seven Deadly Virtues," *Michigan Alumnus Quarterly Review* (Aug. 6, 1955), p. 330.

other's arguments the dignity of an occasional reply."[27] But American elections, he observes, tend to become free-for-alls, and "since everyone is expected to participate, no one is left to be referee."[28]

The problems that would attend efforts to get politicians to accept press conferences, debates, and forums as normal campaign devices are of a different nature. Individual politicians might suffer if these forms of campaigning became normal, but politicians as a class would not. They would simply play the game according to new rules.

At present, candidates often see press conferences as threats, to be avoided if possible, since, as they face each other in press conference, candidates and reporters have contrary objectives. "The official," Leo Rosten notes, "wants to present the information which will reflect most favor upon him. The newspaperman, motivated by the ancient values of journalism, is interested in precisely that type of news which the official is least eager to reveal."[29] Candidates are not without resources to meet the threat, for able press assistants and a news sense can help them to anticipate and prepare for many questions. Nonetheless, there remains room enough for the unexpected to occur, to make California's Whitaker and Baxter list the "press conference debacle" as one of the tactical errors into which a candidate can most easily fall.[30]

Candidates (or at least one of each pair of candidates) normally see the debating situation as threatening also. As in a press conference, the politician in a debate cannot nicely calculate the appeals he will make and decorously avoid discussion of all other matters. He is deprived, moreover, of any ability to win a differential access to the electorate, since, by its very nature, the debate gives rival candidates equal access. Since it tends to reduce the advantage that a better-known candidate or a better-financed candidate would otherwise enjoy, it is not likely to be entered willingly by candidates who enjoy such advantages.[31]

This brief review of the difficulties involved in attempts to

---

[27] H. G. Nicholas, "The Long Morning After, V: Afterthoughts from Abroad," *The Reporter* (May 17, 1953), p. 36.

[28] *Ibid.*, p. 32.

[29] Leo Rosten, *The Washington Correspondents* (1937), p. 65.

[30] Clem Whitaker and Leone Baxter, "Campaign Blunders Can Change History," *Public Relations Journal* (August 1956), p. 6.

[31] Thus Whitaker and Baxter, in a letter to the county and local chairman of their organization to promote the candidacy of Goodwin Knight for Governor of California in 1954, observe: "What about debates? Our candi-

change forms of campaigning shows that such changes will not come automatically, but it does not support the inference that there is no way to change them at all. Action by the press, by legislators, and by citizen groups could do much to encourage a new kind of campaigning.

Newspapers could take action both individually and collectively to promote press conferences as a regular feature of campaigning. Editorial explanation of the value of the press conference would be one form such action could take. Resolutions of the editors' and publishers' associations would be another. Still another would be publicizing the willingness or unwillingness of individual candidates to submit to questioning, as the *Washington Post* and *Times Herald* has done in the case of Cabinet officers. Along with such action, experimentation with varying forms of the press conference might be desirable. Press conferences devoted to cross-questioning candidates on their responses to questions submitted in advance might, for instance, be an improvement on present practices and meet some of the objections candidates have to them at the same time.

Press action should also include more analysis and interpretation of campaign materials and the use of all the techniques that tend to relate the statements of rival candidates and parties to each other. The need for interpretive or depth reporting is now widely recognized among influential newspapermen, partly, one would suppose, because the case for it is persuasive. While press fundamentalists have argued that depth reporting can mean biased reporting, it is equally clear that "objective" reporting can lead readers to badly distorted views of the events reported. Indeed, the fundamentalist view of objectivity often leads to news coverage that is more irresponsible than objective: "[When] . . . a reporter has solid evidence that a statement is misleading," asks Wallace Carroll, "should he merely report that statement or should he give the reader the benefit of his additional knowledge?"[32] If he merely reports, he allows the newspaper to be used, not in the public

---

date is a master in this field, so we regret to say we will schedule no debates with our opponents. We should not permit the stature of the Governor to be utilized to build audiences for his opposition." Murray Chotiner, in a lecture on the techniques and strategies of political campaigning given at U.C.L.A., was similarly wary of debate. His advice for candidates considering participation in forums was: "Always pick your own subject and your own opponent or just don't consider them."

[32] Carroll, *op. cit.*, p. 332.

interest or even in its own, but in that of the propagandist. The economic problems involved in presenting more interpretation and more features could be solved for most papers if the wire services were to furnish them with this kind of material.

Several kinds of measures to stimulate debate in campaigns are available to legislators. They could require a certain number of face-to-face debates between candidates by law. They could make an allowance of time on radio and television, paid for by the government, conditional on its use for debates between candidates. In the voters' pamphlet, they have already provided a medium for partisan argument that has one of the important features of the debating situation—rival candidates enjoy access to the same audience. If such pamphlets were issued several times during the course of a campaign candidates could not only make a general statement of their positions, as they do now, but they could also challenge their opponents and draw distinctions between their positions and those of their rivals.[33]

Legislators could, in any case, alter provisions of existing law that now discourage the use of the airways for debate, for the present effect of Section 315 of the Federal Communications Act is to do just that. A spokesman for the Columbia Broadcasting System told a Senate committee that the network had found "most attractive" suggestions made in 1952 that it sponsor a number of Eisenhower–Stevenson debates. CBS officials felt unable to push such a project in earnest, however, since Section 315 would have required them "at least to give the same amount of time to each of the other 16 candidates."[34] To avoid this complication, the networks have depended largely on noncandidate party leaders to present partisan points of view in their debates and press interview programs. Valuable as these programs may be, they are hardly substitutes for having candidates speak for themselves.[35]

---

[33] This is a proposal made by Louise Overacker in her *Money in Elections* (1932). See pp. 370–71.

[34] Testimony of Richard S. Salant, Vice-President of the Columbia Broadcasting System, in *Federal Elections Act of 1955*, Hearings before the Senate Committee on Rules and Administration, 84 Cong. 1 sess., p. 177.

[35] By taking advantage of the new exemption of news interview programs from the equal time provisions of Section 315, networks can now bring major party candidates together on programs with this kind of format, and Robert Sarnoff has indicated that the National Broadcasting Company will ask the 1960 presidential nominees to appear "side by side" on its "Meet the Press Program" in a six program series to begin in September. (*New York Times*, Apr. 22, 1960.) Adlai Stevenson, has recently proposed that the broadcasting media sponsor regular weekly, back-to-back, half-hour programs

Finally, citizen groups can play an important role in promoting new conceptions of campaigning and in imposing new practices on campaigners. Normally, candidates, not voters, determine the procedures of campaign discussion, but this need not always be so. Voters can turn the tables on politicians if they organize themselves to exact conditions for continuing to listen. A number of citizen groups in various localities have done something very like this and have done it successfully. The voters' service program of the League of Women Voters offers a good example of such action, and one which might well be emulated by other civic groups.

Local League groups carry on several types of activity that contribute to, and condition, campaign discussion. One of the most widespread is the submission of questionnaires to candidates and the publication of their answers. Replies, grouped by office, are prepared for distribution in leaflet form or sometimes as a special feature for local newspapers. In the questionnaires the League solicits information on the candidate's educational, occupational, and other experience. Questions dealing with policy are usually broadly phrased, and candidates are asked to keep their answers brief. The generality of the questions invites generalities in reply, certainly one of the chief shortcomings of this kind of project. The resulting publication does bring together in one place, however, material that can provide the voter with a basis for at least rudimentary comparisons of candidates and their programs.

Candidate meetings are another characteristic part of the voter service activity of the League. The League invites all candidates for a given office to share the platform in a meeting organized by the League and chaired by a League member. Meetings are scheduled only if all candidates accept. If they agree to appear, they are given an opportunity to make brief pleas in their own behalf. The remainder—and usually the greater part—of the meeting is then devoted to a questioning of the candidates by members of the audience. The technique allows and encourages both cross-examination of the candidates and debate between them.[36] In recent years, the League has attempted to bring the benefits of its

---

for major party presidential candidates in the coming election, with a third half hour for rebuttal divided equally between them. ("Plan for a Great Debate," *This Week*, Mar. 6, 1960, p. 14.) If such programs were not to give rise to valid claims for equal time by minor party candidates, however, Section 315 would have to be further revised.

[36] Debate, that is, on policy matters. The League attempts, so far as it is possible, to discourage debate on personal issues in an effort to avoid name-calling and personal attacks.

candidates' meetings to a larger audience through radio and television, and station managers have cooperated by granting public service time. The procedure followed in these broadcasts and telecasts is essentially that of the candidate meeting: a League moderator, joint appearance of candidates, questions from the audience. The most important difference is that the League's inquisitors in these affairs have prepared their questions in advance, and the questioning is, therefore, less spontaneous.

The substantial success the League has had in involving candidates in its programs suggests that the conditions that often lead candidates to avoid questioning and debate are not entirely impervious to conscious efforts to change them. At least two motives incline a candidate toward cooperation with the League, particularly if he is engaged in a close race: the desire for a forum, on the one hand, and fear, on the other, that refusal to cooperate will antagonize an active and articulate group in the community.

SUMMARY

The argument of this chapter can be brought to a close at this point. Its essential outline has been as follows: Contemporary campaign discussion is often of such a character that it is unlikely to help voters much in their efforts to arrive at a wise choice of public officials. It may, in fact, have quite the reverse effect. Campaign propagandists obscure the real differences between candidates and parties by distortion, by evasiveness, and by talking generalities. That they create new and fictitious ones to replace them cannot be regarded as adequate compensation. Many of the forms campaign discussion takes—campaign speeches, spot announcements, advertising, documentaries, "literature," newspaper advertising—both exploit and encourage the fragmentation, passivity, and part-time character of the campaign audience.

Some forms of discussion, however, are much more likely to support rational discourse than others, and this suggests that measures might be taken to increase the contribution of campaign discussion to electoral rationality. Among the measures appropriate to this objective would be: establishing of press conferences as a campaign institution; encouraging interpretative reporting, weekly summaries of campaign news, issue-by-issue feature articles on policy stands taken by candidates, and battle pages; government financing of radio and television debates; revision of Section 315 of the Federal Communications Act to facilitate joint encounters of candidates under the sponsorship of the radio and television networks; government sponsorship of an altered form of the publicity pamphlet; and organizing forums and debates before private associations and citizens' groups. That such measures would work no magic goes without saying, but they should be considered.

CHAPTER FIVE

POLITICAL FEELINGS

VIETNAM SUMMER was an intensive effort, in the summer of 1967, to organize nationwide opposition to the war in Vietnam. Largely a student-led, New Left movement, the program involved at least some of the energies of more than 20,000 people, including some 200 paid workers. The young men and women who ran the National Office, about a dozen of them, were strongly committed to "The Movement" for peace abroad and social change at home; they devoted much more than full time to the task that summer. In the following selection, Kenneth Keniston describes how this group of extraordinarily active citizens felt about their participation.

As Keniston explains in another passage, he is not arguing that personal feelings are all there is to political action. Instead "the study of the psychology of politics is complementary, rather than opposed, to an interest in the sociology, history, and philosophy of these views." A focus on these feelings catches a dimension, an aspect of explanation that would be missed—or simply guessed at—in other types of analyses. Two themes are particularly striking in this report. First, it is clear that Vietnam Summer was not an isolated, strictly "political" segment of life for these persons but was intimately connected with their feelings about many other aspects of their lives. Second, the material shows how activities in the present are significantly affected by the person's memories and expectations, his views of where he has been and where he is going. It is within this moving totality that politics finds a place in life.

YOUNG RADICALS: THEIR POLITICAL COMMITMENT

KENNETH KENISTON

In the summer of 1967, the young men and women who led Vietnam Summer were still in the midst of their personal and political development. More than most of their contemporaries, they considered their lives and their characters changing and incomplete. Most were still deliberately attempting to change themselves as people, to educate themselves as radicals, and to train themselves for greater political effectiveness. And all convincingly described a trajectory of personal growth whose terminus neither they nor I could foresee.

To speak of "the radical commitment" as seen in these young men and women is therefore to try to describe a process rather than an achievement, an evolving style and orientation rather than a finished identity or fixed ideology. The task of this book is to trace some of the interwoven themes—psychological, social, and historical—that enter into the continuing development of this small group of young radical leaders. But what is to be explained is the process of change itself, rather than a group of finished people or a completed Movement. Indeed, one of the central differences between the new and the old radicalism is the fact that process and motion are the essence of today's Movement, a movement of changing young people who deliberately eschew the often rigid personal and ideological positions of the Old Left.

This chapter is an account of who and where these young radicals were during the summer of 1967. One thing they were, of course, was intensely involved in their work with Vietnam Sum-

mer, and, for all, that experience was itself important and forma-
tive. The summer project was by far the largest effort ever organized within the New Left; it not only demanded from its leaders a
high degree of commitment and the full use of skills previously
learned in New Left work, but also the development of new skills
and tactics suited for a large-scale coordinating organization. More
important, it activated and focused the considerable energies of
these young men and women on a project that was sufficiently
successful to prevent the despairs of earlier organizing efforts, and
sufficiently short term to avoid the fragmentations that a more
long-range project might have produced.

The lens of interviews conducted during this summer therefore looked out on a group of young men and women employed to
their fullest, personally and organizationally mobilized for an intensive and short-term effort, intensely and warmly related to each
other, fully activated. Many noted that their mood during the
summer was different from that on previous occasions. The intense
activity of the summer lightened pre-existing gloom; the need for
twelve to sixteen hours a day of focused and engaged work required
putting aside long-range questions about the future; and the effort
to learn how to run a large-scale organization in a style consistent
with the values of the New Left gave these young activists a sense
of personal motion and of challenge. Yet interviews conducted
during the fall of 1967 indicated that the lens of the summer had
not drastically distorted their features. To be sure, in the fall the
intensity and focus of the summer project had been lost, but the
individuals remained much the same, albeit in different settings.

AS SEEN IN INTERVIEWS

That the young men and women I interviewed were extremely
different, one from the other, is not in itself surprising. It is axio-
matic that any given external behavior (like working in Vietnam
Summer) can spring from diverse motives in distinct types of
personality. But the normal expectation of diversity was more than
normally fulfilled with these young radicals. Their most striking
characteristic as a group was their separate "personhood," their
distinctiveness, complexity, and individuality, their colorful, vivid,
and expressive manner—in short, the fact that no two were at all
alike.

I would have preferred to discuss the life histories of several
contrasting individuals at length, thus illustrating concretely their

diversity. But I could find no way of doing this without violating the confidentiality I had undertaken to maintain. In the following chapters, I have therefore used the method of a collective biography, emphasizing those issues that recurred most frequently in the lives of these young men and women. To preserve confidentiality, I have had to summarize or abstract many of the most vivid anecdotes and episodes of their lives. And I inevitably treat these young radicals as a more unified and homogeneous "type" than they are, and thus neglect in practice what I can only assert in principle: that a collective account of these young radical leaders omits many of the special themes that contribute to the intense individuality of each, and that one of the most enduring issues for almost all of them was the ambivalent meaning of that sense of "specialness" they had long possessed.

Some of the most striking characteristics of these activists will be difficult to illustrate in the pages that follow, since they cannot be conveyed in quotations from an interview transcript. For example, as I have noted, I had not expected individuals so open, so unthreatened by my interviews, or so willing to discuss not only the public aspects of their lives, but also the sometimes painfully personal and private. Despite all that has been written about the paranoia of the Leftist—old or new—these young men and women were unusually open, trusting, and candid, at least with me. They are unself-consciously at home with psychological questions and explanations, which they "naturally" apply to their own behavior. Although rarely versed in academic psychology, they take for granted an intimate connection between inner life and social action. Only two of those interviewed had been in psychotherapy, but the remainder discussed themselves with the kind of insight that one normally expects to find from those who have had extensive psychotherapy.[1]

Another quality that cannot be conveyed by interview transcripts is the intensity of feeling they experienced and expressed as they talked about their present and past lives. Talking about an important past event was frequently enough to evoke the emotions

---

[1] One interviewee, reading an earlier draft of this, wrote, "I tend to agree with your point that Movement people are more open . . . than students in general. . . . On the other hand . . . you were received as you were because you were seen immediately as an honest man with good questions. If you had come on as 'Dr. Keniston, the mind expert,' our tense and fractured group would have affirmed its essential solidarity by running you out before the first day."

that had originally accompanied it. The interviewees expressed joy, sadness, anxiety, fear, love, and hate freely as they recounted their development. Several cried briefly in recalling painful (or in one case joyous) experiences. In previous interviewing experience, I have rarely found such readiness to express feelings in a short series of interviews: it suggests unusual emotional openness, whether based on genuine acceptance of feelings, or on a more ominous lack of self-control. In this case, self-acceptance seemed more explanatory than lack of self-control, for another quality of these young radicals was an unusual intellectual coherence, a high degree of cognitive organization, and a capacity to differentiate the distinct aspects of life. Despite the intensity of their feelings, they were able to keep to the point, or to return to the topic at hand after a lengthy digression. Part of this coherence is a function of high intelligence and unusual verbal fluency; another part seems related to a psychological style that involves the capacity for self-control in the presence of intense feelings.

The most graphic demonstration of this control was their reactions to the frequent interruptions in our interviews. The school library where our interviews were conducted was visible through a glass door from the busy main corridor, and we were often interrupted without warning by telephone calls, by letters to be signed, or by lengthy consultations. The young radicals were almost always able to shift from personal and sometimes emotion-laden topics within the interview to the business that had suddenly intruded. And once this business had been dealt with, they could shift back to the narrative of their personal lives.

Despite the intensity of their feelings, almost none of the young radicals attempted to use the interviews as a means of obtaining explicit help, interpretations, support, or reassurance. In many interviewing situations, a proportion of those interviewed request, implicitly or explicitly, some form of therapy from the interviewer, and often develop complex feelings about him that are "transferences" from important early relationships in their lives. But virtually all of these young men and women accepted the role of "co-researcher," treating me as a colleague in a joint inquiry about their personal and political development, in which they were both personally and vocationally interested. While they discussed their past and present problems freely, they seemed to accept the fact that I was in no position to provide them with any psychological help; the focus in these interviews remained the mutually agreed-upon topic of how they had become radicals.

The following account will minimize or neglect much else that was important to the lives of these radicals in the summer of 1967. For example, I will not discuss at any length how these young radicals interacted with each other, the formal and informal group structures they evolved in Vietnam Summer, or the style they developed during the summer. Here, as in other areas, there were enormous individual differences: in group meetings, for example, some preferred the role of silent listener, limiting themselves to an occasional enigmatic comment; while others were active, forceful, and at times directive. Yet what I observed of them in their work was consistent with what they had told me of themselves in interviews, and indeed suggested an unusual integration of private and public life.

ON BEING A RADICAL

No one can predict—and especially not these young men and women themselves—whether, and in what sense, they will remain "radicals." But during the summer of 1967, as during the months that followed, one of their shared characteristics was their deep sense of commitment to the New Left. For each individual this commitment had its idiosyncratic roots. But beyond these important idiosyncrasies, there runs the theme of a deep, shared engagement with the Movement for Social Change and a continuing effort to reshape themselves so as to be more effective in that Movement.

Any interviewer who in effect asks a group of young men and women "How did you come to be what you are?" almost inevitably elicits answers that somewhat artificially integrate and sum up an ongoing process. Such answers must be seen as provisional and preliminary, as progress (or non-progress) reports, as timeslices across a moving flow. Yet such statements are useful, for in them the crucial themes of past and present life are often interwoven. These themes will recur again and again, as I trace the complex development that led these young men and women into the New Left.

One young woman, when I asked her if she had ever considered abandoning her work in the Movement, replied:

No, I've really been very happy. This is one of the things I feel very positive about. . . . One of the things I've learned in the last two years is that you don't need very much to live on. . . . It gives me a completely different perspective on what it is that I decide to go into. I wouldn't mind having a car, but I would have to learn to drive first. I can think of ways to enjoy a nice way of life, but I don't feel obsessed with it. . . .

I sort of feel myself to be open and I feel very happy. It is like I have built a whole new world. It has been a very good transition. I feel like I have a solid foundation. . . . I just saw a friend of mine from ten years ago the other day, and it was very difficult to talk to her. . . . You realize that the people you want to be your friends are people where you don't have to go through the whole process of justifying why you're doing what you're doing. . . . You end up eliminating a lot of your old friends. . . . The kind of people who get involved in the Movement are really people who have a strong need for friendship. . . . I don't feel as politically conscious as maybe I should. Maybe I'm approaching things much more pragmatically. How do you build something? How do you get things done?[2]

In this statement about herself, she introduces issues that will recur in these interviews: her relationship to middle-class monetary and success values, her feeling of openness to the future, her gradual entry into the Movement and her loss of her past friends, her need for friendship, her sense of ideological inadequacy, and finally—and perhaps most important—the questions with which she approaches her own future and the future of the Movement.

For this young woman, as for all of her fellow workers in Vietnam Summer, personality and politics are impossible to separate. Again and again, they stressed the personal origins of political beliefs, and the effects of political involvement in their personal lives. For many, political involvement had been a major catalyst for personal change:

It was only when I first began to do my first political activity, which was—I can't remember, a boycott or peace work or something— but I really started to move personally. I started to put my mind to a project, an activity, a way of thinking. I really started to work hard in terms of learning how to do that stuff. . . . I really put my personality into it. That's what I've been doing ever since. I obviously sublimate a lot of stuff into political activity.

---

[2] All of the quotations in the text are from the young radicals I interviewed in Vietnam Summer. I have changed many personal, organizational, and place names. My own comments or amplifications are noted by brackets. I have used ellipses to indicate deletions from the original spoken narratives. Some quotations have been edited to eliminate unnecessary redundancy or to increase clarity. Apart from these minimal changes, they reflect accurately the spoken style of those I interviewed.

Not only does this young radical underline the personal component of his political life, but he clearly indicates that a major part of the meaning of his radical commitment lies in its role in helping to start "to move personally." Another, summarizing his political development, said:

> The politics came after the people. There was always a personal relationship first. And the most important thing of what you were going to do with a person was personal, not political. The political development came from that background, and from the reading I did.

Here again, the inseparability of the personal, especially the interpersonal, and the political is underlined.

As a rule, formal elaborated and dogmatic ideological considerations were seldom discussed in these interviews; they rarely formed a major part of the radical's presentation of himself to me. No doubt, had I been a political scientist inquiring about political philosophy, statements of formal ideology could have been obtained. But to give great emphasis to such statements would, I believe, falsify the personal position of these radicals, which rests on a set of time-honored principles rather than on any elaborately rationalized ideology. One interviewee, for example, volunteered:

> One of the things that makes it difficult for me to trace where I came from is the fact that I don't have an ideology. If I did, if I knew precisely, I mean if I had clear political goals—well, I have something of an analysis of why certain things happen, and why certain things must happen. But it's not very tightly formulated and I'm very flexible about it. If I did have a rigid view, I would be better able to look back and say, "This is where this and that came from." . . . But I think it's better this way. It's more real, it ties in, it forces you to bring yourself together more as a unified thing rather than to say, "Here are my politics, Dr. Keniston, and this is where they came from. Now if you want to talk to me about a person, that is something else." But things really are together, and that's real. It's so—Things really are together.

And another noted in a similar vein:

> I have never been an ideologue. I always have been a guy who winds up, in terms of ideology, taking it for the excitement of it and really examining it, but I have a lot of difficulty in putting together broad theories. I feel much more humble, I think, than other people do. I think I'm probably wrong about that, but it was always the organizing things that I felt the most at home with. . . .

Formal statements of rationalized philosophy, articulated interpretations of history and political life, and concrete visions of political objectives were almost completely absent in the interviews (and in this respect, as in many others, this is a typically American group). But what did emerge was a strong, if often largely implicit, belief in a set of basic moral principles: justice, decency, equality, responsibility, non-violence, and fairness. The issue of "tactics," too, was often discussed—the utility of demonstrations, community organizing, electoral politics, or "resistance" as instrumentalities for the New Left. But the primary orientation to basic principles, although one of the most important issues in their lives, was so taken for granted by them (and to a large extent at the time by me as well) that it was rarely emphasized in these young radicals' summaries of themselves. And questions about tactics seemed to them so much a pragmatic matter of effectiveness that they did not include them in their self-descriptions.

Convinced that the personal and the political were linked, and emphatically anti-ideological in their ideologies, these young men and women usually emphasized the personal satisfaction they derived from Movement activities. One individual, when asked why he planned to persist as a radical, said:

Part of it is that it's something that I do well. I wouldn't like to have to get up at 9:00 o'clock every morning and finish work at 5:30 and be under somebody's authority. [Laughs] . . . and then one is contemporary with the mainstreams of society. One feels on top of things.

Another spoke in comparable terms about the "motion in the Movement":

I've had a lot of help, because you know there's motion in the Movement. There are people doing things, there are things happening, there are all kinds of exciting people. That helps. That helps a lot.

Still another sustaining force for some of these young radicals is the conviction that they are part of a rising tide of radicalism that is increasingly required by modern American society. For example, one young man, after having discussed his own father's growing impatience with American society, said:

It's happening now on a national basis, some of the people who are old liberals in the analysis of American society are increasingly radical.

For example, Gunnar Myrdal, who back in the fifties had a kind of "growing pains" analysis—you know, America is young and is having growing pains—his analysis is different now: something has got to be done. And I found this also among people like my father, intellectual types, that they are getting the same type of response. A lot of people of your generation or my father's generation, and from your discipline, are getting drawn into political activities.

One prime source of satisfaction in the radical's commitment, then, derives from the feeling of contemporaneity, of being in motion with others, and of involvement with a changing, growing tide of radicalism.

For others, the satisfactions of Movement work come partly from a feeling of continuity with the values of the personal and collective past. One young man from a radical family summarized his recent development as follows:

It just seems to me that what happened was that I saw a different way of relating to people. When I started to look around at things, I felt that political activity was a vehicle for that. But it wasn't until last year that I really started feeling that I've come all the way back round full circle. Politics was no longer a vehicle, but this was *the thing*. And then I said to myself, "My God, it never *was* a vehicle. This is what you *were*. This is where you're *at*. This is where you've come from. This is how you're made up. And you aren't supposed to be doing anything else. You shouldn't feel badly about not doing this or not doing that. This is what you *are*."

It's just, you know, a nice feeling. It's very, very supportive, both that emotional and intellectual feeling. It helps you on. It's not something that happens once and there's beautiful flowing music. But once you get that feeling, it's there, and when the time comes and you start getting into the dumps, you can say, "Look, this is what you were made to do."

Another young man, this one not from a radical family, described a strong sense of continuity to the basic values of his family:

I had a good solid family, no parental trouble among themselves or with the kids. My old man is very straight with the kids. That's been very important, because it has kept in the back of my mind all the time concepts like responsibility, seriousness: "If you're going to work on this, you can't just do it on weekends." I have this whole complex of ideas about carrying through with what you start, being serious about it, being confident about it. I really never could have come close to just flipping out and becoming totally alienated. . . . It doesn't seem to me that simple. All capitalists don't beat their wives, all workers are not hopeless charlatans. . . . That kind of thing was in the back of my mind, nagging at me: "You're not involved, you're not doing anything." . . .

The values I got from my family, the ones that I've kept, are good. I've pared them and peeled them to fit my own style, but there is a good continuity here. I mean it's a new generation, but there's a lot from my old generation that can't be minimized. Otherwise, I might have flipped out or something like that, or just turned myself off altogether.

This young man, from a relatively apolitical background, links his involvement in the Movement and his escape from "just flipping out and becoming totally alienated" to his continuity with the values of his family.

No summary can characterize the satisfactions of Movement work: for each individual, they are numerous and complex. To return to a central theme in radical development, the crucial sustaining force in the radical commitment is probably an underlying sense of acting on one's basic principles. One individual, for example, who grew up in a religious family, argued that his "basic rhetoric" is a theological one, now translated into secular terms:

I don't get upset about sexual things, and I don't get upset about religious things. But I feel that honesty, among yourselves, is necessary. I feel that people should fulfill their commitments. I feel that one has to be serious, and able to work hard. . . . I feel those kinds of things. It's not that I'm against pot smoking or having great dances or wasting time or watching television—I love all those things. . . . But my vision had always been that all of a sudden a million people would march on Washington, singing "A Mighty Fortress Is Our God," and the government would come tumbling down. I would feel much more identified with that than if a million people marched on Washington singing "The Internationale." . . .

If I let down all of my defenses, I would wind up being Billy Graham or Elmer Gantry. That would be my first impulse, to say, "That's immoral." My basic rhetoric is a very theological one. . . . Maybe if I were born three or four hundred years earlier, I'd be a preacher. I'd say that the people should reform, that they should stop being sinners, that they should realize that the world has to be built on different foundations—" 'Tis the final conflict," "Let each man take his place." [Laughs] . . . My initial thing is to get up and preach to people and expect them to follow me. That's where my impulse is, to speak out to the world.

Here the underlying appeal to moral principle is clearly stated: the call to sinners to reform and repent. He went on to note, however, "My problem is that the basic rhetoric is one that's irrelevant. . . . [It] just doesn't work."

Still another, in the course of discussing whether he should buy a friend's Volkswagen microbus, indicated the importance of his underlying moral commitment:

> It may cost me three hundred dollars, and I *had* been going to give that money to a political organization. I may buy it anyway—I think I probably will. It will be nice to have a microbus, and I will have a long life to give money away to political organizations.
>
> [K. K.: But it's a conflict for you.] Right. [Pause] But right now, it looks like there aren't many more kinds of possessions I would like to have. I don't believe people should go crazy and work sixteen hours a day because the revolution isn't coming tomorrow. It's wrong not to live until then. But I feel very strongly that people with a lot of money should give it. That comes from the same kind of value—you absolutely must do what's good for everyone, not what's good for yourself. It would be impossible for me to do that. . . . I'm not uncommitted. I have meaning in my life, that's not the problem. I have other problems, but that's not one of them. . . . And that's something (it's certainly true that I got it from my parents) that was very valuable.

In asserting that "you absolutely must do what's good for everyone," and in connecting this value to his parents, this young man affirmed both his moral commitment and his link to his past.

Another aspect of the radical commitment involves a sense of having "grown up" through involvement in the Movement. Many noted how much they had changed, in ways they liked, since their involvement in the New Left:

> I started off being very insecure in terms of what I was thinking and what I was saying. I usually felt I was wrong, and that I should follow other people's directions. But then, over the last years, I have realized that I am usually right. . . . It's not a matter of whether my predictions are right, whether Bobby Kennedy will run or not. . . . But I feel much more secure in myself, and I am much more willing at this point to project my alternatives onto people, and to push them very hard. I am more willing now to have people follow my direction and to

take responsibility for it. That means the possibility of failure and getting people angry at you and all kinds of things. That was a very big struggle within myself. . . .

Finally, being committed to the Movement means being involved with other people, not being alone, being part of a meaningful group. The radical, as a member of a small political minority, must continually remind himself and be reminded that he is not alone. One individual, for example, said:

You get these periodic shots in the arm that are very essential. Just like the parties around here. You'd think that in this place you wouldn't feel isolated. But after you get back to your apartment or to wherever you live, you see how few you are, and it gets to be very discouraging. There are billions of *them* out there, and we can't even move the students, we can't even get ten percent of the students. But then, you have a party after the meeting on Thursday night, and you get sixty guys who you really like that are radical, and you say, "All right, sixty is enough." You feel reinspired and reinvigorated. It's the same thing with national meetings. You get people together and they give you a shot in the arm. You figure there are some other people around, and you're ready to go back to your own turf and do something yourself.

In raising the issue of helpless isolation ("There are billions of *them* out there"), and then dispelling it by discussing the importance of personal contact with others in the Movement, this young man pointed to a crucial theme in the political lives and personal histories of most of his fellows.

Yet whatever the sense of solidarity in the New Left, membership in a small, fragmented, struggling, and largely unsuccessful radical movement is clearly difficult to sustain. And sustaining most of those I interviewed was their basic feeling of self-respect or adequacy, a feeling they usually traced back to their families. One young woman, when I asked her how she managed to keep going when times were bad, said:

I don't know. I always had the feeling in the family that I was better than [my siblings]. I was smarter than they were, I didn't have to study as hard, that my mother liked me best. . . . That's a terrible thing to think at times, and I felt guilty about it. And then my mother was very supportive. She was always very supportive, and even though I didn't always trust her, I always fell back to her. If I needed her, she was there. A lot of times I still do that now. . . . And I've been lucky because there has always been somebody there who had said the things that need to be said when I'm in a slump. Those have been my friends and my parents—my mother—even though she has all these bad things, when I'm down in the dumps, she is there, even now. I don't go to her any more, but when I was a kid I always did.

Another, describing himself in general, said:

I'll tell you this much—I have . . . a funny kind of self-confidence. And what it did was probably to accentuate even more my need for what I'm doing now. That is to say, "See, boob, you can really finish something; you can work on it and you can really see it through." And then you can say, "Well, that's good, let's look at what it was you finished, let's look at the part you played, what you did."

For all of their self-confidence and commitment to radicalism, these young men and women also have abundant self-doubts. Some of these are intimate and personal. One young man, discussing the undesirable aspects of his parents' relationship with each other, said:

I find that I seem to be duplicating that relationship. I seem to be just moving irrationally into that, using my parents' relationship as a model for my relationship with Judy. In a sense, she puts more value—I do too, but I don't move naturally in that direction—on a *relationship* between people. And I put much more emphasis on the family being an arena from which you go out and do things . . . for instance, my father doesn't do any work around the house, and Judy gets angry at me because I don't take out the garbage or wash the dishes. It's not that I don't think I should, it's just that I've never seen it like that before. . . . That makes me very upset because I consider my father a failure.

This young man's most pressing self-doubts center on his fear of being like his father, a fear that is unusually intense in him, but that has echoes in others with whom he worked.

Others questioned their competence for the work they set out to do. One, discussing the after-effects of a recent meeting that depressed him, said:

I began to question a lot in terms of myself, about where I am in the Movement. Every so often that happens. The whole question came up of which tools I have at my disposal to do the job I want to do. Sometimes I feel that they are very very lacking. . . . I feel I should read more, but I feel I have worked so long and I'm so exhausted that I just can't. Or I read something that's non-political. I'm very very shoddy

about it. It's very depressing to me, because I used to like to read like
crazy when I was younger and I was in college. But now I don't. . . .
I've never read a basic economics book. How about that?

It may be very odd—I say odd because I can't find a better word—I
really knew a hell of a lot for an eighteen- or nineteen-year-old kid. . . .
In terms of politics, I had been doing a lot of reading. I knew a pretty
good deal. The problem is that (this may not be true) I haven't made
three years' progress in three years' time in certain areas of knowledge.
I have developed very well certain abilities, really pushed them almost
to the limit of their development at this stage of my life. Yet there are
other things which I need to have as a background. I need things that
would give me more perspective to help me analyze what it is I've done
and what it is I need to do. I need to know more about economics to
know how that functions. I want to do more reading in history . . . for
example, labor history. I don't know about that. I think if you have a
radical perspective, you really should. I just don't have those things.

But for all of their personal and political self-doubts, and for
all of the changes that have occurred in their lives in recent years,
the most impressive feature of the radical commitment in these
young men and women is the sense of continuity most of them feel
with their pasts. One young man, discussing his parents' desire
that he return to school, said:

This summer they were talking about "Are you thinking about
going back to school? We're proud of you and of what you're doing, and
we don't want to push you, but let's sit down and talk about this." And I
said, "Hey, great, let's *do* talk about it." I'm looking forward to really
trying to explain to them the kinds of things I feel, that I am a very
personal embodiment of what they are, what they created in a son, and
what they brought me up to be. The thing I want to say to them is, "If
you feel you've made a mistake, then tell me so. But *I* feel this is the
way you brought me up. This is the way you and all the other influences
that you put before me in life, that you provided for me—directly and
indirectly—[that you] helped make me." I'd like to sit down and really
talk with them.

Here again, two important issues are joined: the inner conflict
between the Movement and the Academy, and the view of radicalism as an outgrowth of the core values of the past.

To these young men and women, then, being a radical means
many things. It of course means a general commitment to the
general goals and tactics of the New Left. But for all, this commitment is more personal and moral than dogmatic or formally ideo-

logical; and in telling me, a psychologist, who they were, they invariably underlined the correction between the private and the political in their lives. Being a radical means a commitment to others, to a Movement "in motion," and to some kind of effort to create a viable radicalism in America. The radical commitment rests on a set of basic moral principles and instincts more than on any formal and elaborated philosophy. And these principles were invariably felt to be continuous with the people and the principles of the personal past. Finally, being a radical meant being open to an indeterminate future.

THE OPENNESS OF THE FUTURE

In late August, 1967, fewer than half of those interviewed in Vietnam Summer knew for sure what they would be doing on September 15. Those who did know were planning to continue or resume their educations, and had no plans beyond the completion of their studies. Indeed, some were not sure that they *would* complete their studies at all. A sense of openness and indeterminacy toward the future characterized them all. They repeatedly insisted that the future must, in some way, involve continuing work with the Movement; but they could never specify precisely how, where, and in what capacity.

One thing, however, was clear: the conventional options open to this group of intellectually able and personally forceful young men and women attracted them little. One young woman, for example, who had recently spent a year in graduate school, said about her future:

I don't really know what I'm going to do. I feel very open to respond. I've talked to enough people to have a feeling that they just move through college and graduate school without knowing what is going on, and I don't know how much they profited from the academic work they were doing. I'd like to do something that was at least relevant, to feel that at least I'm learning something. . . .
[She talks about her experiences at graduate school.] It was hard to have to say this again, to say that I still had no one to talk to. There *were* a few people. But I mean, when I became *the* expert on Negro history, it was a very sad state of affairs. There are very few academics who see some kind of relationship to what's happening in the world. I don't want to be a scholar, but at some point, I feel a responsibility to bring education to bear on my world.
I would like to teach people to be people—that is more important

than writing a paper. And I got scared when I looked at these kids twenty-eight years old, married with two kids, sitting in the stacks and throwing away time for five or six years. Their thesis is on the Abolitionist Movement, but they have no idea of what has been taking place in America in the past twenty years. They have their deferments, and they read a newspaper once in a while, but they don't really feel concerned. That really frightened me.

The issues mentioned by this young woman recur in the comments of others: academic life is the great temptation, yet is also a symbol of irrelevance and irresponsibility; continuing involvement in the Movement is essential, but precisely how and where the radical commitment can be realized remains unclear. Yet somehow she rejoices in (or at least accepts) the openness of the future.

The tension between academic life and radical work is understandably strong for these intellectually able young men and women. In talking about the future, they almost always discuss academic life in order to reject it. One young radical, asked about his future plans, replied:

It'll be in political organization one way or the other. I don't see myself going into the academic world, although I do a great deal of reading and writing and I think I can operate in that environment okay. . . . But I don't think I would be happy in it. . . . I don't want to take a job . . . where I have to "operate." I mean I want to be part of something where I don't have to worry about what I'm going to say and what I'm going to do, or about whether I have to keep things silent and the rest. . . . I don't enjoy it, it's too manipulative, and it doesn't give me a sense of satisfaction. Or maybe I wouldn't mind doing it, as long as I was part of a primary group that was doing it. But I don't want to be isolated. . . . I just don't like to get the feeling that I'm all alone and I'm doing something to everybody else. I like to have the feeling that there are fifty of us or five hundred or ten thousand that are doing it together. And I want to feel that I have friends and that I'm in a spirit of comradeship with them. . . .

The implicit picture of academic life is clear: it requires "operating," manipulation, and isolation, in contrast to this young man's perception of the New Left.

Another young man was unusual because he hoped to resolve the tension between radicalism and the Academy by combining the two, although his basic commitment is to the Movement.

I don't know what I am going to do. I don't think I want to be a full-time politico . . . and I don't see academics as in the center of things. Especially in this country, the left wing has been very isolated in the academic community. . . . [Also] it is clear that students by themselves can't be a revolutionary, a decisive revolutionary, force. So I guess it's for that same reason that I don't want to be an academic. On the other hand, I don't think I could become a truck driver—I'm too far gone for that. . . . And it's very important for me to live among people I can communicate with. Because, you know, for a long time I was lacking in that. . . . Yet I don't think I would want to do political work full time, because, for one thing, it is always so frustrating and unsuccessful. You know, the revolution isn't going to be here in a few years, and we should all be sane when it happens. 　.　　.　　.　　.　　.

Another rejected option is immersion in conventional middle-class life. Some young radicals are very explicit about their desire to define an alternative to Establishment America, and about the difficulties they have in doing so. One young woman said, for example:

One thing that took me a long time to learn is that there are models of marriage and adult life, but that they don't work. . . . My friends have helped, because all of them saw that: it was the same with them. The Movement brought people together who see things not working, and we have many hang-ups in common. Maybe the hang-up is between living and not knowing what you're going to be doing, and knowing but not having it work. Maybe that's what makes it so intense. It keeps you trying to find your way. I think it's highly probable (and then again it's not) that I might end up living like my mother. It could go like that very easily. But on the other hand, the things I see are so cruddy. Every now and then the cruddiness comes through. . . . I don't think I want to live like that, but I don't know of anyone who has found another way yet. I haven't found any other model. . . .

The fear of middle-class life is especially strong in this young woman because of her rejection of the materialism in her mother's life. (But her mother was also an intensely political woman.) Her problem in finding models of adult life is common to many others. She continues:

There is that whole conflict about being a professional, leading a middle-class life which none of us have been able really to resolve. How do you be an adult in this world? . . . It's very easy to get caught back up in it, especially when you don't know what you're going to be doing over the next years. . . . I don't want to get caught up in that whole professionalism and lose something of what has been built into me. . . . I'm not that secure myself: I'm afraid I'll fall back. I know the feeling. In a lot of people, especially people that are doing professional organizing work, there is a huge conflict . . . about being middle-class, about having things, and all that means. . . .

But most young radicals feel less acutely endangered by middle-class life than does this young woman. One young man said of his years in secondary school:

One thing I found at school was that I never had much sympathy for executive life or suburban life. It is partly because I read all of the Babbitt books, and secondly because my forte has never been an ability to get along with other people in a "ha-ha" kind of way. I was too impassioned and too angry and too individualistic. I knew I couldn't do it. . . . I would be very unhappy. Second of all, I sort of have the thought that those kinds of pretensions [of upper-middle-class business executives] don't belong in a democracy, that they are completely wrong, and that you shouldn't be associated with them.

One alternative to academic or professional life, of course, for the radical, is organizing work of some kind, whether it be local community organizing or, as is increasingly the case, organizing "resistance" groups concerned with the draft, civil disobedience, or other forms of non-legal political action. One young radical turned toward draft-resistance work after the summer; another said, when I asked her what she thought lay ahead for her:

If we go ahead, we can only go so far. [Laughs] . . . In terms of my own development, I feel that I've developed administrative skills, and I can run an office, I can set up a seminar, I can set up a regional conference with a great deal of ease. But I lack a kind of community experience I need. I would really prefer to do that for awhile. . . . There are probably about ten or fifteen people, maybe more, who have said (maybe who have not said, but are thinking): "We are going to be working in the South for the rest of our lives." And we are beginning to dig in now. . . . There's not a deliberate plan, no one sat down and mapped it out. . . . But it's there, and those are the people that I'm going to be working with for a long time. I'm still very close to them. I consult with them, and don't make plans in isolation.

Several of the Vietnam Summer leaders turned again in the fall to full-time organizing work. But still others undertook to continue their educations in some context where relevance and responsibility could be better combined with learning than—as they saw it—in the typical college or graduate school. Thus, schools with "progressive" curricula and strong work-study programs, institutions like the New School for Social Research or the Institute for Policy Studies, drew several of these radicals. And even the one interviewee enrolled in a graduate program in a conventional university had so arranged his schedule that he almost completely escaped normal course work. In all of their efforts at continuing self-education, these young radicals consciously sought to define some new form of learning in which relevance and theory, action and reflection, could be combined.

Several themes unite these statements about the future. As I have noted, the personal future is open, fluid, undefined, and indeterminate. Immersion into middle-class academic or professional life is clearly rejected, but in its place the young radical often finds it difficult to define clearly an alternative role, way of life, or style. As the young woman quoted above put it, "I haven't found any other model." Yet all of those I interviewed agreed that somehow the future must involve a continuation of Movement work. One said:

> In ten years, I definitely don't want to be away from this. That's the only sure thing I can say. I want to continue to be a part of this. I'm not sure what part or what role I could or should play. This is very important to me, the work, the Movement. What I'm saying is that I really hope it's going to be possible for me to be whatever I want to be when I "grow up" [laughs] without breaking the ties. I want to show that it really can be done, that I don't need to burn all these bridges behind me, as part of my past. So I definitely know that I want to be connected with Movement activities. In what way and what form I don't know, I can't tell. Who knows what the Movement is going to be like in ten years. . . .

Somehow all seemed to manage to tolerate the uncertainty and ambiguity of the future. This is partly because they feel caught up in the "motion in the Movement," and partly because of a more basic self-confidence that assures them that they can respond as needed to whatever is needed in the future. To an unusual degree, selfhood in these young men and women, although highly defined and individualized, is also tied in to a loosely defined Movement for Social Change, integrated in solidarity with small groups of other young radicals to whom they turn for guidance and counsel, and dependent upon a series of social and historical changes that the radical seeks to effect. Who, indeed, "knows what the Movement" —or for that matter American society and the world—"is going to be like in ten years"?

The ability to tolerate indeterminacy, then, is related not only to the self-confidence of these young radicals, but to their sense of involvement in a social, political, and historical process that is itself indeterminate. The result is that these young adults show surprisingly little anxiety and apprehension about what they will do: on the contrary, many have learned to enjoy the openness. Of the future, one said:

> For the first time, I have not felt the need to have something certain there that I could go into, that I could stay with, and say, "I am this-and-this man, I am working for this." Now I welcome the uncertainty. I welcome the choice. I welcome the thinking that that forces. That's one of the things that's really keeping me going now.

This young man, like some of his co-workers, has come to identify in part with the change and process of the Movement and of his surrounding world, rather than with the achievement of clearly defined future goals. Animated in part by a dim and rarely articulated vision of a revolutionary changed world, he is sustained even more by the conviction that what he is doing is right, both psychologically and ethically. From such an inner sense of rightness come self-affirmations like the following:

> I've taken a lot of shit for the work I've done. When I was a kid, there were family problems, and then later, for being involved in Movement things. But I wouldn't trade it. It just seems to me that I have had what I consider great fortune—to grow up with the people I grew up with, and the situations I did, with the perceptions I have, and with the feelings that I have. I still feel very proud of the fact that I can cry, that things can really dig me up inside, that I can cry when I'm happy. [He tells about an evening the previous week when he had started out feeling depressed, was with friends he liked, sang, and played the piano.] Afterward, I just went upstairs and my eyes filled up, I felt so good. I felt so turned on and I hadn't touched anything all evening. I got so high, so turned on, just being able to do that—it really digs me, being able to be happy.

It is on personal feelings such as these that the radical commitment is built. Facing a problematic and indeterminate future, members of a small, fragmented, and often confused Movement, tempted by, but determined not to succumb to, the lures of conventional middle-class or academic life, these radicals stand on their own feelings of inner rightness, and in the last analysis identify themselves with that process of social and historical change that their Movement seeks to effect. For all of their many doubts about themselves and their effectiveness, for all their inner conflicts, they express little doubt about their commitment to radicalism:

When *they* drop out, when *they* wind up being associate professors here and there, I'm going to keep on going. . . .

CHAPTER SIX

HOW OPINIONS HELP
PEOPLE

Citizens do not just have opinions; they use them. In fact, political opinions are not apt to be very intense or very long-lasting unless they serve important, persisting needs. Our low-key politics does not often generate strong opinions among most people, but when and where they appear citizens with intense views about politics have a significance beyond their numbers. The opinionated man is more likely than his cooler neighbor to be an activist who tries to persuade others. So it is important to understand how opinions connect with the personal needs of the few militants as well as the many more casual people.

The next selection by the psychiatrist Robert Coles can be taken as an illustration of at least three ways opinions help the opinionated. They help him make sense of a confusing world, by providing categories and frameworks for classifying political phenomena. They help a person relate himself to other people (positively *and* negatively), by the agreement and disagreement his opinions represent in the social context. And opinions may help with the management of inner tensions, partly by pushing personal troubles out onto the political world.

In this account of a segregationist's life and thoughts we can also see the reciprocal character of these relationships. Intense opinions grow out of personal experience; in that sense, we view opinions as affected by needs. On the other hand, strong opinions, once adopted, stimulate new cognitive, social, and emotional needs. Thus there is an interplay, not a strictly one-way relation, between one's way of life and one's political feelings.

WHAT SEGREGATION MEANS
TO A SEGREGATIONST

ROBERT COLES

. . . I first met John, as I shall call him, while he was protesting the Archbishop's decision to admit some children who were Negro, but also Catholic, to the parochial schools of New Orleans. It was a warm, faintly humid early spring day, a Saturday too, and next year's school opening hardly seemed a timely worry. Up and down he walked, tall, husky from the rear, an incipient belly in front. He wore a brown suit, slightly frayed at the cuffs, and on its right shoulder rested his sign, wrought and lettered by himself: "Fight Integration. Communists Want Negroes With Whites." His shirt was starched and he wore a tie. He had brown eyes. He was bald but for the most meagre line of black hair on his neck—it must have happened early and fast. His face was fleshy and largely unlined, and I thought "forty or forty-five."

Several of those marching seemed unaware of the people they attracted. John, however, was the most engaging. Looking at people directly, he would talk with them if they showed the tiniest interest. He moved faster than the others, and seemed to be in charge, now signalling a new direction for walking, later approving or suggesting luncheon shifts.

We moved along the pavement side by side, he and I. Would I want a sign—he had several in reserve. I would rather talk with him; I was very much interested in his opinions. I felt it important that he, that they, not be misunderstood, and I would do my best to record fairly what he thought and wanted. I am a physician, I told him, a research physician specializing in problems of human adjustment under stress. A little amplification of this, and he laughed

Reprinted from Robert Coles, "Public Evil and Private Problems: Segregation and Psychiatry," *Yale Review*, Vol. LIV (June, 1965), No. 4, pp. 516–530, by permission of the author.

—it *was* a strain, the police and the scoffing people, and those reporters with the sly, obviously unfriendly questions. He would talk with reporters, though, any of them, so long as they were not niggers, not Communists, because he wanted to be heard. It was important to be heard or nothing could be accomplished. He wanted to do something, not merely have his say, therefore he would surely talk with me if I were a teacher, if I wanted to report the truth to the educated. They needed his truth. I agreed. He was visibly impressed with certain credentials which, in my nervousness, I had offered: cards, pieces of paper which I now know were unnecessary for his cooperation. We began that day, later in the afternoon, signs put aside, over coffee. I arranged to meet him regularly, weekly, for several months, at his home, or over our coffee in a diner; and he told me about himself and his life, about what he believed and for how long. He liked to talk about himself, and he was grateful for a chance.

He is a passionate segregationist ("You can put down 'the strongest,' the strongest it's possible to be"). He has plans. He would like to exile most Negroes to Africa, perhaps sterilize a few quiet ones who would work at certain jobs fitting their animal nature, itself the work of God, he would emphasize. He would strip Jews of their fearful power, sending them off also, but to Russia, where they came from and yearn to return. There are other suspicious groups, Greeks, Lebanese—it's a port city, they can leave their boats. Unlike the niggers and Jews, whose clear danger to his city he had formulated for some time, he had not determined his exact position on those other people, or his solution for them.

He was born in central Louisiana, say for example the town of Acme in Concordia Parish. The state is split into its southern, Catholic and French area and a northern section, basically Protestant and Anglo-Saxon. A representative son, his father was the former and his mother Scotch-Irish, a wayward Baptist who embraced the Roman Church (the only term used for the Catholic Church in certain areas of the so-called Bible Belt) a few weeks before her marriage. Born their second child in the month America entered the First World War, he was sickly and fatherless his first year of life. While his father fought in Europe the boy was taken with what we now call "allergies," a timid stomach which mostly rejected milk, a cranky skin which periodically exploded red, raw, itchy, and was often infected by his responsive scratches. His sister was five years older, and she remembered all this. She and his mother, still alive, have told him about his fretful infancy, and he knew it well enough to be able to tell their memories. *His* first memory was a whipping from his father's strap. With his father home from war, a second son and last child was born when John was three. He had pinched the infant, done enough wrong to the child's skin to cause a cry and then his father's punishing attention. That was to happen many times, though he held a special place in his mind for this earliest occasion: "My brother and I started off on the wrong track, and we've never got along with one another."

His brother is tall and thin, ruddy-faced and blue-eyed like his mother, wears a white shirt to a bank teller's job near their home town. He, dark and shorter like his father, has several "blue-shirt" skills which at various times he has used. "I can build a house myself" was his way of summarizing them: carpentry, electric work, plumbing, even brick-laying.

As children the development of the boys forked: one neat, precise, his mother's favorite as well as her physical reflection; the other, by his own description, naughty, often idle or busy being scrappy. John in short was an overlooked and troubled middle child. He resembled his father, yet hated him as far back as he can remember. Oddly though, his manner, his temperament, sound like the father's as he describes the man, shows pictures of him, now ten years dead, a large blustery fellow, open, opinionated, rumpled, a mechanic preoccupied with automobiles—under them daily, reading magazines about them by night. He had storms within him, and they fell upon his middle child, alone and arbitrarily, the boy felt.

Once John and I had talked long and hard, it seemed like a whole day, and I noticed it was nearly three hours, and the length of time measured a certain trust, a certain understanding which was developing between us. I found myself knowing him, recognizing some of the hardships he had endured, not just psychological ones, but the hunger and jobless panic which must have entered so many homes in a decade when I was scarcely born and he yet a child. I felt guilty in a moment, torn between him and the simple, but of course complicated facts and experiences of his life, and him as he now is, a shabby fanatic. He was feeling his own movement toward me, and with considerable emotion in his voice, lifting his right hand in a gesture which might well have been his father's, he interrupted our talk of Huey Long's racial attitudes and how they compared with those of his family: "Daddy (southern fathers can be "Daddy" to their children forever without embarrassment) had a bad temper, and I took it by myself. We had never had much money and bills would set him going, but he wouldn't touch my mother, or my brother or sister either . . . Yes (I had asked), my sister and brother both favored Ma . . . and he'd feel no good because he couldn't get a week's pay . . . Oh, he was for Huey boy all the way, except Huey was soft on niggers, but I think Daddy was, too. He used to say they were children, and we should protect them. But if they're like kids, they're like bad ones, and, just like animals, they've got to be watched over . . . You wouldn't let a wild animal go free in your home or in school with your kids, would you? It's right crazy how we forget that sometimes. Look at Harlem, and what happens when they let them go. They rape and kill our women and dirty the whole city up. I've been there and seen it . . . No (prodded again), I don't blame Daddy, because, you see, in those days we had them firm under our grip, so it was different and you didn't have to worry about them. But look at now." We did talk about current events for a few minutes, but each of us tired suddenly, and hardened.

Of course, from those old times to the present had been an eventful period for him as well as for the Negro race. He almost died twice. At seven he had a serious bout of pneumonia which, without antibiotics, nearly killed him. He recalled gratefully a Negro maid who cared for him through this, one of those, few now, who knew and willingly lived in her "place." She died shortly after he recovered. Abruptly and looking still young ("I think she was around forty, but you can't tell with niggers") she collapsed before his very eyes while preparing supper for him. It was, by his description, probably a stroke that took her, and she proved irreplaceable. They had given her a pittance, but she had stayed with them for lack of better. About that time several Negro families started moving North, while others trekked south to New Orleans. Though his father had not really been able to pay Willi-Jean her established wages for many months, it was only death which would end her loyalty and their comfort. "I got pneumonia again when I was twelve, and so did my brother. It nearly killed Ma taking care of us . . . She used to try to keep everything in its place, I think that's why it was so hard without Willi-Jean, and with us sick on top of it, she almost didn't get through it all, she got so nervous."

In telling him of my interest in his medical history, I asked him several times to describe in further detail his fits of illness, and the care given him during these times. It seemed clear that he had, in fact, suffered badly at his mother's hands, neglected by her for his sister or brother, blamed for getting sick. The Negro woman's sudden death was actually a severe, a deeply resented blow to him. His affections for her were hastily buried with her. He had to keep his guard, more directly confront his mother's personality, now no longer buffered. During one of our last recorded talks he said, "You know, Doc, I think I *did* have a bad time with sickness when I was a kid. When I was twelve I almost died of pneumonia, and then I broke my leg a few weeks after that and lost that year of school." He had tried to run away from home before he contracted pneumonia, and after his recovery, too, until his lame leg made such attempts impossible for a while.

If his mother was nervous, oppressively ritualistic, and far from his advocate, his father was a heavy drinker, temper-ridden, and fearfully unpredictable. When drunk he was moody. He also became assaultive, and his middle son was his customary target. Declaring a truth too painful to see precisely, John once reflected, "I never figured why Daddy picked on me. We got along fine when he was sober, but when he got liquored up, I got it first and hardest. I looked like him and helped him most in fixing things around the house, but he never remembered things like that when he was drunk." Not that his parents weren't "the nicest parents anyone could ever want." Any vision into their problems, any criticism of them, had to be followed eventually by the atonement of heavy sentiment. He had long ago learned how dangerous it was to speak his mind. Perhaps his life, as we now see it, has been a quest for that very possibility. "I used to be afraid to say anything for fear it'd get someone upset at home, so I just kept quiet and ran my trains." Trains were his chief hobby for a little longer than is usual, well into the early teens. He warmed while telling me about his empire of them, and he became wistful afterwards. I wanted to hear of his childhood interests, and in speaking of them, he said a bit ambiguously, "I knew trains better than anyone in town."

By the last two years of high school he had found an easier time. His mother became menopausal, yielded in her war against dust and for order, and became cheerless and distant. His father now drank less, but had to struggle hard with another form of depression, an economic one which he shared with his country. A rich nation had somehow gone wrong in its ability to produce and distribute its wealth. Amid all this, John curiously prospered. His sister married poorly, a marginal farmer soon dispossessed of his land. Slothful and malignant, he quickly fathered two children by her, while beating her regularly, and left shortly thereafter. She never remarried and has had to work hard to keep her two children fed and clothed. His brother had trouble with learning. He left high school after one year, and for a time, nearly penniless, he drew food and small coin from government relief programs. Recently he has managed a job in a bank, but his wife is a heavy drinker, maybe worse, and they have five children. John says they "live like pigs," and apparently this state of decay set in very rapidly after their marriage. His brother's cleanest, most organized moments are at work.

John, however, graduated from high school, the first to do so in his family, and went beyond that by securing a rare job in the local hardward store. He had come to know its owner and his daughter, too. Always interested in fixing things—bicycles, injured cars, faltering plumbing, stray wires—he began in the hardware store as a willing and unpaid helper. The mysterious new radio was his love, and he tinkered endlessly with the various models. The store had many other gadgets, and it also had his girl-friend, the owner's daughter. He determined to marry her at about fifteen and did so at twenty. At the time of his marriage he was a relatively prosperous man, now come upon a white collar, regularly paid in dollars increasingly powerful out of their scarcity for many. ("My folks said I married real well, especially for those days.")

To hear him talk, the twelve months on either side of his wedding day were his best time. He remembers the pleasure and hope, but his nostalgia is brief, and is always tinctured with the bitterness which soon followed. His father-in-law's business, the star of John's rise, fell reluctantly, joining the domain of the few creditors who seemed to be gathering the entire countryside into their control. These provincial financiers, with their small banks all over the state, were controlled by Big Power and Big Money, both in New Orleans. Governor Huey had said so, and they killed him. John, with wife and a boy of three months, had no choice but to try Huey's gambit, follow the Power, follow the Money: "We just up and moved. An uncle of my wife's thought he could get me work repairing radios . . . they were like TV now. No matter how poor you were, you needed some relaxation."

He knew the radio, realized its uses and comforts. He obtained and held on to his job. He started by going into homes to repair wires or replace tubes. Soon he was selling them, all shapes and sizes on all kinds of payment plans. He was an exceptional sales-man, seeing the radio as a box of easily summoned distraction for weary, uncertain people. He aimed at first not to sell but to explain, tracing with the future customer the webs and tangles of copper, informing his listener of their connections and rationale, pressing hard only at the end their whetted appetite, their need. ("Mostly they were people without cash.")

However, by the time a second world war was underway most Americans had radios, and his work slackened, a credit to him and those like him, and one measure of the nation. In early 1942 he was the father of a four-year-old son, a two-year-old daughter. He owned a comfortable house in a distinctly middle-class area of white frame houses, each bulky, yet each a bit different. Most, though, had green shutters, high ceilings, thick walls, large, long windows, but no garage, all expressions of a warm, wet climate. More likely than not every residence had a single car so that the streets, palmy, well-paved, were lined on both sides just as, from a plane's view, the roofs asserted rows of radio antennae.

He still lives there, though many of his former neighbors have moved. For some the neighborhood was out of keeping with what they had newly become. They left for one-storied new houses in sprawling developments outside the city. They were replaced by others for whom the same neighborhood's value was defined by what they had just left. There are, however, a few who still prize these old houses, see their faintly shabby gentility and cherish their age and the memories they inspire. For John it is this way: "Those ranch houses are too expensive . . . Funny thing with a lot of the nigger-lovers, they move out into the suburbs and then tell us how we should open our streets to them . . . I won't leave and I'd shoot to kill if they ever tried to buy a house nearby . . ." (He cannot afford to leave. "They" are 2.4 miles away at their nearest.)

The war came, happily. The economy was stagnant, floundering with too many unemployed. Poor people had bought their radios, and he was feeling the pinch. ("Even the niggers had them. Some of them even had two.") Actually, he had sold many to Negroes in the years of such work. He had collected money from them and taken his showers after he came from their houses. Balancing such services for Negroes was his participation in lynchings. He'd been in two. His words: "We'd go home to see our folks, and you know in the country things are more direct, and there's no busybody reporters around. Once I heard one being organized, so I dropped by to see it." The other time was a rather spontaneous and informal affair. He noted that they "did it real quick like, the way you should. When you draw them out it makes it hard because you might get bad publicity . . . there are still lynchings around in farm country, I don't care what they tell you in the papers. We know how to take care of them when they get wise . . . We don't use rope, it's true, and get the crowds up we used to . . . we may not always kill them, but we scare the Jesus out of them . . . you know the buckshot shootings you read about every now and then, it's the same thing. They know what'll happen if they get smart." Did he object at all to this? "Hell, no."

The Negroes were working for the Communists, any he would want to kill; I must know that. Had there been Communists in his town when he was a boy, during the twenties and thirties when lynchings were more public and common, some of them seen by him as a youth? Of course. The Communists took over in 1917, he knew the autumn month, but some of them had been working in this country even before that. He wasn't sure how far back, but he thought maybe twenty or thirty years, and they wanted to take this country, its free economy, for their prize. John was capable of broad, apocalyptic strokes: "This is a war between God and His Commandments and the Devil, and we may lose." I broached the subject of loss. How could God lose? "To punish us." Why would he want to do that? "We disobeyed him." Just an example or two—I was interested in them. "Nigger-loving."

In any case, he was accumulating unpaid bills, and was glad to go to war in 1942. He yearned for the East—he wanted to go fight the Japs. He wasn't so sure about why we were fighting the Germans, who were combating the Reds, and might be our allies if we would but have them. Hitler's enemies were his, the Jews, money-eyed, slyly alien, and the main support of the Negroes, inferior lackeys who did their bidding for small reward. This was all Communism, personified in those hundreds of thousands of hook-nosed or black-skinned natives who were in New York, in Hollywood. They were the capitalists, too; they controlled publishing houses, banks, and the stock exchanges, their voices commanded a crippled, traitorous President's ear, bought the votes of errant, susceptible Congressmen. "I was never against the Germans. I was proven right. Look at us now. They're our best protection against the Commies." Still, he added, the Germans would be of small help if the UN and Integration took over America.

He never fought, though he helped others fight. He worked at an army camp in New Jersey, a very small distance from Manhattan's subversion, perversion—and fascination. He went there all the time, to look, to see his enemy. He would always tell his friends how well he knew his New York enemies, and to my observation his friends always seemed interested and stimulated by the details he supplied.

From all those furloughs to Union Square, Harlem, and Greenwich Village he managed to return home alive, heavier by fifteen pounds, and his balding completed. He worried about work after his discharge with good reason. He came home to older children, a wife with moderate rheumatoid arthritis ("Her joints are stiff all the time"). He was now irascible and sullen. His wife usually wanted to stay away from him—out of pain, out of lack of response. She was withdrawing into her world of routine care of the home and the symptoms of a chronic, slowly crippling disease. To help her she had a young Negro, a high school girl, less experienced, but less expensive. (The price of Negroes was rising, along with all other postwar costs.) A mulatto, as thin and lissome—I gathered from pictures I saw of her with his children—as her mistress was fattening and severe, she stayed with them for three years, five part-time days a week, until her marriage bore unexpectedly heavy demands of her own in twin sons.

During those few years John developed his own hardening, a fixing and tightening of his mind's thinking. He tried television repair work, but couldn't connect with it as with radio. He drew unemployment relief for a while, spare in the face of consuming inflation. Finally, nearly drowning in doctor's bills, in debt even for essentials like food and the most urgently needed clothing, his home heavily mortgaged, he found rescue in his state government, a clerk's job in a motor vehicle registration office. Now, barely secure, in his mid-thirties, he was free to settle into concentrated, serious suspicion and hate. It was, after all, the decade of the fifties, when many of his countrymen would seek far and wide for subversives, and when the Supreme Court would declare segregated schools unconstitutional.

I met him, of course, well along in such zeal and well into actions based upon it. From our first meeting it was clear that he relished talking, and was a good talker. He had found comfort for his views from his employer, a state government whose legislature, in its very chambers, had carried on a mock funeral of a federal judge, a native son who had ordered four Negro girls into two elementary schools in New Orleans. The governor was a man whose chief quality seemed to be that of a banjo player and singer. His theme song was "You Are My Sunshine."

John dips constantly into the literature of segregation for

companionship. It includes a range from the remarks of a scattering of biologists about a purported inferiority of the Negro on the basis of a supposedly lighter, smoother brain (fewer lines on the all-important frontal lobes) to the saddest rot of the disturbed. He reads in such allied fields as the frantic anti-Communism which holds the President and Supreme Court contaminated victims, even agents. There are always such diversions as the menacing effect of fluoridation in the quickening erosion of America's freedom.

He has a commanding way with his friends, just as he is a rather distinctive kind of father. One of the first questions he had hurled at me, in our early tentative moments, was about his son. The young man was contemplating marriage and, a loyal Catholic, was about to attend a pre-marriage instruction course offered by their local church. The church was hell-bent on integration, however, and John feared the worst for and of his son. Did I believe "in integrated marriage courses"? I wanted to know more about this. Well, he would kill his son if a Negro came into such a class and he, John Junior, remained. His customary composure cracked (one of the few times I was ever to see this, even when I knew him much better) and he shouted loud enough that I doubted for a while that *he* would be one "reasonable enough" for me ever to know "reasonably well." Yes, he'd kill his own son, I was to know that. Would I? I thought not. Still, I told him I wanted to hear more about integrated marriage classes. Well, if I wanted to hear more, he would oblige.

The real truth was that he and his son hadn't managed together for a long time, and for that matter he and his wife weren't now "together" as they used to be. Just as once with his mother, menopause along with arthritis had come to his wife, heightening with its flashing signals her sense of decline, pulling her from her husband into a separate bed. Once scornful of even a aspirin, she now juggled and swallowed seven separate encapsulated remedies. Their daughter, her father's great delight for years, had rewarded him with excellent school work and high achievement in pre-college tests. Yet her success, in the form of a full scholarship, had eventually transported her away from home. Now it was their son, an office worker by day and part-time college student by night, who was about to leave. His family was dissolving, his marriage disintegrated. He was lonely.

"My boy is a fool, and he always has been." He became angry at first, but later appeared to regret his own remark. His son, it seems, cared little about Negroes and their threatening postures.

He and his son had fought about ways of dressing, table manners, and hobbies; had fought all along as the boy tried to be his own person and John resisted, tried to pinion the lad, fashion him in his father's image. Murderous thoughts by a father at the shameful possibility of his son's marriage class in a church being attended by a Negro were but a final, public expression of long, private turmoil.

It was against a background of such family problems that he ardently pursued a world as white and shadowless as possible. His work for most of the fifteen-odd years since the war had been uncertain or dull. He tired of temporary work selling in stores, then became bored with the security but confinement and meagre pay of his state position. About a year before I met him he had run for a significant political office, claiming he would ferret out Communists in his district, export Negroes north or across the Atlantic, deprive Jews of any local, if hidden sovereignty, and keep a careful, alert eye upon Washington and New York. He lost, but polled a good vote. In the course of the campaign he met a gas station owner sympathetic to his ideals and also successfully burdened by too many stations to control by himself. ("He liked to watch the help, just like me. You can't trust a nigger out of the reach of your eye.") John, who prided himself on his sharp vision, purchased one of these stations, mortgaging his house further, even against his wife's stiff opposition—her arthritis worsened, a connection caught by him unaided by any sophistication in psychosomatic medicine. Selling fuel has been a tough, slimly profitable venture; a fortunate arrangement, however, because he was able to inform a fellow gasoline vendor, fast and angrily, about a Negro employee working for him whose child was one of the handful to initiate school desegregation. After all, John had helped organize the mobs around the school. Vocal and persistent in his attentions to these nearly deserted and embattled buildings where a few Negro and white children stubbornly persisted in getting educated together, he could scarcely allow one of the Negro families a weekly wage. To help fire the Negro was actually as heartening an experience as he had enjoyed in a long time, and he referred back to this moment of accomplishment frequently. He liked disorder in the streets, but he was not one to pass up a private spite or intrigue either, whether familial or racial.

In time, after acquaintance, we begin to understand the design of a life, how old threads appear in seemingly new patterns. Remember him while very young, a dark and sulky boy whose black-haired, ill-humored father preferred his fair wife, daughter, and younger son. He knew, knew all too well, arbitrary discrimination coming without apparent cause other than that of appearances. He was born in a state split among many lines—I catalogued them earlier—northern, Anglo-Saxon, lighter skinned, Protestant farmers, and southern, Catholic, Mediterranean types, many of the thousands who lived in a wicked, international port city. His parents brought these different traditions together in an uneasy marriage, and the boy grew up sensing, and a victim of, this delicate arrangement. How accidental is it to find him, years later, moodily resenting dark people?

Our psychiatric evaluations find him oriented and alert, in no trouble about who or where he is, his name, the date and place of our talks. His mind works in understandable fashion. He does not hallucinate, and, though we may consider his beliefs delusional, they are held in company with thousands, and do not seem insistently private or as incomprehensible as those in schizophrenic delusional systems. His thinking is not psychotic, flowing in orderly and logical steps, given certain assumptions which again are shared by many others and thus are social rather than predominantly idiosyncratic.

He is intelligent, beyond question so, grasping issues, relating them to others, seizing upon problems, analyzing them, and implementing proposed solutions. He has read widely, if with self-imposed restrictions, deeply, but only where he is allowed by his own mind. Much of what he reads gives him real encouragement. Full of references to God and Country, emphasizing virulent racism, submitting violence as possibly necessary in some future Armageddon of white-black, Gentile-Jew, biblical patriotism-atheistic internationalism, this "literature" seeks an America which we hope will never exist, but it also gives its readers fellowship. One can call *all* these people crazy, but it is a shared insanity. John works, has a family and friends. He is fitful, alternately glum or buoyant. He is not a shy or withdrawn person, and he is in definite contact with many people, and responds to their feelings. Can we call him "sick"?

In one of those compact appraisals of an individual person we might say that John is not insane, not psychotic in any operational sense of the word; neither retarded nor delinquent. He has no police record, has committed no crimes as his society defines them, is even careful to obey laws on picketing or demonstrations where they exist or are enforced. (*His* kind of demonstrations are often encouraged by many officials of his state.) Absurdly xenophobic, an anti-Semitic, anti-Negro "paranoiac"? Yes, along with many, many thousands in his region. A frustrated, defeated man, a some-time political candidate, a feckless sidewalk crank who is unworthy of our attention, harmless if occasionally irritable? Right now, yes, but far from alone.

Born in a region long poor and defeated, to a family itself humble and moneyless, often at the mercy, therefore, of capricious economic, social, or political forces, the boy at home faced those first insecurities, those early rivalries, hates, and struggles which set the pattern for later ones. A split country or state was for him a split family. White man against black was for him all those child-hood hatreds, all those desperate, anxious attempts of children to find themselves, locate themselves and their identities amid the strivings of siblings, amid the conscious and unconscious smiles and grudges, animosities and predilections of their parents. He was an active child, a fighter who survived perilous disease and hard times. When grown he temporarily had some modest success at home and at work, only to return from a war into a sliding, middle-aged, hardly covert depression, a personal one, but certainly a familial and economic one also, all of these happening simultane-ously, probably all of them connected with one another in his mind. Individual psychopathology, social conflict, and economic instability, each has its separate causes. On the other hand they can stimulate one another reciprocally and keenly.　　.　　　.　　　.

CHAPTER SEVEN

POLITICAL PERSUASION

I<small>T DOES NOT TAKE MUCH RESEARCH</small> to show that political persuasion is complex. Studies of communication make clear that political messages flow and drip and bubble through many connected channels, and that they may fall on fertile or barren soil. This complexity is a challenge to research in political behavior that aims to uncover regularities rather than simply to display complications.

The startling figures on the hours Americans spend watching television and the confidence people say they have in television point to the potential importance of media for persuasion, but they tell us little of what actually comes across. In particular, it is difficult to relate the message to action, the appeal for a vote with voting. The following selection from a first-rate study of specialized communication adds another dimension. Here we see in the midst of mass persuasion a set of citizens—businessmen—receiving, interpreting, and passing on messages few people understand: communications about international trade policies. The authors show how variations in social structure and in the salience of an issue for a particular audience shaped the main communications patterns and related to patterns of political action.

COMMUNICATION THROUGH THE BUSINESS STRUCTURE

RAYMOND A. BAUER
ITHIEL DE SOLA POOL
LEWIS ANTHONY DEXTER

The media read by businessmen contained copious information, at least about the main course of debate over major pieces of trade legislation. Yet we found that, among the heads of the smallest firms, only about half professed knowledge of the Randall report, the most widely publicized event concerning foreign-trade policy in the previous months. It is not stretching things to say that to have avoided learning about the Randall report may have taken a little effort. Such selectivity of attention, recall, and response will appear repeatedly as we look at specialized communications dealing with foreign-trade problems. The mass media reached everyone in our sample, forcing some information even on readers without an active interest. The specialized media came only to those individuals who felt some need for information on foreign-trade policy.

The notion of "information concerning foreign-trade policy" defies precise specification. For American businessmen it may include topics as broad as the political stability of foreign countries and as narrow as the decisions of customs authorities on the procedure for counting the jewels in watches. In our own research group, we found that each of us had a slightly different perspective on what was relevant to the study. All, of course, would be interested in the Swiss reaction to watch tariffs and in the speeches of Oscar Strackbein. But one of us might clip an article on the health of a particular congressman because it bore on the potential mem-

Reprinted from R. A. Bauer, I. de S. Pool, and L. A. Dexter, *American Business and Public Policy: The Politics of Foreign Trade* (New York: Atherton Press, 1963), pp. 179–95, by permission of Atherton Press, Inc. Copyright © 1963, Massachusetts Institute of Technology.

bership of the Ways and Means Committee. Another might note a drought in Brazil which could affect coffee imports. A third would read a report that Japanese cameras had improved in quality.

The above is by no means far-fetched. Our informal interviews clearly established the fact that American businessmen in the years 1953–1955 viewed information concerning foreign-trade policy in many and varied ways, ranging from the broadest of policy considerations down to the most narrowly technical details. For businessmen, information on tariff and foreign-trade policy is far from being exclusively information on newsworthy matters.

We asked our respondents what they considered the best sources of information on tariff and foreign-trade policy, however they defined that subject matter for themselves. Their answers to this question are characterized in Table 1. The distribution of responses offers an interesting contrast to the sources from which they had learned about the Randall and Eisenhower messages. The vast majority of men who knew of the Eisenhower message reported having heard about it in general news media. However, our respondents, when asked about their preferred sources of news on

TABLE 1

SOURCES OF INFORMATION ON TARIFF AND FOREIGN-TRADE POLICY RESPONDENT CONSIDERED BEST

Source	Size of firm		
	Large	Medium	Small
A. General public printed sources			
1. Newspapers	15%	15%	21%
2. News magazines	15	15	15
3. General business magazines	13	11	19
4. Other general publications	4	6	6
Total public printed sources	47	47	61
B. Special sources			
1. Individual business associates, including foreign-trade specialists	13	17	8
2. Communications from business and trade associations and lobbying groups	43	31	27
3. Political figures	3	4	4
4. Government agencies, reports, and officials	30	25	22
Total special sources	89	77	61
Total all sources	136	124	122

whatever they called matters of tariffs and foreign-trade policy, replied by naming highly specialized sources. They were presumably thinking of tariff policy as embracing a narrower and more technical domain than that of the public policy statements embodied in the Randall report and Eisenhower message.

Men from large firms, in particular, voted confidence in specialized sources. In this preference, they reflected their greater need for, their better access to, and their superior knowledge of such detailed and thorough information media. Many more, for example, have foreign-trade specialists in their firms to whom they can turn. They have more communications directed at them from industry specialists, lobbyists, and the like. They have better contact with government agencies. They are more knowledgeable themselves and are aided by better and larger staffs.

There is an anomaly in the fact that men from the smaller firms are more likely to prefer general media. Use of general sources might be taken to imply less concern with the narrower and more technical features of foreign-trade policy and more concern with matters of broad policy. But breadth of interest does not characterize the men from small firms. They are, on the contrary, less concerned with issues of wide public policy. Another factor in this instance overrode the usual proclivity of small businessmen to read trade publications rather than those dealing with national affairs, and that factor was indifference. Being less involved with foreign trade policy, they had less demand for detailed technical information. Those few small businessmen who were actively involved in the issue had a frame of reference generally narrower than that of the men from the larger firms. Those more interested small businessmen, along with their colleagues from larger firms, thought of rather specific business consequences when they thought of foreign-trade policy, and, accordingly, they preferred specialized sources for information on the subject; but they were a minority.

TALKING ABOUT TARIFFS AND FOREIGN-TRADE POLICY

The media are inputs into the business community. The Randall report, the President's message, and the vast majority of the articles read and speeches heard originated outside that community, in government or in the professions. Reviewing now more focused communications, we turn first to a type which occurs largely within the confines of the business community—conversations.

We asked our respondents three questions: whether in the preceding month they had talked to any persons in their organization specially designated to handle matters concerned with foreign trade, whether they had talked about trade to other persons within their company, and whether they had talked with persons outside their company. The proportions of men who had talked about foreign-trade matters under any of these three conditions is summarized in Fig. 1.

The amount of conversation reported was surprisingly large. In the large and medium firms, over 60 percent of the men had talked about tariffs and foreign-trade policy in some circumstances. The men from the small firms were conspicuously less active. Note, also, that twice as many members of the business community had discussed the issue face-to-face in the previous month as had read or heard some particular article or speech on it (Fig. 2). The system of communication about trade matters was to a large degree an oral one. But participation in it was highly selective. Fig. 1 indicates that some men talked a great deal and some not at all. Except in the smallest firms, if a man talked at all, he was more likely than not to have talked both inside and outside the firm.

About 40 percent of all discussion inside a man's firm took place with someone in charge of foreign-trade matters. To some extent, talking with such a man was a function of his availability, and we find that such foreign-trade specialists were much more likely to be found among the larger than among the smaller firms (74, 63, and 41 percent, respectively). Discussion with other persons within one's firm almost always meant talking with other top officers. A few men talked with representatives of the sales department, and still fewer with a scattering of staff personnel.

Discussion outside the firm was also often with business contacts (about three-fifths of the time for large and medium businessmen and half the time for the smallest businessmen, who had a less elaborate structure around them with which to interact). In other words, the issue was more apt to appear to leading businessmen as a business topic appropriate for discussion within his industry and with suppliers and customers than it was to present itself as a political issue for citizen consideration, appropriate for civic

FIGURE 1
TALK ABOUT FOREIGN TRADE IN PRECEDING MONTH

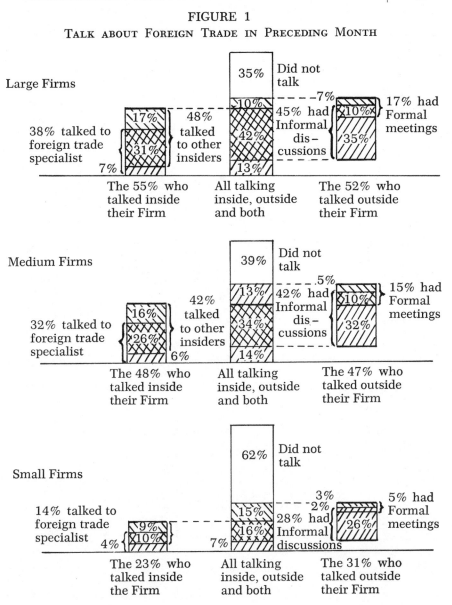

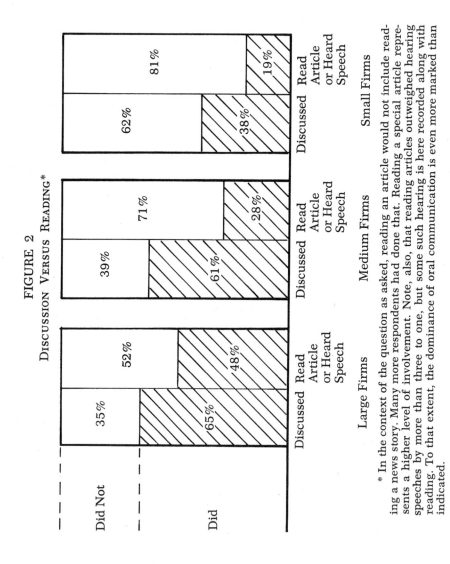

FIGURE 2
DISCUSSION VERSUS READING*

* In the context of the question as asked, reading an article would not include reading a news story. Many more respondents had done that. Reading a special article represents a higher level of involvement. Note, also, that reading articles outweighed hearing speeches by more than three to one, but some such hearing is here recorded along with reading. To that extent, the dominance of oral communication is even more marked than indicated.

groups, neighbors, and the breakfast table (Fig. 3). . . . A businessman or a congressman was less likely to have a sense of how a geographical constituency felt than of how an industry felt. Furthermore, those who attempted to promote expression of civic feelings about the issue had less success than those who attempted to organize representation of direct business interests.

Most of the outside talking consisted of informal discussion. Yet one-sixth, except in the small firms, had discussed foreign trade at a formal meeting within the previous two weeks. Some men attended repeated meetings, and others attended none; yet, over a period of a year, many of our respondents would find themselves at a meeting where foreign-trade policy was discussed.[1]

We have already pointed out that foreign-trade policy extends over a wide range of issues from general policy to the narrowly technical problems of a specific business or industry. Discussions inside a firm are likely to be focused on the problems of that firm. Discussions outside may either continue such focus on the specific problems agitating the firm or industry or they may be couched in symbols of ideology or national interest. We asked which way the discussions outside the firm had gone. When we look at the men who talked only outside their firms and compare them with the men who had talked both inside and outside their firms, we discover that the men who had talked only outside their firms were likely to have entered into general discussions, whereas men who had talked also inside their firms were more likely to have talked about matters affecting their firms specifically, even in their outside conversations.

We have now established, at least in a sketchy way, who talked to whom and what they talked about. What significance did such conversations have? We take talking about foreign-trade policy to be an indication of involvement in the subject. Note as evidence on this point that talking about foreign-trade matters is correlated with reading about them, too.

Talking is also correlated with knowledge. Indeed, men who were active by any communications criterion showed consistently more knowledge concerning the men and organizations involved in foreign-trade policy. For example, those who had discussed foreign

---

[1] About half those meetings were called specially for the purpose. Cf. Bauer and Pool, *American Businessmen and International Trade* (New York: Free Press, 1960), p. 41.

FIGURE 3

DISCUSSION OF FOREIGN TRADE WITH BUSINESS
ASSOCIATES OR WITH OTHERS

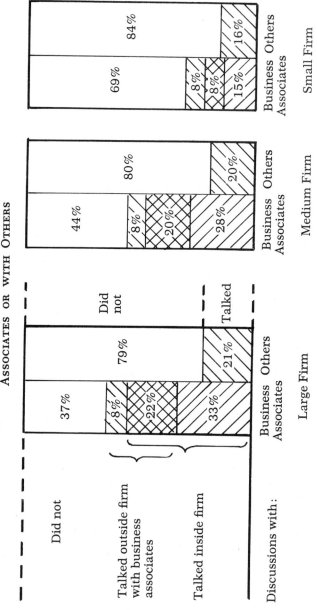

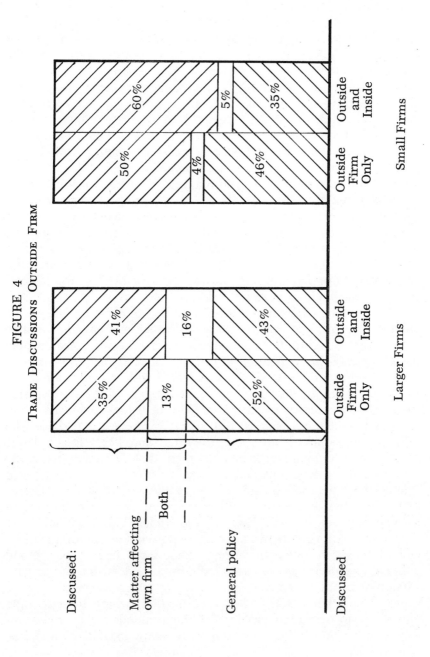

FIGURE 4

TRADE DISCUSSIONS OUTSIDE FIRM

trade were more likely to know the views of their congressmen—among the larger firms by about two to one.

Communications activity with respect to foreign-trade policy may thus clearly be treated as an indication of interest. We can rule out the alternative hypothesis, that communicators on the trade issue were simply men who communicated on everything. There is no clear indication that having discussed foreign-trade policy (holding size of firm constant) is generally related to total newspaper-reading, magazine-reading, and so on. A high level of communication on foreign trade is in general specific to the issue.

This talk was more than idle chatter. Arising from a real interest in the issue, it often led to action. Fig. 6 presents the relationship between talking and reading about foreign-trade policy and the probability that a man will have communicated with his congressman on trade matters in the years immediately preceding our 1954 survey. The most dramatic contrast is between those who did no talking and those who talked both inside and outside their firms. Among the nontalkers, only a negligible number communicated with Congress. Among the most active talkers, the proportions approach a quarter or a third.

Reading or hearing mass-media material without further discussion of it produced little action. Conversations outside the firm were perhaps slightly less related to action than were those inside. A small but highly revealing difference appears when we compare Figs. 5 and 6, a difference of a sort which will be confirmed again in other results. In Fig. 5, we see that persons who talked outside the firm were more likely to read articles or listen to speeches than those who talked only inside. But, in Fig. 6, we see that those who talk only inside are, if anything, the ones more likely to act. To be more precise, among bigger businessmen, those who talk inside the firm and those who talk outside are equally likely to act, even though those who talk outside are more likely to inform themselves by reading, too. Among smaller businessmen, those who talk inside the firm are even more likely to act, though less likely to read.

This result reveals two alternative patterns of communication. One of these, in which the foreign-trade issue figures as a broad political question, involves use of the published media and of conversations in the broad civil community of which the respondent is a part. The other pattern of communication, where foreign trade figures as an operating problem of the respondent's business, involves much oral communication with fellow executives and less

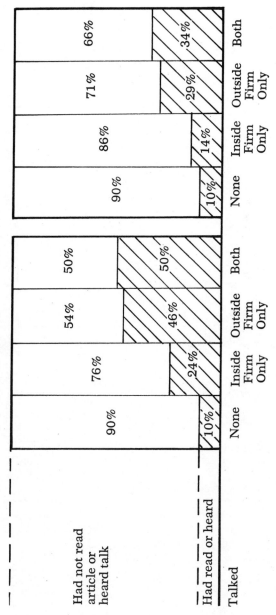

FIGURE 5

Proportion of Respondents Having Read Article or Heard Speech Specifically about Foreign-Trade Policy Related to their Patterns of Discussion

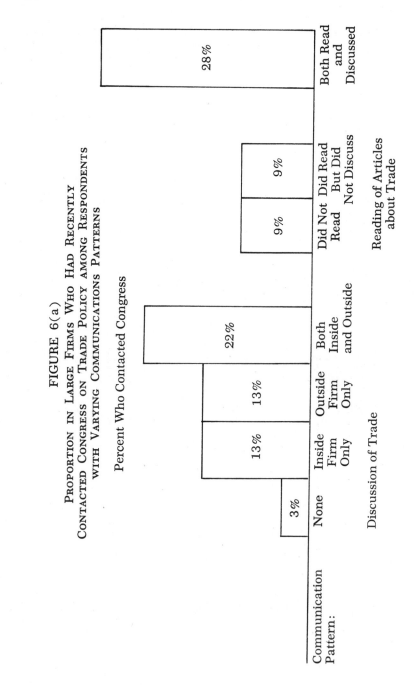

FIGURE 6(a)

PROPORTION IN LARGE FIRMS WHO HAD RECENTLY
CONTACTED CONGRESS ON TRADE POLICY AMONG RESPONDENTS
WITH VARYING COMMUNICATIONS PATTERNS

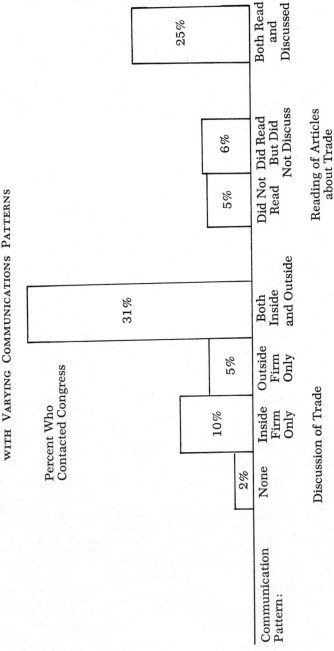

FIGURE 6(b)

PROPORTION IN SMALL FIRMS WHO HAD RECENTLY
CONTACTED CONGRESS ON TRADE POLICY AMONG RESPONDENTS
WITH VARYING COMMUNICATIONS PATTERNS

use of published media. Such a pattern was the more conducive to action.[2]

Sociological studies in recent years have repeatedly established that oral communication with reference persons located in the immediate social environment of an individual is far more likely to lead to action by him than will mass media material alone. This has been found to be so among farmers,[3] housewives,[4] physicians,[5] and others. We find it again among business executives, and that is not surprising.

Furthermore, the whole organization of business is geared to producing action easily and quickly on any current business problem. It takes much more initiative for the executive to act as a private citizen outside his office, where he has no secretary, staff, in-box, and out-box. Executives of the kind we were interviewing arrive at the office to face a neatly arranged pile of mail and memos. A first precept is that every letter must be answered and every proposal get some action decision. A staff is waiting to discuss and facilitate decisions. (Discussions with staff are some of the conversations which appear in our data.) If a letter to an executive is a plea from a business colleague to write Congress about a particular difficulty of the industry, he must either present reasons for declining—devise an "out," such as referring it for study—or send the requested letter, and that usually within a few days. Although a form request from a trade association may simply go unanswered, the option of letting the problem slide by sheer indecision is not approved for proposals more weighty than that.

Many of the letters sent by our respondents to their congressmen arose out of this compulsion for action. A case in point is one in which the major Eastern railroads came to the support of fuel-oil quotas, though their self-interest was not at all clear. Nonetheless, they responded to a request in almost all cases by agreeing to sign a

---

[2] Note that causality goes two ways. The usual interpretation in the literature is that word-of-mouth communication has a greater causal impact on action than do written media. It is probably also true, however, that, when a man is ready to act, he is prone to talk about the topic.

[3] Everett Rogers and G. M. Beal, "The Importance of Personal Influence in the Adoption of Technological Changes," *Social Forces*, 36 (1958), No. 4, 329–335; Bryce Ryan and Neal Gross, *Acceptance and Diffusion of Hybrid Seed Corn in Two Iowa Communities* (Ames, Iowa: Iowa State College of Argiculture and Mechanic Arts, Research Bulletin #372, 1950).

[4] Elihu Katz and Paul Lazarsfeld, *Personal Influence* (Glencoe, Ill.: The Free Press, 1955).

[5] Elihu Katz and Herbert Menzel, "Social Relations and Innovation in the Medical Profession," *Public Opinion Quarterly*, 19 (1955), 337–352.

statement. Had their diesel-fuel suppliers approached them first, they might have been found on the other side.

The initiators of the low-tariff lobby were conscious of the advantages of using business channels and of relating themselves to operational problems of firms. But, as we shall have occasion to relate, that strategy was replaced in 1954–1955 by civic appeals through lectures, luncheon meetings, and public exhortation. Whatever educational value those activities may have had, and in the long run that may have been very great indeed, they did not produce much immediate action. In 1962, the strategy of making individualized appeals to businessmen with foreign markets was revived with good effect.

The fact that generalized views find expression less readily than special demands may be demonstrated by reference to the otherwise-puzzling figures on letter-writing to Congress. Although both business and public opinion strongly favored a liberal-trade policy, the weight of the mail was the contrary. We had no opportunity to systematically sample congressional mail, but a few congressmen opened their files to us, and some mail clerks gave us estimates. That left us with the impression that the mail was perhaps ten-to-one for protection. Even if one subtracts the stimulated campaigns of a few organized industries, which accounted for perhaps two-thirds to four-fifths of all the mail, the majority of the mail still consisted of pleas for protection. Especially if one subtracts that portion of the residual mail from other than businessmen—for example, that from members of the League of Women Voters—the majority of business mail was clearly protectionist. It became apparent, as we spoke to congressmen about situations that we knew, that the discrepancy was to a large extent explained by letters from businessmen who in our interview would have been rated as liberal traders and, indeed, were that. But they wrote their congressman, not about their general feeling on foreign trade from home in their capacity as citizens, but from their offices, as executives, about some particular problem of customs classification or administrative procedure which was hurting their competitive position. In the environment of Congress, these letters were read as protectionist.

Thus, the structure of the communications system favored the propagation of particular demands. Internal consultation in a company generally preceded action. Outside discussion and reading often followed. Just as the man who has bought a new car reads the advertisements for it both to reassure himself and because of his newly found interest in that brand, so, too, a businessman who had written his congressman often talked about that act and read articles supporting what he had done. He also discussed and read in advance of his action, as he sought to inform himself better about the issues which faced him. But reading and general conversation alone, without the final stimulus of discussion within an institution geared to action, were unlikely to lead to an action in the short run.

THE GENESIS OF COMMUNICATIONS ACTIVITY— INTEREST AND ATTITUDE

What makes some heads of firms more likely to talk about foreign-trade policy than others? We often take issue with simple notions of economic self-interest, but never to deny that it is an effective motive to action. Our reservations have to do with the difficulty of arriving at an unequivocal criterion. Yet, having entered these reservations, we find that there is a positive correlation between communications activity on foreign-trade policy and virtually any criterion of economic self-interest which we may employ.

Men who said that tariffs were important for their firms were more likely than others to have talked about foreign-trade policy in the previous month. Similar relationships hold between talking (also reading or hearing a particular article or speech) and other subjective criteria of self-interest, such as the importance of foreign competition and export markets. But statements that tariffs, export markets, foreign competition, and the like are important to one's firm—that is, subjective criteria of self-interest—though to some extent unquestionably reflecting objective facts, may be contaminated by the respondent's personal involvement (or lack of it) in the issues.

Let us take the existence of a foreign-trade specialist in a firm as objective, prima facie evidence that the firm has an interest in foreign-trade policy. We find that, among firms which have a foreign-trade representative on their staff, the chief officer of the firm is twice as likely as otherwise to have talked about foreign-trade policy to members of his firm other than his foreign-trade specialist (Fig. 7).

It may well seem self-evident that men with an interest in a topic would be likely to talk about it. It is not equally obvious, however, that the amount of discussion should be related to the

FIGURE 7

DISCUSSION OF FOREIGN-TRADE POLICY AS A FUNCTION
OF ITS IMPORTANCE TO THE FIRM

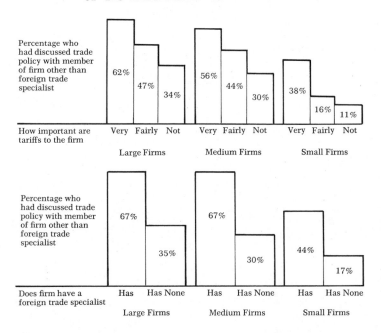

direction of a man's interest, but we see in Fig. 8 that it is so related. The self-interest of our respondents' industries are consistently related to whether they have talked and read about trade matters. Regardless of the criterion of activity or of size of firm, the men from high-tariff industries are most active, those from mixed industries come second, those from low-tariff industries are next, and in all instances those from no-interest industries are least active. High-tariff interest seems to be conspicuously more effective in stimulating communications than is low-tariff interest. In almost all cases, the low-tariff group is closer in its reported activity to the no-interest group than it is to the high-tariff group. The protectionist component of a mixed interest apparently makes even that group more active than the low-tariff group.

There is one difference between the smaller and the larger firms that should be noted. Company interest had more impact in producing communication about foreign trade in the smaller firms. More accurately, among the heads of smaller firms, attention to the

FIGURE 8

PERCENTAGE TALKING AND READING ABOUT FOREIGN-TRADE
POLICY AS A FUNCTION OF THE OBJECTIVE TARIFF INTEREST
OF THE INDUSTRY

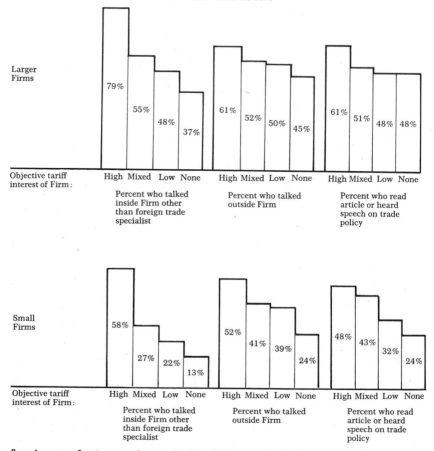

foreign-trade issue depends heavily on their having some direct business interest in the matter. Among the heads of larger firms, the foreign-trade issue often attracted their attention even in the absence of special business involvement. It attracted their attention also in their general reading and sometimes involved their participation in civic affairs outside their firms. The heads of large businesses more often than those of small saw themselves as having a responsibility for the general condition of the national economy. The head of a giant insurance company could hardly say, as could a small-town manufacturer, that the state of dollar balances or of national economic policies was none of his affair. He could not see himself as a little man, having to accept whatever national trends the economy produced. He had, and recognized that he had, channels by which his voice could affect any national policy of significance to him, even if its significance arose through its impact on the position of the nation in the world. The heads of large firms therefore participated more than those of small firms in the public affairs of business through such organizations as the Committee for Economic Development, the International Chamber of Commerce, and the Committee for a National Trade Policy and through reading and discussing foreign trade as a national policy issue, independent of their own firms' special interests.

Despite this difference of degree between large and small firms, we may conclude that any interest is likely to increase communications activity, though a high-tariff interest is markedly more effective in evoking action than is low-tariff interest. A high-tariff interest is particularly effective in stimulating discussion inside the firm and by implication, therefore, of its own problems, in contrast to broad matters of policy. It is thus all the more conducive to action.

This conclusion is buttressed by Fig. 8, where talking about foreign-trade policy is compared to objective tariff interest. Those who advocated raising tariffs did the most talking, especially within their firms. Fewest did no talking. More talked both inside and outside their firms. But few talked only outside their firms. If they did not talk both outside and inside, then they talked inside only.

A high-tariff interest and/or attitude proved a more effective stimulus to action than did a low-tariff interest, because, in part, a high-tariff interest and/or attitude stimulated discussion within a firm along lines directly concerned with its specific interests, rather than discussion of general policy.

CHAPTER EIGHT

CITIZEN POWER AND COMMUNITY CULTURE

Leaders are leaders because followers follow them. A leader may be strikingly effective in one political setting and fall flat when he tries the same appeals in a different setting. So to grasp the central meanings of political leadership (or power or influence) in a community we need an understanding of the interests and values of the people being led and why they are attracted to particular leaders. This is the empowering process, a kind of cultural equivalent for natural selection.

The empowering process is more than a matter of individual citizens, one at a time, deciding to fall in line behind a leader. It is a profoundly *social* process. For example, one reason people are attracted to join a following may be that others like themselves—with similar histories and values and expectations—are in the group. The purposes a leader personifies to the public must fit their purposes. In democratic electoral politics, the leader who deviates from his following too far or too fast risks his political life. So does the leader who fails to deliver on the expectations he has aroused.

The contemporary crisis of the cities shows this interplay between community culture and leadership. The mayors of many large cities walk a tightrope between mass violence and repressive control as they struggle for accomodations among conflicting groups. At the heart of that struggle is race. Millions of Negro citizens, new to the city and hoping to find a better life there, are surrounded by white neighborhoods where fear of change conflicts with the spirit of communitywide cooperation. In the following selection, three recent big-city elections are analyzed to show how the patterns of community support for new leaders affects their chances for success in gaining office and in governing once elected.

THE MAKING OF THE NEGRO MAYORS 1967

JEFFREY K. HADDEN
LOUIS H. MASOTTI
VICTOR THIESSEN

Throughout most of 1967, black power and Vietnam kept this nation in an almost continual state of crisis. The summer months were the longest and hottest in modern U.S. history—many political analysts even felt that the nation was entering its most serious domestic conflict since the Civil War. Over a hundred cities were rocked with violence.

As the summer gave way to autumn, the interest of the nation shifted a little from the summer's riots to the elections on the first Tuesday of November. An unprecedented number of Negroes were running for office, but public attention focused on three elections. In Cleveland, Carl B. Stokes, a lawyer who in 1962 had become the first Democratic Negro legislator in Ohio, was now seeking to become the first Negro mayor of a large American city. In Gary, Ind., another young Negro lawyer, Richard D. Hatcher, was battling the Republican Party's candidate—as well as his own Democratic Party—to become the first Negro mayor of a "medium-sized" city. And in Boston, Louise Day Hicks, a symbol of white backlash, was conducting a "You know where I stand" campaign to capture the mayorality.

Normally, the nation couldn't care less about who would become the next mayors of Cleveland, Gary, and Boston. But the tenseness of the summer months gave these elections enormous significance. If Stokes and Hatcher lost and Hicks won, could

Reprinted from *Trans-action*, Vol. 5 (January-February 1968), No. 3, pp. 21–30. Copyright © 1968 by *Trans-action* magazine, St. Louis, Mo.

Negroes be persuaded to use the power of the ballot box rather than the power of fire bombs?

Fortunately, November 7 proved to be a triumphant day for racial peace. Stokes and Hatcher won squeaker victories, both by margins of only about 1500 votes; in Boston, Kevin H. White defeated Mrs. Hicks by a 12,000 plurality. Labor leader George Meany was exultant—"American voters have rejected racism as a political issue." Negroes in the three cities were also jubilant. In Gary, the most tense of the cities, Richard Hatcher urged the mostly Negro crowd at his headquarters to "cool it." "I urge that the outcome of this election be unmarred by any incident of any kind. . . . If we spoil this victory with any kind of occurrence here tonight, or anywhere in the city, it will be a hollow victory." The evening *was* cool: joyous Negroes danced and sang in the streets.

But beyond the exultation of victory remain many hard questions. Now that Cleveland and Gary have Negro mayors, just how much difference will it make in solving the many grave problems that these cities face? Will these victories cool militancy in urban ghettos next summer, or will the momentum of frustration prove too great to put on the brakes? A careful analysis of *how* these candidates won office may help provide the answers.

The focus of this report is on Cleveland because:

● As residents of Cleveland, we are more familiar with the campaign and the election.

● Cleveland is unique because, in 1965, it had a special census. By matching voting wards with census tracts, we can draw a clearer picture of voting behavior than we could in the other cities, where rapid neighborhood transitions have made 1960 census data quite unreliable in assessing voting patterns. Having examined Cleveland in some detail, we will draw some comparisons with the Gary and Boston elections, then speculate about their significance and implications.

CLEVELAND—CITY IN DECLINE

Cleveland has something less than 2,000,000 residents. Among metropolitan areas in America, it ranks eleventh in size. Like many other American cities, the central city of Cleveland is experiencing an absolute decline in population—residents are fleeing from the decaying core to the surrounding suburbs. The city certainly ranks high both in terms of absolute and proportional decline in the central-city population.

Between 1950 and 1960, the population of the central city declined from 914,808 to 876,050, a loss of almost 39,000. By 1965 the population had sunk to 810,858, an additional loss of 65,000. But these figures are only a partial reflection of the changing composition of the population, since new Negro residents coming into the central city helped offset the white exodus. *Between 1950 and 1960, nearly 142,000 white residents left the central city, and an additional 94,000 left between 1960 and 1965—nearly a quarter of a million in just 15 years.*

During the same period the number of Negro residents of Cleveland rose from 147,847 to 279,352—an increase from 16.1 percent to 34.4 percent of the city's population. There is no evidence that this dramatic population redistribution has changed since the special 1965 census. Some suburbanization of Negroes is beginning on the east and southeast side of the city, but the pace is not nearly so dramatic as for whites. In 1960, approximately 97 percent of the Negroes in the metropolitan area lived in the central city. This percentage has probably declined somewhat since then —16,000 Negro residents have moved to East Cleveland. But the basic pattern of segregation in the metropolitan area remains. The development in East Cleveland is little more than an eastward extension of the ghetto, and the older, decaying residential units the Negroes have moved to are hardly "suburban" in character.

While the population composition of Cleveland is changing rapidly, whites are still a significant majority—about 62 percent. Again like many other central cities, a significant percentage of the white population comprises nationality groups that live in segregated sections, with a strong sense of ethnic identity and a deep fear of Negro encroachment. (In 1964, the bussing of Negro students into Murray Hill, an Italian neighborhood, resulted in rioting.)

In 1960, the census classified 43 percent of the central city's white residents as "foreign stock." In that year, five groups—Germans, Poles, Czechs, Hungarians, and Italians—had populations of 25,000 or greater; at least 20 other nationality groups were large enough to have to be contended with in the political arena. But today these ethnic groups—although unwilling to admit it—have become less than the controlling majority they constituted before 1960.

The Cuyahoga River divides Cleveland, physically as well as socially. When Negroes first began to move into the city, during World War I, they occupied the decaying section to the south and east of the central business district. As their numbers grew, they continued pushing in this direction and now occupy the larger part of the eastside (except for some ethnic strongholds). There are no stable, integrated neighborhoods in the central city—only areas in transition from white to black. To the west, the Cuyahoga River constitutes a barrier to Negro penetration.

Ever since 1941, when Frank Lausche was elected, Cleveland has had a succession of basically honest but unimaginative Democratic mayors. These mayors have kept their hold on City Hall by means of a relatively weak coalition of nationality groups. At no point in this 26-year Lausche dynasty did a mayor gather enough power to seriously confront the long-range needs and problems of the city.

By early 1967, the city had seemingly hit rock bottom. A long procession of reporters began arriving to write about its many problems. The racial unrest of the past several years had, during the summer of 1966, culminated in the worst rioting in Cleveland's history. This unrest was continuing to grow as several militant groups were organizing. Urban renewal was a dismal failure; in January, the Department of Housing and Urban Development even cut off the city's urban renewal funds, the first such action by the Federal Government. The exodus of whites, along with business, shoved the city to the brink of financial disaster. In February, the Moody Bond Survey reduced the city's credit rating. In May, the Federal Government cut off several million dollars of construction funds—because the construction industry had failed to assure equal job opportunities for minority groups. In short, the city was, and remains, in deep trouble. And while most ethnic groups probably continued to believe that Cleveland was the "Best Location in the Nation," the Negro community—and a growing number of whites—were beginning to feel that Cleveland was the "Mistake on the Lake," and that it was time for a change.

Carl Stokes's campaign for mayor was his second try. In 1965, while serving in the state House of Representatives, he came within 2100 votes of defeating Mayor Ralph S. Locher. Stokes had taken advantage of a city charter provision that lets a candidate file as an independent, and bypass the partisan primaries. Ralph McAllister, then president of the Cleveland School Board, did the same. For his hard line on *de facto* school segregation, however, McAllister had earned the enmity of the Negro community. The Republican candidate was Ralph Perk, the first Republican elected to a county-wide position (auditor) in many years. A second generation

Czech-Bohemian, Perk hoped to win by combining his ethnic appeal with his program for the city (Perk's Plan). He had no opposition for his party's nomination. The fourth candidate was Mayor Locher, who had defeated Mark McElroy, county recorder and perennial candidate for something, in the Democratic primary.

It was in the 1965 Democratic primary that the first signs of a "black bloc" vote emerged. The Negroes, who had previously supported incumbent Democratic mayoral candidates, if not enthusiastically at least consistently, made a concerted effort to dump Locher in favor of McElroy. There were two reasons:

● Locher's support of his police chief after the latter had made some tactless remarks about Negroes. Incensed Negro leaders demanded an audience with the mayor, and when he refused, his office was the scene of demonstrations, sit-ins, and arrests. At that point, as one of the local reporters put it, "Ralph Locher became a dirty name in the ghetto."

● Stokes, as an independent. His supporters hoped that the Democratic primary would eliminate the *stronger* candidate, Locher— for then a black bloc would have a good chance of deciding the general election because of an even split in the white vote.

Despite the Negro community's efforts, Locher won the primary and went on to narrowly defeat Stokes. Locher received 37 percent of the vote, Stokes 36 percent, Perk 17 percent, and McAllister 9 percent. Some observers reported that a last-minute whispering campaign in Republican precincts—to the effect that "A vote for Perk is a vote for Stokes"—may have given Locher enough Republican votes to win. The evidence: The popular Perk received only a 17 percent vote in a city where a Republican could be expected to poll something closer to 25 percent. Had Perk gotten anything close to 25 percent, Stokes would have probably been elected two years earlier.

Although he made a strong showing in defeat, Carl Stokes's political future looked bleak. No one expected the Democratic leaders to give Stokes another opportunity to win by means of a split vote. Nor were there other desirable elected offices Stokes could seek. Cleveland has no Negro Congressman—largely because the heavy Negro concentration in the city has been "conveniently" gerrymandered. The only district where Stokes might have had a chance has been represented by Charles Vanik, a popular and liberal white, and as long as Vanik remained in Congress Stokes was locked out. Stokes's state senate district was predominantly white; and a county or state office seemed politically unrealistic because of his race. So, in 1966, Stokes sought re-election to the state house unopposed.

Between 1965 and 1967, Cleveland went from bad to worse, physically, socially, and financially. With no other immediate possibilities, Stokes began to think about running for mayor again. The big question was whether to risk taking on Locher in the primary—or to file as an independent again.

THE PRIMARY RACE

In effect, Stokes's decision was made for him. Seth Taft, slated to be the Republican candidate, told Stokes he would withdraw from the election entirely if Stokes filed as an independent in order to gain the advantage of a three-man general election. Taft had concluded that his best strategy was to face a Negro, *alone,* or a faltering incumbent, *alone,* in the general election. But not both. In a three-man race with Locher and Stokes, Taft correctly assumed that he would be the man in the middle with no chance for victory. (Taft would have preferred to run as an independent—to gain Democratic votes—but the county Republican leader threatened to file *another* Republican candidate unless Taft ran as a Republican.)

Meanwhile, Locher committed blunder after blunder—and Democratic party leaders began to question whether he could actually win another election. In the weeks before filing for the primary, Democratic leaders even pressured Locher to accept a Federal judgeship and clear the way for the president of the city council to run. But the Democratic leaders in Cleveland are not noted for their strength or effectiveness, as is evidenced by the fact that none of the Democratic mayors since 1941 were endorsed by the party when they were first elected. When Locher refused to withdraw, the party reluctantly rallied behind him.

Another Democratic candidate was Frank P. Celeste, former mayor of the Republican westside suburb of Lakewood. Celeste established residency in the city, announced his candidacy early, and—despite pressure from the Democratic Party—remained in the primary race.

There was always the possibility that Celeste would withdraw from the primary, which would leave Stokes facing Locher alone. But the threat of Taft's withdrawal from the general election left Stokes with little choice but to face Locher head-on in the primary. A primary race against Locher and a strong Democrat was more appealing than a general election against Locher and a weak Republican.

Now, in 1965 Stokes had received only about 6000 white votes in the city in a 239,000 voter turnout. To win in the primary, he had to enlarge and consolidate the Negro vote—and increase his white support on the westside and in the eastside ethnic wards.

The first part of his strategy was a massive voter registration drive in the Negro wards—to reinstate the potential Stokes voters dropped from the rolls for failing to vote since the 1964 Presidential election. The Stokes organization—aided by Martin Luther King, Jr. and the Southern Christian Leadership Conference, as well as by a grant (in part earmarked for voter registration) from the Ford Foundation to the Cleveland chapter of CORE—did succeed in registering many Negroes. But there was a similar drive mounted by the Democratic Party on behalf of Locher. (Registration figures are not available by race.)

The second part of the Stokes strategy took him across the polluted Cuyahoga River into the white wards that had given him a mere 3 percent of the vote in 1965. He spoke wherever he would be received—to small groups in private homes, in churches, and in public and private halls. While he was not always received enthusiastically, he did not confront many hostile crowds. He faced the race issue squarely and encouraged his audience to judge him on his ability.

Stokes's campaign received a big boost when the *Plain Dealer,* the largest daily in Ohio, endorsed him. Next, the *Cleveland Press* called for a change in City Hall, but declined to endorse either Stokes or Celeste. But since the polls indicated that Celeste was doing very badly, this amounted to an endorsement of Stokes.

More people voted in this primary than in any other in Cleveland's history. When the ballots were counted, Stokes had 52.5 percent of the votes—he had defeated Locher by a plurality of 18,000 votes. Celeste was the man in the middle, getting only 4 percent of the votes, the lowest of any mayoral candidate in recent Cleveland history.

What produced Stokes's clear victory? Table 1 reveals the answer. The decisive factor was the size of the Negro turnout. While Negroes constituted only about 40 percent of the voters, 73.4 percent of them turned out, compared with only 58.4 percent of the whites. Predominantly Negro wards cast 96.2 percent of their votes for Stokes. (Actually this figure underrepresents the Negro vote for Stokes, since some of the non-Stokes votes in these wards were cast

TABLE 1

	City Totals			Negro Wards			White Wards			Mixed Wards		
	1965 General	1967 Primary	1967 General	1965 General	1967 Primary	1967 General	1965 General	1967 Primary	1967 General	1965 General	1967 Primary	1967 General
Registered Voters	337,803	326,003	326,003	103,123	99,885	99,885	159,419	152,737	152,737	75,261	73,421	73,421
Turnout	239,479	210,926	257,157	74,396	73,360	79,591	111,129	88,525	119,883	53,962	49,105	57,113
% Turnout	70.9	64.7	78.9	72.1	73.4	79.7	69.7	58.0	78.5	71.7	66.9	77.8
Stokes Votes	85,716	110,769	129,829	63,550	70,575	75,586	3,300	13,495	23,158	18,866	26,699	30,872
% Stokes Votes	35.8	52.5	50.5	85.4	96.2	95.0	3.0	15.2	19.3	35.0	54.4	54.1

by whites. Similarly, the 15.4 percent vote for Stokes in the predominantly white wards slightly overestimates the white vote because of the Negro minority.)

Newspaper and magazine reports of the primary election proclaimed that Stokes could not have won without the white vote. Our own estimate—based on matching wards with census tracts, and allowing for only slight shifts in racial composition in some wards since the 1965 special census—is that Stokes received 16,000 white votes. His margin of victory was 18,000. How would the voting have gone if the third man, Celeste, had not been in the race? Many white voters, feeling that Stokes could not win in a two-man race, might not have bothered to vote at all, so perhaps Stokes would have won by an even larger margin. Thus Stokes's inroad into the white vote was not the decisive factor in his primary victory, although it was important.

Stokes emerged from the primary as the odds-on favorite to win—five weeks later—in the general election. And in the first few days of the campaign, it seemed that Stokes had everything going for him:

● Stokes was bright, handsome, and articulate. His opponent, Seth Taft, while bright, had never won an election, and his family name, associated with the Taft Hartley Act, could hardly be an advantage among union members. In addition, he was shy and seemingly uncomfortable in a crowd.

● Both the *Plain Dealer* and the *Cleveland Press* endorsed Stokes in the general election.

● The wounds of the primary were quickly (if perhaps superficially) healed, and the Democratic candidate was endorsed by both the Democratic Party and Mayor Locher.

● Labor—both the A.F.L.-C.I.O. and the Teamsters—also endorsed Stokes.

● He had a partisan advantage. Of the 326,003 registered voters, only 34,000 (10 percent) were Republican. The closest any Republican mayoral candidate had come to winning was in 1951, when —in a small turnout—William J. McDermott received 45 percent of the vote.

● Stokes had 90,000 or more Negro votes virtually assured, with little possibility that Taft would make more than slight inroads.

● Perhaps most important, voting-behavior studies over the years have demonstrated that voters who are confronted by a dilemma react by staying home from the polls. Large numbers of life-long

Democrats, faced with voting for a Negro or a Republican by the name of Taft, were likely to stay home.

Had this been a normal election, Democrat Carl Stokes would have won handily. But this was not destined to be a normal election. During the final days of the campaign, Stokes knew he was in a fight for his political life. Those who predicted that the cross-pressures would keep many voters away from the polls forgot that the variable "Negro" had never been involved in an election of this importance.

On Election Day, an estimated 90 percent of those who voted for Locher or Celeste in the Democratic primary shifted to Taft—many pulling a Republican lever for the first time in their lives. Was this clearly and unequivocally bigoted backlash? To be sure, bigotry *did* play a major role in the election. But to dismiss the campaign and the election as pure overt bigotry is to miss the significance of what happened in Cleveland and the emerging subtle nature of prejudice in American society.

THE NON-ISSUE OF RACE

A closer look at the personal characteristics and campaign strategy of Seth Taft, the Republican candidate, reveals the complexity and subtlety of the race issue.

In the final days of the Democratic primary campaign, Taft repeatedly told reporters that he would rather run against Locher and his record than against Carl Stokes. On the evening of the primary, Taft appeared at Stokes's headquarters to congratulate him. As far as he was concerned, Taft said, the campaign issue was, Who could present the most constructive program for change in Cleveland? Further, he said he didn't want people voting for him simply because he was white. A few days later, Taft even presented a strongly-worded statement to his campaign workers:

The Cuyahoga Democratic party has issued a number of vicious statements concerning the candidacy of Carl Stokes, and others have conducted whisper campaigns. We cannot tolerate injection of race into this campaign. . . . Many people will vote for Carl Stokes because he is a Negro. Many people will vote for me because I am white. I regret this fact. I will work hard to convince people they should not vote on a racial basis.

Seth Taft's programs to solve racial tensions may have been paternalistic, not really perceptive of emerging moods of the ghetto. But one thing is clear—he was not a bigot. Every indication is that he remained uncomfortable about being in a race in which his chances to win depended, in large part, upon a backlash vote.

Whether Taft's attempt to silence the race issue was a deliberate strategy or a reflection of deep personal feelings, it probably enhanced his chances of winning. He knew that he had the hardcore bigot vote. His task was to convince those in the middle that they could vote for him and *not* be bigots.

Stokes, on the other hand, had another kind of problem. While he had to draw more white votes, he also had to retain and, if possible, increase the 73 percent Negro turnout that had delivered him 96 percent of the Negro votes in the primary. Stokes's campaign leaders feared a fall-off in the voter turnout from Negro wards—with good reason. The entire primary campaign had pushed the October 3 date so hard that some Negroes could not understand why Carl Stokes was not mayor on October 4. Full-page newspaper ads paid for by CORE had stated, *"If you don't vote Oct. 3rd, forget it. The man who wins will be the next mayor of Cleveland!"* So Stokes felt he had to remobilize the Negro vote.

The moment came during the question-and-answer period of the second of four debates with Taft in the all-white westside. Stokes said:

> The personal analysis of Seth Taft—and the analysis of many competent political analysts—is that Seth Taft may win the November 7 election, but for only one reason. That reason is that his skin happens to be white.

The predominantly white crowd booed loudly and angrily for several minutes, and throughout the rest of the evening repeatedly interrupted him. Later, Stokes's campaign manager revealed that his candidate's remark was a calculated risk to arouse Negro interest. Stokes probably succeeded, but he also gave Taft supporters an excuse to bring the race issue into the open. And they could claim that it was *Stokes*, not Taft, who was trying to exploit the race issue.

To be sure, *both* candidates exploited the race issue. But, for the most part, it was done rather subtly. Stokes's campaign posters stated, "Let's Do Cleveland Proud"—another way of saying, "Let's show the world that Cleveland is capable of rising above racial bigotry." A full-page ad for Stokes stated in bold print, "Vote for Seth Taft. It Would Be Easy, Wouldn't It?" After the debate, Taft was free to accuse Stokes of using the race issue—itself a subtle way of exploiting the issue. Then there was the letter, signed by the leaders of 22 nationality clubs, that was mailed to 40,000 members in the city. It didn't mention race, but comments such as "protecting our way of life," "safeguard our liberty," and "false charges of police brutality" were blatant in their implications. Taft sidestepped comment on the letter.

No matter how much the candidates may have wanted to keep race out of the picture, race turned out to be the most important issue. Both Taft and Stokes could benefit from the issue if they played it right, and both did use it. And although the Stokes's remark at the second debate gave white voters an excuse to vote for Taft without feeling that they were bigots, many whites probably would have found another excuse.

TAFT AS A STRATEGIST

· The fact is that Taft, for all his lackluster qualities, emerged as a strong candidate. He was able to turn many of his liabilities into assets:

• Taft was able to insulate himself against his Republican identity. He successfully dissociated himself from his uncle's position on labor by pointing to his own active role, as a student, against "right to work" laws. At the same time, he hit hard at Stokes's record as an off again-on again Democrat. This strategy neutralized, at least in part, Taft's first political disadvantage—running as a Republican in a Democratic city.

• A second liability was that he came from a wealthy family. Taft was an Ivy League intellectual, cast in the role of a "do-gooder." He lived in an exclusive suburb, Pepper Pike, and had bought a modest home in Cleveland only a few weeks before declaring his candidacy. How, it was frequently asked, could such a man understand the problems of the inner-city and of the poor? Almost invariably the answer was: "Did John F. Kennedy, Franklin D. Roosevelt, and Nelson Rockefeller have to be poor in order to understand and respond to the problems of the poor?" Taft's campaign posters were a side profile that bore a striking resemblance to President Kennedy. Whether he was consciously exploiting the Kennedy image is an open question. But there can be little doubt that when Taft mentioned his Republican heritage, he tried to project an image of the new breed of Republican—John Lindsay and Charles Percy. This image didn't come across very well at first, but as he became a seasoned campaigner it became clearer.

• Another liability was that Taft had never held an elected office. His opponent tried to exploit this—unsuccessfully. Taft could point to 20 years of active civic service, including the fact that he was one of the authors of the Ohio fair-housing law. Then too, the charge gave Taft an opportunity to point out that Stokes had the worst absentee record of anyone in the state legislature. Stokes never successfully answered this charge until the last of their four debates, when he produced a pre-campaign letter from Taft commending him on his legislative service. But this came moments *after* the TV cameras had gone off the air.

• Still another liability emerged during the campaign. Taft's strategy of discussing programs, not personalities, was seemingly getting him nowhere. He presented specific proposals; Stokes, a skilled debater, succeeded in picking them apart. Stokes himself discussed programs only at a general level and contended that he was best qualified to "cut the red tape" in Washington. His frequent trips to Washington to confer with top Government officials, before and during the campaign, indicated that he had the inside track.

Taft, realizing at this point that his campaign was not gaining much momentum, suddenly switched gears and began attacking Stokes's record (not Stokes personally). Stokes had claimed he would crack down on slumlords. Taft discovered that Stokes owned a piece of rental property with several code violations—and that it had not been repaired despite an order from the city. He hit hard at Stokes's absenteeism and his record as a "good" Democrat. He put a "bird dog" on Stokes and, if Stokes told one group one thing and another group something else, the public heard about it.

The upshot was that in the final days of the campaign Taft captured the momentum. Stokes was easily the more flashy debater and projected a superior image; but Taft emerged as the better strategist.

SHOULD TAFT HAVE WITHDRAWN?

One may ask whether all of this discussion is really relevant, since the final vote was sharply divided along racial lines. In one sense it *is* irrelevant, since it is possible that a weaker candidate than Taft might have run just as well. It is also possible that a white racist might actually have won. Still, this discussion has buttressed two important points:

• Taft was not all black, and Stokes was not all white. Taft proved a strong candidate, and—had he been running against Locher

TABLE 2

PERCENT STOKES VOTE BY WARD

WHITE WARDS	% Negro	1965 General	1967 Primary	1967 General
1	.6	3.2	17.2	20.5
2	.3	1.9	12.8	17.4
3	.9	2.5	13.6	22.1
4	.3	3.0	18.2	20.9
5	.6	1.7	11.8	17.8
6	.8	2.3	15.1	16.7
7	.6	3.4	16.5	23.7
8	3.0	6.1	24.7	29.3
9	.2	1.9	12.4	16.4
14	1.4	1.1	12.7	13.0
15	1.4	1.2	9.2	14.1
22	5.7	8.1	22.5	26.3
26	1.1	2.8	16.3	19.9
32	2.4	2.9	10.0	15.3
33	.3	2.5	17.7	21.4
Average		3.0	15.2	19.3
NEGRO WARDS				
10	91.3	88.7	97.3	96.7
11	91.8	86.3	95.9	96.0
12	82.7	76.9	90.4	90.5
13	75.2	75.8	90.7	88.4
17	99.0	86.6	98.1	97.9
18	89.3	84.0	96.0	95.7
20	91.0	83.0	95.0	92.8
24	92.6	90.6	98.1	98.1
25	90.9	91.3	98.4	98.2
27	85.7	85.2	95.6	94.0
Average		85.4	96.2	95.0
MIXED WARDS				
16	56.6	50.7	69.9	70.1
19	25.3	29.2	48.0	39.9
21	61.1	55.2	66.3	68.9
23	20.3	9.8	18.2	23.2
28	28.5	26.5	54.8	57.3
29	24.4	26.8	43.2	42.3
30	51.7	51.5	75.3	71.4
31	21.8	16.9	31.8	39.0
Average		35.0	54.4	54.1

instead of Stokes—he might have amassed strong support from Negroes and defeated Locher.

● By being a strong candidate, Taft made it much easier for many white Democrats, who might otherwise have been cross-pressured into staying home, to come out and vote for him.

Some people felt that Taft should have withdrawn and let Stokes run uncontested. But many of the same people also decried white liberals who, at recent conferences to form coalitions between black-power advocates and the New Left, let black militants castrate them. It is not traditional in American politics that candidates enter a race to lose. Taft was in to win, and he fought a hard and relatively clean campaign—as high a compliment as can be paid to any candidate.

Yet all of this doesn't change the basic nature of the voting. This is clear from the evidence in Table 2. Stokes won by holding his black bloc, and increasing his white vote from 15 percent in the primary to almost 20 percent in the general. An enormous amount of the white vote was, whether covert or overt, anti-Negro. It is hard to believe that Catholics, ethnic groups, and laborers who never voted for anyone but a Democrat should suddenly decide to evaluate candidates on their qualifications and programs, and—in overwhelming numbers—decide that the Republican candidate was better qualified. The implication is that they were prejudiced. But to assume that such people perceive themselves as bigots is to oversimplify the nature of prejudice. And to call such people bigots is to make their responses even more rigid—as Carl Stokes discovered after his remark in the second debate with Taft.

This, then, is perhaps an important lesson of the Cleveland election: Bigotry cannot be defeated directly, by telling bigots that they are bigoted. For the most part Stokes learned this lesson well, accumulating as many as 30,000 white votes, nearly five times the number he received in 1965. But another slip like the one in the second debate might have cost him the election.

A few words on the voting for Stokes ward by ward, as shown in the table. Wards 9, 14, and 15—which gave Stokes a comparatively low vote—have the highest concentration of ethnic groups in the city. Not only is there the historical element of prejudice in these areas, but there is the ever-present fear among the residents that Negroes will invade their neighborhoods. (This fear is less a factor in ward 9, which is across the river.)

Wards 26 and 32 also gave Stokes a low percentage of votes, and these wards are also the ones most likely to have Negro migration. They are just to the north of East Cleveland, which is currently undergoing heavy transition, and to the east of ward 27, which in the past few years has changed from white to black. In these two wards, then, high ethnic composition and a fear of Negro migration would seem to account for Stokes's 19.9 and 15.3 percentages.

The highest percentage *for* Stokes in predominantly white areas was in wards 8 and 22. Ward 8 has a growing concentration of Puerto Ricans, and—according to newspaper polls—they voted heavily for Stokes. Ward 22 has a very large automobile assembly plant that employs many Negroes. Now, in 1965 the ward was 5.7 percent Negro—a large increase from 1960. Since 1965, this percentage has probably grown another 2 or 3 percent. Therefore, if one subtracts the Negro vote that Stokes received in this ward, the size of the white vote is about the same as in other wards.

'IMMINENT DANGER' IN GARY

The race for mayor in Gary, Ind., was not overtly racist. Still, the racial issue was much less subtle than it was in Cleveland. When Democratic chairman John G. Krupa refused to support Richard D. Hatcher, the Democratic candidate, it was clear that the reason was race. When the Gary newspaper failed to give similar coverage to both candidates and sometimes failed to print news releases from Hatcher headquarters (ostensibly because press deadlines had not been met), it was clear that race was a factor.

Even though race was rarely mentioned openly, the city polarized. While Stokes had the support of the white-owned newspapers and many white campaign workers, many of Hatcher's white supporters preferred to remain in the background—in part, at least, because they feared reprisals from white racists. Hatcher didn't use the black-power slogan, but to the community the election was a contest between black and white. And when the Justice Department supported Hatcher's claim that the election board had illegally removed some 5000 Negro voters from the registration lists and added nonexistent whites, the tension in the city became so great that the Governor, feeling that there was "imminent danger" of violence on election night, called up 4000 National Guardsmen.

Negroes constitute an estimated 55 percent of Gary's 180,000 residents, but white voter registration outnumbers Negroes by 2000 or 3000. Like Stokes, Hatcher—in order to win—had to poll some white votes, or have a significantly higher Negro turnout.

The voter turnout and voting patterns in Cleveland and Gary were very similar. In both cities, almost 80 percent of the registered voters turned out at the polls. In the Glen Park and Miller areas, predominantly white neighborhoods, Joseph B. Radigan— Hatcher's opponent—received more than 90 percent of the votes. In the predominantly Negro areas, Hatcher received an estimated 93 percent of the votes. In all, Hatcher received about 4000 white votes, while losing probably 1000 Negro votes, at most, to Radigan. This relatively small white vote was enough to give him victory. If Stokes's miscalculation in bringing race into the Cleveland campaign gave prejudiced whites an excuse to vote for Taft, the glaring way the Democratic Party in Gary tried to defeat Hatcher probably tipped the scales and gave Hatcher some white votes he wouldn't have received otherwise.

THE SCHOOL ISSUE IN BOSTON

The Boston election, unlike the Cleveland and Gary elections, didn't pose a Negro against a white, but a lackluster candidate— Kevin White—against a 48-year-old grandmother who had gained national attention over the past several years for her stand against school integration. On the surface, Mrs. Hicks seems to be an obvious racial bigot. But she herself has repeatedly denied charges that she is a racist, and many who have followed her closely claim that this description is too simple.

Mrs. Hicks, perhaps more than any other public figure to emerge in recent years, reflects the complex and subtle nature of prejudice in America. Her public denial of bigotry is, in all probability, an honest expression of her self-image. But she is basically unaware of, and unwilling to become informed about, the way her views maintain the barriers of segregation and discrimination in American society. In 1963, when the NAACP asked the Boston School Committee to acknowledge the *de facto* segregation in the schools, she refused to review the evidence. Meeting with the NAACP, she abruptly ended the discussion by proclaiming: "There is no *de facto* segregation in Boston's schools. Kindly proceed to educational matters." Later, when the State Board of Education presented a 132-page report on racial imbalance in Massachusetts schools, she lashed out at the report's recommendations without bothering to read it.

Mrs. Hicks, like millions of Americans, holds views on race that are born out of and perpetuated by ignorance. John Spiegel, director of Brandeis University's Lemberg Center for the Study of Violence, has summed up the preliminary report of its study of six cities:

> . . . the attitude of whites seems to be based on ignorance of or indifference to the factual basis of Negro resentment and bitterness. . . . If white populations generally had a fuller appreciation of the just grievances and overwhelming problems of Negroes in the ghetto, they would give stronger support to their city governments to promote change and to correct the circumstances which give rise to strong feelings of resentment now characteristic of ghetto populations.

Prejudice is born not only out of ignorance, but also out of fear. There is much about the Negro ghettos of poverty that causes whites, lacking objective knowledge, to be afraid, and their fear in turn reinforces their prejudice and their inability to hear out and understand the plight of the Negro in America.

In Boston, the voter turnout was heavy (71 percent) but below the turnouts in Cleveland and Gary. White accumulated 53 percent of the vote and a 12,000 plurality. Compared with Stokes and Hatcher, he had an easy victory. But considering Mrs. Hicks's lack of qualifications and the racial overtones of her campaign, Boston also experienced a massive backlash vote. Had it not been for the final days of the campaign—when she pledged, unrealistically, to raise police and firemen's salaries to $10,000 without raising taxes, and came back from Washington with "positive assurance" that nonexistent Federal monies would cover the raises —she might even have won. But throughout the campaign Mrs. Hicks repeatedly revealed her ignorance of fiscal and political matters. Mrs. Hicks had another handicap: She is a woman. The incredible fact that she ran a close race demonstrated again the hard core of prejudice and ignorance in American society.

Now let us consider the broader implications these elections will have on the racial crisis in America. To be sure, the immediate implications are quite different from what they would have been if Stokes and Hatcher had lost and Mrs. Hicks had won. If the elections had gone the other way, Summer '68 might well have begun November 8. As Thomas Pettigrew of Harvard put it a few days before the election, "If Stokes and Hatcher lose and Mrs. Hicks wins, then I just wonder how a white man in this country could ever look a Negro in the eye and say, 'Why don't you make it the way we did, through the political system, rather than burning us down?' "

THE MEANING OF THE ELECTIONS

But do these victories really alter the basic nature of the racial crisis? There is, true, some reason for hope. But to assume that anything has been fundamentally altered would be disastrous. First of all, it is by no means clear that these elections will pacify militant Negroes—including those in Cleveland, Gary, and Boston. In Boston, some militants were even encouraging people to vote for Mrs. Hicks—because they felt that her victory would help unify the Negro community against a well-defined foe. In Cleveland, most militants remained less than enthusiastic about the possibility of a Stokes victory. Of the militant groups, only CORE worked hard for him. In Gary alone did the candidate have the solid support of militants—probably because Hatcher refused to explicitly rebuke Stokely Carmichael and H. Rap Brown, and because his opponents repeatedly claimed that Hatcher was a black-power advocate.

If the Stokes and Hatcher victories are to represent a turning point in the racial crisis, they must deliver results. Unfortunately, Hatcher faces an unsympathetic Democratic Party and city council. Stokes has gone a long way toward healing the wounds of the bitter primary, but it remains to be seen whether he will receive eager support for his programs. Some councilmen from ethnic wards will almost certainly buck his programs for fear of alienating their constituencies.

Stokes and Hatcher themselves face a difficult and delicate situation:

● Their margins of victory were so narrow that they, like Kennedy in 1960, must proceed with great caution.

● Enthusiasm and promises of change are not the same as the power to implement change. And the two mayors must share power with whites.

● They must demonstrate to Negroes that their presence in City Hall has made a difference. But if their programs seem too preferential toward Negroes, they run the risk of massive white resistance.

This delicate situation was clearly seen in the early days of the Stokes administration. Of his first ten appointments, only two were Negroes. Although relations with the police has been one of the most sensitive issues in the Negro ghetto, Stokes's choice for a new police chief was Michael Blackwell, a 67-year-old "hard liner." This appointment was intended to ease anxieties in the ethnic neighborhoods, but it was not popular in the Negro ghetto. Blackwell, in his first public address after being sworn in, lashed out at the Supreme Court, state laws, and "publicity-seeking clergy and beatniks" for "crippling law enforcement." Cleveland's Negroes are already beginning to wonder whether a Negro in City Hall is going to make any difference.

Some observers believe that Stokes is basically quite conservative, and point to his sponsorship of anti-riot legislation. To be sure, Stokes's position on many issues remains uncertain, but what does seem fairly clear from his early days in office is that his efforts to gain support in white communities is going to lead to disaffection among Negroes. How much and how quickly is a difficult question.

Race relations is only one of many problems that these two new mayors must face. Stokes has inherited all of the problems that brought national attention to Cleveland last spring—poverty, urban renewal, finance, transportation, air and water pollution, and so on. Hatcher faces similar problems in Gary, and must also cope with one of the nation's worst strongholds of organized crime. If they fail, the responsibility will fall heavier on them than had a white man failed. Some whites will generalize the failures to all Negro politicians, and some Negroes will generalize the failures to the "bankruptcy" of the American political system.

Almost certainly, Washington will be a key factor in determining if these two men succeed. The national Democratic Party has a strong interest in making Stokes and Hatcher look good, for it desperately needs to recapture the disaffected Negro voters before the 1968 national election. But how much can the party deliver? The war in Vietnam is draining enormous national resources and Congress is threatening to slash poverty programs. Even if Federal monies were no problem, there is the question whether *any* of Washington's existing programs are directed at the roots of ghetto unrest. Many informed administrators, scientists, and political analysts feel they are not. And the chances for creative Federal programs seem, at this moment, fairly dim.

Another clear implication of these elections is that white resistance to change remains large and widespread. More than 90 percent of the Democrats in Cleveland who voted for a Democrat in the primary switched, in the general election, to the Republican candidate. Now, not many American cities are currently composed of as many as 35 percent Negroes; the possibility of coalitions to elect other Negro candidates appears, except in a handful of cities, remote. Additional Negro mayoral candidates are almost certain to arise, and many will go down to bitter defeat.

Stokes and Hatcher won because black voter power coalesced with a relatively small minority of liberal whites. It was not a victory of acceptance or even tolerance of Negroes, but a numerical failure of the powers of discrimination, a failure that resulted in large part because of the massive exodus of whites from the central city. The election of Stokes and Hatcher may break down white resistance to voting for a Negro, but this is, at best, problematical. Also problematical is how bigoted whites will react to the election of a Negro mayor. Their organized efforts to resist change may intensify. As we have already indicated, the pace of white exodus from the central city of Cleveland is already alarming. And an acceleration of this pace could push the city into financial bankruptcy.

AMERICA HAS BOUGHT A LITTLE TIME

In short, while the implications of the November 7 elections are ambiguous, it does seem that the victories of Stokes and Hatcher, and the defeat of Mrs. Hicks, have kept the door open on the growing racial crisis. America has, at best, bought a little time.

On the other hand, we do not find much cause for optimism in those elections—unlike George Meany, and unlike the *New York Times*, which, five days after the election, published a glowing editorial about "the willingness of most voters today to choose men solely on personal quality and impersonal issues." To us, it would seem that the elections have only accelerated the pace of ever-rising expectations among Negroes. And if results don't follow, and rather rapidly, then we believe that the Negro community's frustration with the American political system will almost certainly heighten.

The hard task of demonstrating that Negroes can actually achieve justice and equality in America still lies ahead.

CHAPTER NINE

POLITICAL CHANGE

MOST OF THE NATION'S POOR are white. Most of them live in the countryside. They share with the Negro poor in the cities, not the burden of race prejudice, but a poverty as searing as that of the ghetto. Yet by any accounting of national political attention, the contemporary white, rural poor are neglected. The reasons for this neglect and the possibilities for overcoming it are instructive topics for the student of political change.

The following selection describes—without systematic interpretation—contemporary conditions in the Cumberland Plateau of eastern Kentucky. The author, Harry M. Caudill, finds those conditions appalling; he is an advocate, not a census-taker. His account is included here as material for you, the reader, to analyze and interpret. Up to this point, your main task has been to develop an understanding of some methods and concepts of political behavior, through careful attention to the finished works of social scientists. To move beyond appreciation and criticism of other analyses to the invention of your own is the purpose of this and the following selection.

Caudill's account, then, is raw material for developing a systematic interpretation of political change in a specific setting. This interpretation should include, at a minimum, an ordering of the major factors which sustain the present situation and the factors which you consider, in the light of what you have learned of citizen political behavior, potentials for organized change.

NIGHT COMES TO THE CUMBERLANDS

HARRY M. CAUDILL

The present crisis is compounded of many elements, human and material. They have produced what is probably the most seriously depressed region in the nation—and the adjective applies in much more than an economic sense. They have brought economic depression, to be sure, and it lies like a gray pall over the whole land. But a deeper tragedy lies in the depression of the spirit which has fallen upon so many of the people, making them, for the moment at least, listless, hopeless and without ambition.

The essential element of the plateau's economic malaise lies in the fact that for a hundred and thirty years it has exported its resources, all of which—timber, coal and even crops—have had to be wrested violently from the earth. The nation has siphoned off hundreds of millions of dollars' worth of its resources while returning little of lasting value. For all practical purposes the plateau has long constituted a colonial appendage of the industrial East and Middle West, rather than an integral part of the nation generally. The decades of exploitation have in large measure drained the region. Its timber wealth is exhausted and if its hillsides ever again produce arrow-straight white oaks, tulip poplars and hemlocks new crops of trees will first have to be planted and allowed to mature. Hundreds of ridges which once bulged with thick seams of high-quality coal have been emptied of all that lay in their vitals and their surfaces have been fragmented for the pitiful remnants in the outcrop. While billions of tons still remain undisturbed they lie in inferior seams and are of poorer quality. The magnificent veins through which Percheron horses once hauled strings of bank cars have been worked out.

Reprinted from Harry M. Caudill, *Night Comes to the Cumberlands* (Boston: Atlantic-Little, Brown and Co., 1963), pp. 325–41 and 352–61, by permission of Atlantic-Little, Brown and Co. Copyright © 1962, 1963 by Harry M. Caudill.

Even more ruinous than the loss of its physical resources is the disappearance of the plateau's best human material. Most of the thousands who left were people who recognized the towering importance of education in the lives of their children, and craved for them better schools than Kentucky afforded. Too many of those who remained behind were without interest in real education as distinguished from its trappings. If their children attended the neighborhood schools the parents had done their duty. Too often they were far less ambitious and such ambition as they possessed was to evaporate in the arms of Welfarism and in the face of repeated failures.

From the beginning, the coal and timber companies insisted on keeping all, or nearly all, the wealth they produced. They were unwilling to plow more than a tiny part of the money they earned back into schools, libraries, health facilities and other institutions essential to a balanced, pleasant, productive and civilized society. The knowledge and guile of their managers enabled them to corrupt and cozen all too many of the region's elected public officials and to thwart the legitimate aspirations of the people. The greed and cunning of the coal magnates left behind an agglomeration of misery for a people who can boast of few of the facilities deemed indispensable to life in more sophisticated areas, and even these few are inadequate and of inferior quality.

Only one facet of the industry ever sought to return to the region any substantial part of the wealth it produced. The United Mine Workers' program of health, welfare and retirement benefits funneled back to the coal counties millions of dollars otherwise destined for the pockets of distant shareholders. To compound the tragedy of the plateau, even this program is today showing unmistakable signs of breakdown and failure. The union and the trustees of its fund were headed for inevitable trouble after the end of the second boom in 1948. Its seeds germinated in the same soil that sprouted the difficulties of the late 1920s: the industry was grossly overexpanded and was prepared to produce twice as much coal as its markets could consume. In 1948 the tremendous new truck-mining industry was overgrown and, hard though they struggled to mechanize their mines with the cast-off relics of their big competitors, the little operators were never really able to compete. A widespread double standard blanketed the coalfields. The big rail mines were sternly forced to comply with the wage and hour contracts negotiated year after year with the United Mine Workers, but John L. Lewis and his associates looked the other way where the truck mines were concerned. Fearing that if these small pits were shut down the resulting labor surplus might break the contracts in the big mines, they tolerated clandestine wage cuts. It became customary for the truck-mine operator to sign the contract and then ignore it. He paid his workmen five or ten dollars per day less than the scale wage and sent only a token contribution to the Health and Welfare Fund. Thus the truck mines existed for a decade, by sufferance of the union.

Then in the spring of 1959 the United Mine Workers undertook to change all this. Wages in many of the truck mines had sunk to ridiculous levels and in others the miners were "gang working" as partners and dividing the meager profits equally. But however they managed and toiled, many were earning no more than eight dollars a day and some as little as four dollars. Despite the pious provisions of the Federal Wage and Hour Law most operators paid as little as the miners could be persuaded to accept. But for a man with a wife and "a gang of young-'uns," with no money, no property and nowhere to go, any income is better than none. Thus when the union suddenly attempted to force the small pits to comply fully and faithfully with the contract their efforts ended in ignominious defeat. The miners in the little "dog-holes" had lost faith in the "organization." It had let them work at ever-lessening wages for ten years, preaching automation and higher pay to men who grew increasingly desperate with each passing year. In their cynical eyes John L. Lewis, once their hero and idol, had become a traitor to their interests.

When the 1959 strike was called, the response was far from uniform. Some of the workmen quit and picketed those who attempted to work. The strike dragged on for months amid recurrences of violence reminiscent of the 1930s. Men were slain, ramps and tipples were blasted and burned, and eventually the state's National Guard was sent into the troubled counties to preserve order. But the strike failed. In the long run practically all the truck miners deserted the union and went back to work. Today they mine many trainloads of coal daily but pay nothing into the Welfare Fund. Their miners no longer pay union dues. Their locals have folded up and disappeared. In retaliation against them the U.M.W. Fund trustees canceled their hospital cards and Welfare benefits and thousands of truck-mine laborers are now stranded at the mercy of their employers and the customers who buy their coal. It is a harsh world for everyone, but in all America there is no worker —not even the imported Mexican "wetback"—who occupies a position more exposed and helpless than the men who dig coal in these little pits.

The Federal Government makes only a token effort to enforce the minimum wage requirements of the Fair Labor Standards Act. Almost always when complaints are called to the attention of the United States Attorneys they are too busy to deal with them and the miner in question receives a form letter advising him to bring suit for back-wages in "a court of competent jurisdiction." But lawsuits cost money and the miner has none, so the suit is not brought, the delinquency is not collected and the low wages continue. His union has ostracized him as a yellow dog and a scab. Some of the magnificent union hospitals stand half-empty while their skilled physicians resign in disgust because there are so few patients to attend.* The truck-mine operator is earning little on the coal he sells and competition from the increasing numbers of strip and auger companies constantly deflates the price of his product. While other Americans are enjoying prosperity, planning expensive vacations in new automobiles and buying corporate stocks in unprecedented numbers, the truck miner who is fortunate enough to have a job works for minuscule wages and wonders from payday to payday whether his employer will be able to pay even the pittances for which he has contracted.

Even worse, the Federal Government treats him as a second-class citizen when it comes to safety. Of all the things John L. Lewis can boast of having accomplished for his followers, the Federal Mine Safety Code is the most important. But Congress gave Lewis only half a loaf, specifically restricting the act's application to mines employing fifteen or more men. Small pits were left to the tender mercies of their bosses and of state inspectors; the carnage continued in them unabated. Most of the plateau's coal counties now go two or three years at a time without a fatal accident in a railroad mine, but the dreary reports of dead and mangled bodies continue to filter with chilling frequency from the little operations. Truck mines produce approximately 12 percent of the plateau's coal output and 33⅓ percent of its killed and injured miners. Strangely enough the state's senior senator, himself an eastern Kentuckian, is an outspoken defender of this industrial mayhem, and

---

* In October of 1962, the trustees of the Fund announced that four of its hospitals in the plateau would be permanently closed on June 30, 1963.

for several years has almost single-handedly staved off Federal safety enforcement in the smaller coal mines.

So the miners, the employed workmen who by hundreds make a skimpy living in the truck mines of the plateau, live on a downward spiral which for several years has appeared to be nearing rock bottom. With low wages, lack of union membership and protection, and in most instances without even Workmen's Compensation coverage, such a miner is fortunate to keep corn bread and beans on the dinner table in the poor shack he so often calls home.

So trifling were his wages that in many instances the "dog-hole miner" could not survive without the free food doled out to him monthly from the great stores of the United States Department of Agriculture. Though his situation was unusually severe, a miner recently remarked to me that for eleven eight-hour shifts of work he collected twenty-nine dollars in wages. It is apparent that he, his wife and three children would starve to death if his labor afforded their only support. It is true that some truck mines are so efficiently organized and have grown so large that they are able to pay decent wages, though few attempt the union scale. The largest ones, however, mine as much as a thousand tons a day and their owners pay twenty dollars for an eight-hour shift. Their miners live reasonably well but it should not be inferred that they set the standards for the industry. In most areas truck mining has degenerated into a ghastly economic mire which holds miner and operator alike enchained. Often the employer is fortunate if he can earn twenty dollars a day for himself, and his employees are lucky if they take home eight or ten dollars. In those pits in which the miners work as partners they are practically unsupervised by safety bosses. Each co-worker thinks of himself as his own boss and of equal voice in the management of the mine and, in consequence, none can enforce safety discipline. Yet they continue to dig coal from the thinning seams, producing it for incredibly low prices and adding to a coal glut which can only depress prices, earnings and wages still further.

Here and there a few rail mines still operate. During the last fifteen years there has been a relentless consolidation as the bigger companies steadily bought up the smaller ones. With roaring machines and shrunken crews, these corporate giants continue to pour coal from the black veins into the clattering tipples. But where nearly eight thousand men once toiled for United States Coal and Coke Company in the Big Black Mountain, fewer than seventeen hundred are now at work. Where five thousand miners once went under the hill for Consolidation Coal Company at Jenkins and McRoberts, nine hundred survivors are still on the payroll. But at neither place has coal production lessened. To the contrary, with advancing mechanization it has steadily swollen.

These fortunate hundreds earn a basic union wage in excess of twenty-four dollars a day and enjoy all the benefits the union contract bestows. They present a sharp contrast to the pauperized dog-hole miners. The two, and frequently they are blood brothers, are prince and pauper. The workman for Inland Steel, Bethlehem Mines, International Harvester and United States Steel owns his home in a camp or in one of the rural areas. He has improved the house and installed a furnace and plumbing. His home is neat and well-painted. He drives and owns a late-model automobile and his children attend school regularly. He hopes to send at least some of them to college, perhaps to the University of Kentucky. He has a thousand dollars or so on deposit in a local bank. The magnificent facilities at the Miner's Memorial Hospitals exist primarily for his care. When he or any member of his family is ill or injured, doctors, surgeons and hospitalization cost him nothing. The trustees have lowered the retirement age and when he reaches his sixtieth birthday he can leave the mines and draw from the Fund a monthly retirement check of seventy-five dollars. The mine in which he works is well-ventilated and under the orders of Federal Safety Inspectors has been made as safe as human ingenuity can vouchsafe. If, despite the precautions, he is injured, compensation benefits up to a total of $15,300 await him. His union shelters him from coercion by company officials and has long since forced the closing of the scrip office. In most camps the company store is little more than a memory.

But there are portents of trouble for these union miners and their organization. The United Mine Workers has shrunk its membership and raised the living standards of those who remain. In so doing it has kept abreast of progress because progress is bigness, efficiency, technological advancement and organization. At the same time, it has created a favored class, a sort of blue-collar royalty amid a populace of industrial serfs. The combination of giant companies and giant union is driving the truck mines from the scene. Each spring the beginning of the lake trade finds fewer truck mines in operation. Within a few more seasons, the rail-mine operators can confidently expect the last of their small competitors to have been relegated to the scrap heap of history. But they are confronted with competition from other quarters—savage rivalry they cannot dispose of in so cavalier a fashion.

The rising crescendo of strip and auger mining is pouring growing quantities of extremely low-priced coal onto the market. So long as unspoiled ridges invite the bulldozers and big screws, the Big Bosses will face a gruesome dilemma. At great cost to their stockholders they have made ready to market clean and high quality coal. Ironically, this product is now becoming old-fashioned. The trend is toward lower prices and quality, and therefore the huge complex washeries may be little more than outmoded symbols of a departed time. In consequence, the union and its members are losing their economic and political importance. When coal was dug by simple tools and machines the many men who operated them could give fiscal chilblains to industrialists and government officials across the land. The nation was dependent upon coal, and hence on the miner's skills, but this dependence is seeping fast away. In coal production the cornerstone is still the dust-blackened, blue-collar miner, but he is surrendering his primacy to the white-collar expert whose skill and cunning has worked a far-reaching revolution in so short a time. The growing petroleum glut and the network of natural gas pipelines lessen coal's importance with each passing season. Within a few years tireless atomic reactors will provide much of the electric power now made from coal. Though the nation will surely grow steadily, coal is unlikely ever again to be a prime industry. Its path is downward, and the men and communities who are dependent upon it are tied to a descending star. Since coal is, for all practical purposes, the plateau's only industry, the region and its people are tied to an industrial albatross.

In a state where politics is the essence of life, success is measured by the ability to deliver votes. The union once possessed great influence at the polling places, but this too is evaporating. For fifteen years after the union drives were successfully concluded politicians sought the support of union chiefs, and while the rank and file never blindly followed the wishes of their leaders, such endorsements were worth many votes. A great many miners quietly "went along with the organization" and stamped their ballots for candidates who were approved as friends of labor. But such political influence as the shrunken locals still possess is shriveling still further. With the truck miners almost entirely nonunion and thousands of other diggers jobless, the rolls of bona fide, active union members are now relatively small. Too, the once-numerous union pensioners are disappearing fast. The hosts of charter members who retired in the late 1940s have been thinned by death, and most of the survivors are close to eighty years of age. Though they still pay union dues and are grateful to the organization for their monthly checks, they take little interst in the affairs of the locals. They are out of contact with the younger men and are seldom seen at union meetings. They pay little attention to political recommendations, and often fail to vote.

The pendulum has swung so far that union endorsement is now as often a hindrance as a help. The truck miners and their employers are bitterly antagonistic toward the union they once worked so hard to promote. Many miners who scrimped through long strikes in the 1940s to support the great union struggle for shorter hours, higher wages, Federal Safety regulations and the Welfare Fund now view the union with aversion. They are more likely to oppose than to support a candidate the U.M.W. has approved.

In fact, the union may be fighting for its very life. In the spring of 1961 a Federal Court in Tennessee awarded damages in the sum of $280,000 to a truck-mine operator who alleged the U. M. W. had conspired with the big operators to force the small pits out of existence. If the judgment is confirmed on appeal, it may well lead to such attrition by lawsuit as to sap ruinously an already seriously weakened organization. So much "nonunion coal" is now on the market that for the last two years the fund has collected much less money than it has disbursed. In the fiscal year ending on June 30, 1961, receipts dropped to 10 percent under those for the preceding year, and disbursements exceeded income by $16,300,000. Already the trustees of the depleted Fund have been compelled to reduce monthly retirement pensions from one hundred to seventy-five dollars and further reductions may soon be necessary. Thus the region's one union—and the only counterpoise to its one industry—is rushing rapidly toward a severe crisis in its affairs. It is by no means inconceivable that within a few more years the U. M. W. will disappear from the plateau, or, at best, be reduced to impotence with small islands of membership in only a few communities.

In community after community one can visit a dozen houses in a row without finding a single man who is employed. Most are retired miners and their wives who live on social security and union pension checks. Hundreds of other houses are occupied by aged widows, some of whom have taken in a grandchild or other youngster for "company" in their old age.

One row of camp houses has twenty-one residences. Seven are occupied by widows, the youngest of whom is fifty-two years of age and four of whom are more than seventy. Five are the homes of aged couples. Four shelter unemployed miners in their early fifties —men "too old to get a job and too young to retire." Three families draw state aid because the men are disabled from mining accidents. Only two houses are supported by men who still have jobs in a nearby mine.

One may walk the streets of camps and wander along winding creek roads for days and rarely find a young man or woman. For years the young and the employable have turned their backs on the plateau. Each spring when warm weather begins to enliven the land the more energetic and ambitious of the young men and women develop a yen for a more hopeful region. One by one they slip away. A year after high school diplomas are distributed, it is hard to find more than 4 or 5 percent of the graduates in their home counties. In the autumn of 1960 one high school principal assured me that not a single graduate of his school in 1958, 1959 or 1960 was living in the county. A couple of dozen are in military or naval service, but 70 percent had found jobs (or at least lodgment) in Ohio, Indiana and Michigan. The others were scattered over New York, Illinois and California.

When citizens leave the region at such an early age they rarely return except for short visits. Within a few years they have found spouses, homes and friends elsewhere. Occasionally they come back to attend a funeral or a family reunion, but after a few years such visits generally stop altogether. Poor though its schools are by national norms, the pleateau is educating its children almost entirely for other and wealthier parts of the nation. The one thing it needs most desperately is an educated and energetic cadre of leaders—imaginative and challenging men and women to grapple with its encrustations of problems and shortcomings. As matters now stand there is little likelihood it can develop such leadership, and its destiny is likely to remain in the hands of the absentee wreckers and their apologists.

The 1960 census discloses some breathtaking facts about the metamorphosis now under way in the character of the Kentuckian and his state. The preceding decade was one of unparalleled dynamism and growth for the nation. While Arkansas, Mississippi and South Dakota lost population, most states, including Kentucky, managed to make at least some population gains. For California,

Oregon, Washington, Utah, Arizona, Florida, Ohio, New York and Pennsylvania it was a decade aglow with prosperity. New citizens poured in from other areas. Cities sprang up in waste lands. Some portions of Kentucky—the western and northern areas—shared in the national growth. On the whole, however, the state's census statistics are chilling because of the dreary picture they portray. The total population of Kentucky rose from 2,944,806 in 1950 to 3,038,156 in 1960. The rural population as a whole decreased 9.4 percent while the urban population rose 24.8 percent, reflecting the general nationwide movement from the countryside into the incorporated town. A sustained exodus from the state persisted throughout the decade. Most of the emigrés were between twenty-five and twenty-nine years of age. For the state as a whole, that age bracket lost 21.7 percent, but for the plateau counties the loss ran much higher.

The state as a whole lost 14.6 percent of its citizens between twenty and twenty-four years of age, but again the loss rate from the Cumberland Plateau was more than twice this figure.

During the same years the number of people eighty-five years of age or older increased in the Cumberlands by 61.8 percent!

While the energetic, the ambitious and the hopeful were leaving the state, those who remained behind were not idle. The number of children increased by 16.7 percent. The plateau counties sustained a "fertility ratio" much higher than that of the rest of the state. The poverty-stricken mountain area produced nearly twice as many children per thousand women as did the wealthy and stable Bluegrass. The fertility ratio is determined by the number of children under five years of age per thousand women. In Leslie County this figure was 790. The other pleateau counties did not fall much below that level.

Nor should we assume that even the relatively educated highland youth is faring well at the hands of the outside world. Even those with high school diplomas find many doors shut to them. Unfortunately the region's poor schools and the limited cultural facilities have produced whole crops of high school graduates who are poorly prepared when compared with students who have been educated in good public or private schools elsewhere. Despite twelve years in elementary and high school a majority of the proud young graduates are scarcely literate. They have read little outside their pallid textbooks and have made no real effort in composition. The mathematics classrooms have long been the "sideline" domain of the football and basketball coaches. Physics, chemistry, calculus, algebra and geometry have been so neglected that in some institutions they have practically vanished. Latin and foreign languages, too, disappeared from many curricula during or soon after the Second World War and few students can comprehend a word of any foreign tongue. Infinitely more tragic is their inability to comprehend the best expressions of their own language. Shakespeare and the other poets and playwrights, old and new, are mysterious citadels whose walls few of them have attempted to breach. For years I have talked with high school students in an effort to discover their knowledge of English and American poetic literature. I can number on the fingers of one hand the few students who have been able to recite from memory even a single stanza from Shakespeare, Shelley, Keats, Browning, Wordsworth, Tennyson, Poe or Whitman. The great novels which spellbound other generations of scholars are regarded as laborious chores to be struggled through out of sheer necessity.

But while genuine learning—where it existed at all—has withered, athletics have found no dearth of official and public support. Rare is the high school whose football coach is not paid far more than its chemistry, mathematics and English teachers. Though decades passed without the building of new classrooms or laboratories the administrators managed to finance gymnasia. In school systems too poor to buy library books, money was always discovered for basketballs and playing floors. In 1947 one school board discussed at length the rising cost of maintaining a chemistry class in each of the county's high schools. Finally, with supreme generosity, the board budgeted fifty dollars for each chemistry teacher to spend on laboratory equipment and supplies. The chemistry teachers were voted annual salaries of $2250. Then, with this vexatious problem disposed of, the board voted to sell bonds in order to spend $257,000 for a gymnasium. The superintendent declared and the board agreed that a strong athletics program would bring the school vigorous support from the community and would keep in the classrooms many students who otherwise might be tempted to go North in quest of jobs.

The region's school system is still hopelessly bogged in politics. Elected school board members hire the superintendents. School board elections occur every two years and invariably the superintendent is one of the most powerful political figures in the county. Almost without supervision by the state he spends hundreds of thousands of dollars annually, all of which can be dispensed to political as well as educational advantage. In 1960 the Legislature enacted a long overdue general 3 percent sales tax, devoting nearly two thirds of the money to the public schools. This huge and abrupt rise in appropriations has financed substantial salary raises for teachers, and a modest building program.

It has also enabled the school politicians to fortify themselves with massive patronage dispensations. As a rule the school clique is interwoven with the courthouse political machine which spends county funds and discreetly oversees the local management of the State Aid programs. These powerful allies are thus so well-financed and entrenched that they are extremely difficult to overturn and their foremost objective is political perpetuation. They keep the schools enmeshed in endless political brawls. The tensions generated by the politicians are reflected in cynical teachers who know they are more often hired for their vote-getting power than for their teaching skill. Even more tragically, it is mirrored in dilapidated school buildings, tattered collections of books posing as libraries, comparatively palatial gyms and recurring crops of educationally stunted high school graduates.

The Selective Service system deals daily with the products of the weak and politically oriented schools. One county of approximately thirty thousand people (a county in most respects typical) boasts five high schools and is generally rated as having one of the plateau's more effective school systems. In 1960 Selective Service examined one hundred and four young draft registrants from the county. All of them were under twenty-three years of age. Only two failed for physical reasons, but twenty-six failed because they could not pass the mental tests. They were "functional illiterates" who were unable to read or comprehend satisfactorily ordinary printed matter such as newspapers and magazines. Even more shocking, four high school graduates volunteered and two of them were rejected for the same reason. Selective Service rejections for mental and educational reasons are running from 25 percent in the "better" counties to as much as 50 percent in the worst.

A fifty-six-year-old jobless miner summed up the hopelessness the shoddy schools sometimes engender. He sat in my law office one rainy Saturday afternoon and described his plight:

I hain't got no education much and jist barely can write my name. After I lost my job in 1950 I went all over the country a-lookin' fer work. I finally found a job in a factory in Ohio a-puttin' televisions inside wooden crates. Well, I worked for three years and managed to make enough money to keep my young-'uns in school. Then they put in a machine that could crate them televisions a whole lot better than us men could and in a lot less time. Hit jist stapled them up in big card-board boxes. I got laid off again and I jist ain't never been able to find nothing else to do.

But I kept my young-'uns in school anyway. I come back home here to the mountains and raised me a big garden ever' year and worked at anything I could find to do. I sold my old car fer seventy-five dollars and I sold all the land my daddy left me and spent the money on my children. They didn't have much to eat or wear, but they at least didn't miss no school. Well, finally last spring my oldest boy finished up high school and got his diploma. I managed to get twenty-five dollars together and give it to him and he went off to git him a job. He had good grades in school and I figured he'd git him a job easy. He went out to California where he's got some kinfolks and went to a factory where they was hirin' men. The sign said all the work hands had to be under thirty-five years of age and be high school graduates. Well, this company wouldn't recognize his diploma because it was from a Kentucky school. They said a high school diploma from Kentucky, Arkansas and Mississippi just showed a man had done about the same as ten years in school in any other state. But they agreed to give the boy a test to see how much he knowed and he failed it flatter than a flitter. They turned him down and he got a job workin' in a laundry. He jist barely makes enough money to pay his way but hit's better than settin' around back here.

I reckon they jist ain't no future fer people like us. Me and my wife ain't got nothin' and don't know nothin' hardly. We've spent everything we've got to try to learn our young-'uns something so they would have a better chance in the world, and now they don't know nothin' either!

That his son is not an exceptional example is borne out by the statistics on college freshmen from the plateau. Some, of course, do excellent work in college and have little difficulty in entering the University of Kentucky or colleges outside the state. Most of the hopeful freshmen, however, are shockingly unprepared for college study. The standard College Qualification Test is given annually to seniors in the state's high schools and in those of other states. The test is prepared by the Psychological Corporation, a New York firm, and seeks to measure the high school graduate's cultural background as well as his scholastic achievement. As its name implies, it is designed to measure the student's preparation for college study. In 1960 students in Virginia and Tennessee averaged above

80 percent on the test. In areas of Kentucky outside the plateau grades averaged between 55 percent and 65 percent out of a possible 100 percent. If this poor showing is startling what, then, must be one's reaction to the results of the same examination in the counties of the plateau? When the high school graduates in a broad belt of the coal counties were given the test in 1960, the average grade was only 17.5 percent.

These undereducated young Americans are the region's fortunate youths, notwithstanding the shortcomings of their schooling. Infinitely worse off are the uncounted children who simply do not go to school. One teacher, for example, began the 1959–1960 school term with fifty-eight enrolled pupils, in four grades. But as the term advanced many difficulties beset her weather-beaten little institution. Some children lived several miles away and had little appetite for the long walk over slippery paths on cold wintry mornings. The drafty building was a breeding ground for cold and influenza viruses and a substantial number were kept away by illness. Most absentees, however, stayed at home simply because their parents could not provide shoes and clothing for them to wear. Consequently, average daily attendance was only thirty-four.

Weak and sporadic elementary school preparation results in crops of high school freshmen who are totally unprepared for further studies. Almost one third of the freshmen of 1956 had dropped out of school in 1959.

The incidence of total illiteracy is startingly high. Every lawyer in the pleateau receives clients almost daily who are unable to sign their names to legal documents. On one occasion I went to a coal camp to obtain the signatures of a miner and his wife. Though they were under thirty-six years of age they could not write their names. Under the law their "marks" required attestation by two witnesses. Neither of their nearest neighbors could perform this simple duty and we were compelled to visit the third house before a man and woman were found who could sign as witnesses.

The physical task of providing decent housing for the region's schoolchildren—a prerequisite without which real improvement is unthinkable—is staggering. Though the new retail sales tax is financing the construction of several hundred new classrooms annually, the building rate cannot begin to equal that at which ancient, rickety buildings have to be abandoned. Speaking of the building program in his own county, Pike County Superintendent C. H. Farley told a congressional committee in March, 1961, that the task of catchingup appeared insuperable without major new sources of revenue. As he termed it, "The hurrieder we go, the behinder we get. Our schools are short on literally everything but children."

The county of approximately thirty thousand people which I have previously mentioned is largely supported by Welfarism of one character or another. As this is written, seven hundred and four Old Age pensioners receive monthly checks from the state capitol. Four hundred and eighty-six families are supported by Aid for Dependent Children checks. Seventy-one blind persons draw checks, and one hundred and twenty-six families are supported because the breadwinner is disabled, has fled or has been imprisoned. Nearly a thousand households receive checks from the United Mine Workers, and more than thirty-five hundred persons draw Social Security checks totalling two million dollars annually. Over a thousand pension and compensation checks reach the county each month from the United States Veterans Administration. At least two hundred families receive compensation checks because the husbands were killed or injured in mining accidents. Two thousand other men are paid unemployment compensation benefits while actively seeking other jobs. On "check days," at the beginning of each month, wastebaskets in county-seat banks are piled high with empty brown envelopes from state and Federal agencies. Sometimes they are inches deep on the floor at the tellers' windows. The millions of dollars thus pumped into the plateau each year keep the people alive and support the merchants and other business establishments. Without such checks a majority of the highlanders would be in abject starvation in a matter of days.

One third of the county's population is on the Commodity Relief rolls. From relatively humble beginnings the commodity distribution program has grown to mammoth proportions. On "give-away" days queues a hundred yards long form in front of the distribution centers and the huge bags and boxes full of staples are carried to automobiles. Sometimes several people will rent a single car to haul their rations, and its luggage compartment will not hold the entire load.

Other Relief recipients arrive in their own vehicles, ranging from pathetic rattletraps to new Buicks. The late-model cars are the property of miners who were recently idled by layoffs at the rail mines. They worked ten or fifteen years at high wages and still drive cars bought or contracted for in happier times. It is incongruous in the extreme to see a man carry his bag of "giveaway grub" out to a bright red late-model Mercury with synthetic leopardskin seat-covers.

Sixteen hundred of the county's men are still employed in the unionized rail mines (at the height of the Big Boom its rail pits hired ninety-four hundred men), and seven hundred and fifty others work two or three days a week in nonunion truck mines. The county and independent school districts hire nearly five hundred teachers, supervisors, bus drivers, lunchroom cooks, librarians and other personnel for nine months out of each year. Banks, stores, garages, filling stations, machineshops, quarries, sawmills, post offices, restaurants, utilities companies, printers, morticians, railroads and other enterprises provide full or part-time employment to another thirteen hundred men and women. The United Mine Workers' hospital employs a hundred and twenty-five others. Approximately one hundred and fifty persons work for municipalities, the county and the state. Together, the employed support fewer than half the county's population.   .   .   .   .

THE POLITICS OF DECAY

In her checkered history Kentucky has had four written constitutions. Beginning with the first in 1792 they were extremely democratic documents, vesting in the voters the power to elect almost every man who governs them or has charge of public affairs. The present constitution, written in 1890, attempted to preserve undiluted the rough frontier equality whose character had been stamped on the state's people a century before. First of all the Constitutional Convention undertook to reserve all real power at the local level. A host of county and city elective officers was established. In a six-year interval the people in a typical plateau county choose the following officials: the state senator, state representative, circuit judge, circuit court clerk, commonwealth attorney, county court clerk, county judge, county attorney, tax commissioner, sheriff, coroner, eight justices of the peace, eight constables and five members of the Board of Education. In addition the people in each municipality elect a mayor, a police judge, five or six members of the Common Council, and, in some towns, a city attorney and marshal.

At the state level they elect a governor, lieutenant-governor, secretary of state, auditor of public accounts, treasurer, commissioner of agriculture, attorney general and seven judges of the

Court of Appeals. Most ridiculous of all they elect a clerk of the Court of Appeals. This official keeps a record of the proceedings of the state's highest court and has to earn his modest salary by electioneering among three million people in forty thousand square miles of territory.

But the state officials are a façade. The real power of government is at the base. Except for the judicial officers all this great host of local servants are paid by fees. The amount of their compensation is dependent upon their ability to collect charges from the general public. The state officials lack power to remove any of these "fee grabbers" other than the sheriffs, and there is no practical means by which malfeasance at the local level can be punished. To all intents and purposes the governor is little more than a presiding county judge. His ability to lead depends upon his capacity to persuade, because once a governor has fallen into the disfavor of the courthouse cliques his days are numbered. Dealing with a faceless multitude of county-centered and often illiterate voters, the county officials can propagandize endlessly to the detriment of a state administration, assuring its political doom regardless of the worthiness of the governor's aims. The courthouses are one hundred and twenty anchors which perpetually hold developments to the political center of the stream at a virtual standstill. At the bottom of this courthouse conservatism is a relentless determination to prevent any change that might replace fees with salaries or dilute the powers of local offices.

And what is the role of the public servant who holds office in such a setting? What kind of people knock at his door and what standards of public service do they demand of him? By what creed do they expect him to serve the holy principles of Liberty and Justice? In this most democratic of all states, how does Democracy fare?

The office of the county judge is the nerve center of the courthouse. In addition to being a judicial official charged with the trial of misdemeanors and minor civil actions, His Honor is the chief executive officer of the county. He presides over the fiscal court, directs the spending of county funds and is generally the chief "contact man" with Frankfort in political matters pertaining to the county.

His office consists of two dingy rooms. The long unpainted walls are peeling and paint hangs in scales from the ceiling. The rays of the sun struggle with small success to pierce the dirty, rain-streaked windowpanes. In the corner of the outer room a tobacco-stained cardboard box serves as a waste can.

The outer room contains the desk of his secretary and a half-dozen chairs are lined up along the walls. No matter how harassed she may be by the constant procession of callers, his secretary never fails to smile ingratiatingly—because even the smallest frown may offend a voter. From 8:30 in the morning when the office opens until 4:30 when the doors are locked, there is seldom a moment when a group of people are not waiting to "see the judge."

A day spent with the county judge in such an office in a plateau county is a revealing experience. It tells a story of the breakdown of Democracy and of the growing dependence and futility of the population. If Democracy is to eventually prevail over totalitarian ideologies the individual citizen must be able to shoulder a multitude of responsibilities and to discharge them out of a sense of duty. To do this he must possess the ability to meet social and economic problems and the willingness to grasp them. Until a generation ago the mountaineer was accustomed to "turn out" for road workings and other undertakings for community betterment. He was not paid and he did not expect to be. His willingness to work on roads and other essential projects was a holdover from the frontier where no government or government largesse existed. However, as government expanded and its benefits multiplied the old sturdiness began to dissolve. Though many frontier modes and outlooks survive and are sharply impressive, the traumas of fifty years have left a lasting imprint on the character of the mountaineer. His forefathers lived by the frontier maxim "root hog or die." They would be astounded if they could return in the spirit to behold their descendants thronging the office of the county judge to implore his assistance in a multitude of situations which, in an earlier time, would have been met by the citizens without its once occurring to them that help from any quarter was either possible or desirable.

A moment after the judge unlocked the door to his office an elderly woman darted in behind him. The judge greeted her with an affable smile and after a moment of small talk about her family and community, he inquired her business. She drew a paper from her purse and displayed it to him. On it was scrawled in longhand: *"We the undersigned persons have contributed to help—who is sick and has to stay at home."* Below this caption four or five courthouse officeholders and county-seat merchants had written their names. Each of them had noted his contribution of $1.00 to the sufferer. The old lady explained that her son had a family and had been sick for a long time. "The doctors," she said, "can't find out what's the matter with him, and, as fer me, I'm almost certain it's cancer. You know, judge, how we've always voted fer you every time you ever run for anything and will again just as shore as you run. If you can help him out now when he's having such bad luck, we shore will appreciate it."

The judge sighed ruefully, because such pleas are routine, but he added his name to the list and handed the woman a dollar bill.

A moment later the secretary arrived and callers began to fill the chairs in the waiting room. Some said they had just dropped by to shake hands with the judge and had no business in particular, but three very determined gentlemen were ushered into his office. Dressed in mud-spattered overalls, they lived on a creek some eleven miles from the county seat. The state had built a rural highway into the community in 1949 and later hard-surfaced it. But long neglect had allowed the road to deteriorate badly. The spokesman for the group, a tall, raw-boned mountaineer, told their story:

Judge, you know what kind of a shape our road is in and that it's prac'ly impossible to travel it. The ditch lines are all stopped up and there are holes all over it big enough to set a washtub in. One feller broke an axle right in the middle of the road last week. Now you know our precinct has always been one of the best in the county and you never come up there electioneering in your life that you didn't git a big vote, but if you can't do something for us now we'll sure as hell remember it if you ever run for anything else again. We ain't got no governor or he wouldn't let the roads get in the shape they're in now. We've just got to have the ditch lines cleaned out and the holes filled up.

The judge attempted to mollify his angry visitors, for this was not their first visit to his office on the same business. He pointed out very courteously, however, that funds were short and that a new coat of surfacing was out of the question. He promised to send a scraper to clean out the drainage ditches, and pledged an application of gravel for the worst places in the road. He warned them, however: "The roads all over this county are going to pieces, and we simply don't have the money to keep them up. We are doing everything in our power to maintain the roads, but we just don't have the money to do a decent job."

Somewhat mollified, the men departed—but not before dropping another threat of retribution at the polls if some effective relief did not ensue.

As they left, the county attorney rapped on the door and then entered the judge's private office. The Grand Jury had adjourned the day before and, as their predecessors had done for a good many years, the jurors had blasted the county officials for allowing the courthouse and jail to fall into filthy ruin. In a report to the circuit judge they declared that they had inspected the jail and found that structure wholly "unfit for human occupancy." The walls were cracked and broken, the roof leaked and the cells were inadequately heated. The commodes were without seats and the coal-black mattresses were without sheets. The entire facility reeked of excrement, urine and sweat. They recommended that the jail be closed and not reopened until completely renovated. They found the courthouse in almost equally foul condition, and said so in scathing terms.

The judge and the county attorney went over the report together line by line and agreed with the sentiments expressed in it. The county attorney remarked that it was a good report. "They would have been a lot more helpful, though," he said, "if they had told us where to get the money to do something about it." The judge reminded him that in several mountain counties the question of a bond issue for the construction of a new jail and courthouse had been referred to the people and sternly rejected at the polls. The county attorney opined: "If the same issue was placed on the ballot in this county you wouldn't get three votes for it out of that grand jury panel."

While he and the judge talked, proof of the jury's criticism was manifested by a vile stench which crept into the office from the public toilet in the basement of the courthouse.

When the county attorney was gone one of the county's justices of the peace brought his son-in-law to meet the judge. The justice pointed out that the fiscal court would soon have to add another man to the county road crew, and that his son-in-law desperately needed the job. The judge and justice were political allies, and His Honor agreed that the jobless son-in-law was ideally suited for the position. When this happy accord had been reached his secretary informed the judge that a deputy sheriff had arrested a speeder and that the culprit was awaiting trail. Whereupon the judge walked into the unswept little courtroom near his office and sat down behind the judicial desk.

A middle-aged man and his wife were sitting on the front bench in the section of the courtroom reserved for spectators. Nearby sat a man in overalls and an open-collared, blue workshirt. He wore a baseball player's cap and an enormous star-shaped badge was pinned to the bib of his overalls. Strapped to his side was a German Luger pistol, a memento of some distant battlefield. The judge cleared his throat and asked the officer the nature of the charge against the defendant. The deputy stood up and came forward.

"Judge," he said, "this man was driving in a very reckless way. I got behind 'im and follered 'im about four mile, and I seen his car cross the yaller line at least three times. I want a warrant chargin' 'im with reckless driving."

His Honor turned to the offender and asked what he had to say. He was from New Jersey and was on his way to visit his son in Virginia. He and his wife had decided to turn aside and see the Kentucky mountains, about whose beauty they had heard so much. They had driven neither recklessly nor rapidly, and if their automobile had crossed the center line at any time it had been done inadvertently and on a relatively straight stretch of road where no other vehicles were in view.

It was obvious that the judge was impressed by the "violator's" sincerity and that he believed what he had said. He paused for a long moment and reflected upon the situation and, to one versed in mountain politics, his silent cogitations left a plainly discernible track. He weighed the fact that on the one hand he was dealing with a deputy who voted in the county and whose kinsmen and friends were equipped with razor-sharp votes. He knew that if the motorist paid no fine the deputy would be offended. The officer made his living from the fees collected in cases such as this one. If the New Jersey motorist paid a fine he must also pay the costs, six dollars of which would go into the pocket of the deputy. The guardian of the public peace would take unkindly to a dismissal of the case after he had gone to the trouble to capture the man and bring him three miles to the county seat. Weighed on the other end of the scale was a stranger who would never be here again and who, even if he paid a small fine, perhaps unjustly, would not suffer irreparably. These considerations produced the inevitable conclusion. His Honor decreed the minimum fine allowed under the statute. The total came to eighteen dollars and fifty cents. When justice had thus been meted out the judge did not return to his office but took advantage of the opportunity to escape for lunch

When he returned at 1:00 P.M. the callers had increased in number and their problems had grown even more vexatious.

A fifty-year-old man, his wife and her father had come to tell the judge that the welfare worker had denied his claim for public assistance. He wanted the judge to talk to her and, if necessary, to go to Frankfort and see if the claim couldn't be straightened out. He said:

Judge, I just can't work. I can't do nary thing. I'm sick and I've got a doctor's certificate to prove it. I worked in the mines for twenty-five years before they shut down but you know I got into bad air and ever since then when I git hot or a little bit tired I git so nervous I can't hardly stand it. I don't have a thing in the world to live on and they've turned down my claim, and I know that if you will get onto the people at Frankfort you can get it straightened out. There's a sight of people in this county that ain't as bad off as I am and they didn't have any trouble gettin' it and I'm sure not a-goin' to give up on it without seeing into it a little further.

At this juncture the man's father-in-law, a gentleman of approximately seventy-five, chimed in. He had lived with his daughter and son-in-law for three years and never had known anybody who was a harder worker. He had seen the man work an hour or two in his vegetable garden and get so nervous that he would spill his coffee when he came into the house to rest. He assured the judge that he would be the first to say so if he thought his son-in-law was "putting on."

The judge heard this tale of woe with deep respect and assured his visitors that they had his sympathy and that he would make every effort to help them. He hedged by pointing out that public assistance is administered by a state agency over which he had no control. The Welfare Department had a lot of stubborn people on its staff, some of whom, unfortunately, were quite unreasonable. He remembered that the sick man had always been his friend and had stood by him in bygone years. He summed up his gratitude with the assertion, "You've scratched my back in the past and I'll try to scratch yours now. You know, turnabout is fair play."

Highly gratified, the nervous man, his wife and his father-in-law left, after again reminding the judge that they sure would appreciate his help.

The next caller had been drawing State Aid but his check had been discontinued because his children had not been attending school regularly. He explained that his young-'uns had been sick.

"Not sick enough to have a doctor, but feelin' bad and I just couldn't make 'em go to school a-feelin' bad. As soon as they got to feelin' better they went right back to school, and I don't know what we'll do if we don't git some help fer 'em again."

He promised that if the judge could prevail upon the welfare worker to restore his check he would make an affidavit to send his children to school on each day when they were well enough to go.

About 3:30 in the afternoon the county truant officer (known officially by the horrendous title of Director of Pupil Personnel) made his appearance. A warrant had been sworn out charging a father with failing to send his children to school and the trial was set for that hour. The defendant was already present in the little courtroom. A few moments later the county attorney appeared to prosecute the case for the state. The truant officer explained that the defendant was the father of six children, all of whom were of elementary school age. They had not been to school in the preceding month despite his pleas that the father keep them in regular attendance. The county attorney asked the court to impose a fine or jail sentence. The judge asked the defendant why he had not been sending his children to school. The man stalked forward and gazed around him with the uncertainty of a trapped animal. He was dressed in tattered overalls to which many patches had been affixed. He was approximately forty-five years old and it was obvious from his huge hands and stooped shoulders that he had spent many years under the low roof of a coal mine. He pleaded his defense with the eloquence of an able trial lawyer. With powerful conviction he said:

I agree with everything that's been said. My children have not been going to school and nobody wants them to go any more than I do. I've been out of work now for four years. I've been all over this coalfield and over into Virginia and West Virginia looking for work. I've made trip after trip to Indianny, Ohio and Michigan and I couldn't find a day's work anywhere. I drawed out my unemployment compensation over three years ago and the only income I've had since has been just a day's work now and then doing farm work for somebody. I sold my old car, my shotgun, my radio and even my watch to get money to feed my family. And now I don't have a thing in the world left that anybody would want. I'm dead-broke and about ready to give up. I live over a mile from the schoolhouse and I simply don't have any money to buy my children shoes or clothes to wear. I own a little old four-room shanty of a house and twenty acres of wore-out hillside land. Last spring the coal company that owns the coal augered it and teetotally destroyed the land. I couldn't sell the whole place for five hundred dollars if my life depended on it. Me and my oldest boy have one pair of shoes between us, and that's all. When he wears 'em I don't have any and when I wear 'em he don't have any. If it wasn't for these rations the gover'ment gives us, I guess the whole family would of been starved to death long afore now. If you want to fine me I ain't got a penny to pay it with and I'll have to lay it out in jail. If you think puttin' me in jail will help my young-'uns any, then go ahead and do it and I'll be glad of it If the county attorney or the truant officer will find me a job where I can work out something for my kids to wear I'll be much abliged to 'em as long as I live.

At the conclusion of this declaration the judge looked uneasily around, eying the county attorney and the truant officer in the hope that some help would come from that quarter. Both gentlemen remained silent. At length the judge plied the defendant with questions. The man had a third-grade education. He had worked in the mines for a total of twenty years and had spent three years as an infantry soldier in the war against Japan. He had been fortunate, however, and had received no wounds. Consequently, he drew no pension or compensation from the Veterans' Administration. The factories to which he had applied for employment had insisted on men with more education than he possessed. They also wanted younger men. Finally the county attorney demanded to know whether he had any skill except mining coal. The answer was an emphatic "No." Then he blurted out:

Judge, I'm not the only man in this fix on the creek where I live. They's at least a dozen other men who ain't sent their children to school for the same reason mine ain't a-goin'. They can't send 'em cause they can't get hold of any money to send 'em with. Now the county attorney and the truant officer are trying to make an example out of me. They think that if I go to jail for a week or two the rest of 'em will somehow find the money to get their kids into the schoolhouse.

He looked intently at the truant officer and demanded, "Ain't that so?" to which the truant officer hesitantly assented.

The judge mulled the problem over for a moment or two and then "filed away" the warrant. He explained that it was not being dismissed, but was being continued upon the docket indefinitely. "If the case is ever set for trial again I will write you a letter well in advance of the trial date and tell you when to be here," he said. "In the meantime go home and do the best you possibly can to make enough money to educate your children. If they don't go to school they'll never be able to make a living and when they get grown they'll be in just as bad a fix as you are in now."

The defendant thanked the judge, picked up his battered miner's cap and walked to the door. There he paused and looked back at judge, attorney and truant officer for a long moment, as though framing a question. Then he thought better of it and closed the door behind him. His Honor had had enough for one day, and decided to go home. While he was locking the door I glanced at the headlines on the newspaper the morning mail had brought to his desk:

FEDERAL AID TO EDUCATION BILL DIES IN HOUSE COMMITTEE

BILLIONS APPROVED FOR FOREIGN AID

JOBLESS MINER KILLS SELF IN HARLAN

CHAPTER TEN

THE DARKER SIDE
OF CHANGE

A FOCUS ON THE FUTURE has a special effect on the student of political behavior. It pushes him beyond analysis—breaking down past situations into their components—to synthesis—adding up the components to assess their political implications. We like to think the future can be shaped or at least affected by conscious choice and deliberate action. Yet that depends on our ability to discern—in advance—the probable dimensions of choice and the probable effects of action.

David Riesman wrote the following selection in the midst of the Nixon–Humphrey–Wallace campaign of 1968. His argument is diagnostic and predictive, stressing the identification of key trends and the developments they seemed to indicate for the election and its aftermath. In the fall of 1968 a national turn toward the right appeared to be accelerating. Riesman undertook the difficult job of estimating where that was taking us. His own preferences are made clear and are clearly related to his view of the facts.

As with the last selection, this one invites the exercise of the student's own powers of diagnosis and prediction. How does Riesman's estimate of trends fit the evidence you have encountered so far? What has happened since he wrote that tends to support or contradict his interpretation? And if you were to make a similar estimate as of now, what significant political trends do you see developing beyond tomorrow?

AMERICA MOVES TO THE RIGHT

DAVID RIESMAN

When Barry Goldwater was defeated by a large majority in the electoral college in 1964, many liberals and radicals concluded that the right wing had been similarly defeated. I thought then that they were too euphoric, overlooking the substantial numbers who had voted not only for the Republican party but specifically for Goldwater, and especially the many enthusiastic young people who brought to the Goldwater crusade an intensity of passion, an anarchic attitude toward bigness in government and, often, in business, and a quasi-conspiratorial view of its enemies similar to what we see now on the extreme left. The left and the right, of course, differ very much in the objects of their compassion and concern: the left cares about the non-white world, about the weak and powerless and the victims of militarism at home and abroad; the crusaders of the right, far less compassionate to begin with, are concerned about William Graham Sumner's original forgotten man: the middling white man who works hard, pays taxes, likes sports more than ideas and finds the modern world bewildering. (There are also a number of extremely wealthy, though provincial, sponsors of right-wing thought who, as Daniel Bell has observed, nevertheless feel dispossessed because they have more wealth than standing or understanding.) On the right wing, there are a number of people who are psychologically predisposed to authoritarianism, admiring the strong and despising the weak, fiercely chauvinistic vis-a-vis their race, their country, their definition of the American way. However, people of this dispensation, although more than sufficient to staff a totalitarian regime, account for only a fraction of the support for right-wing political candidates. How, then, is one to explain the persistence and growth of right-wing sentiment in

America, to the point at which a quarter of our young people have become supporters of George Wallace, a brilliant demagogue where Goldwater was genial and perhaps the most capable right-wing politician since Huey Long?

To begin with, it must be recognized that the United States through most of its history has been a profoundly conservative country. However, the conservative majority for much of our national existence has been apathetic, reasonably generous and good-natured and willing to put up with change if it did not come too fast and if it did not appear to threaten the majority's definition of what America stood for and what they themselves represented. Revisionist historians of Jacksonian America (Richard Hofstadter, Lee Benson, Marvin Meyers) have argued that, despite Populist rhetoric, neither Jackson nor his followers were radicals, nor did their movement have radical consequences, even for the civil service. Lincoln was no radical, nor was Woodrow Wilson, nor yet Franklin Roosevelt. Indeed, even in the Depression of 1929 and subsequent years, Communists, Trotskyites and national-Populists were mistaken in supposing that vast unemployment and an apparent failure of capitalism offered opportunities to mobilize people for revolutionary political change. On the whole, Americans have favored equality of opportunity, not equality of result, although there has been a slowly increasing willingness to put a floor under misery, if not a ceiling over aspiration and accomplishment.

The conservative majority has not been especially interested in politics, particularly at the national level. It has distrusted politicians, by which is meant professional politicians, not generals or celebrities whose previous reputations made it possible for them to appear to be above politics. Some national leaders, and many members of national elites, have been liberal or even radical; their views have gradually influenced Americans without ever establishing a permanent liberal hegemony. What has resulted is a blend of traditions: a conservatism about American values coupled with an interest in innovation and, when people have felt unthreatened, a certain measure of mutual tolerance for different ways of life. Correspondingly, when cumulative changes have presented the conservative majority with definitions of American life sharply at odds with their own, the result has often been what Prof. Joseph Gusfield terms symbolic crusades to extirpate the strange and the stranger and to set the country back on the right track.

Gusfield points out, for example, that the temperance movement was a way in which Protestant small-town America defined beer-drinking Germans in Milwaukee or whisky-drinking Irishmen in Boston not as an interesting contribution to cultural pluralism but as a threat to their America, just as the hippies appear to some today not as an exotic curiosity but as a threat to masculine dominance and family stability. Even when the national climate is moderately liberal, many such battles are fought locally, with the victory going to the conservatives. There are, for instance, the many recent referenda on the fluoridation of water in New England and elsewhere. Fluoridation comes to be defined as an interference with God's water, a conspiracy between the Communist party and the aluminum company to poison good Americans. Beyond that, it is seen as one more example of the intrusion of the national scientific elite into local affairs—and the vote against fluoridation has often been a vote against those well-educated, smooth people who have come into one's town and who seem to understand the modern world and even profit from it.

The natives can score similar victories over such people (and over the young as well) by voting down school bond issues or school budgets; such negative votes have been endemic in the last few years. To understand them better, one has to appreciate the fact that geographic and social mobility have the effect of forcing change on those who stay put as well as those who move. Stay-putters feel threatened by new people who come from elsewhere to run the new light industries, teach at the new colleges, preach at the more liberal Catholic and Protestant churches and otherwise bring the tolerant messages of the college-educated, national upper-middle class to previously isolated locales—messages which include staying up later at night, treating children more permissively, spending more on their education and introducing foreign movies. Hence a vote against fluoridation or a school bond issue may express resentment against a style of life that is costlier and at the same time more articulately defended than that of the indigenous stay-at-homes; such a vote also may be a gesture of impotent defiance against the big and feared powers: big government, big business, big labor—and the media. In the South, a similar politics of resentment has operated on the issue of race and in many communities has permitted a counter-establishment to develop in opposition to traditional moderate upper-class and upper-middle-class paternalistic whites who do not feel endangered by Negroes but who can be pushed out of authority by less affluent segregationists.

It is only under certain conditions, such as an unsatisfactory war, that these local pockets of right-wing and defensive conservatism coalesce into any kind of national movement. Father Coughlin represented such a movement at the time of the Depression, Senator Joseph McCarthy at the time of the Korean War. Like George Wallace today, and like Huey Long, the late Joseph McCarthy espoused some Populist attitudes, speaking on behalf of the little people against all the big powers, eventually including the Army itself. Opportunistically, he sought victims, not an agenda for change or even an effort to turn America back to the point where older people could feel that things made sense again. Joseph McCarthy helped to throw liberals and the left off balance by bullying individuals and by making dramatically visible the extent of resistance to change. Furthermore, as a Republican Irish Catholic, he helped cement a new tacit alliance of Catholic and Protestant fundamentalism—an alliance that became still more evident in the Kennedy–Nixon election, when a minority of conservative Catholics opposed Kennedy and allied themselves with Southern Baptists; it is often forgotten how near they came to winning, how tenuous Kennedy's victory was.

It has been almost as difficult for the various fragments on the extreme right to unite as for those on the extreme left, thanks to the suspiciousness and distrust that is one of the characteristics of right-wing attitudes. Among many other groups, the John Birch Society has been one which, as it were, could keep in storage some of the more well-to-do secular fundamentalists during a period when the right wing was on the defensive nationally, even while the society's members could be given practice in domestic counter-insurgency in crusades against UNESCO or Earl Warren or Polish hams in supermarkets. Its extreme economic conservatism and aura of wealth deprived the society of the Populist support that Joseph McCarthy had. Its weight, along with that of other endemic right-wing sects, could be felt only locally. However, at a time when the less well-to-do working class and the lower-middle class —stirred up by the Negro revolution, South and North, and by its liberal and radical white supporters—are ready to respond to someone like Wallace, who speaks to them directly as one of them, the wealthier and already organized right-wing cadres can serve as clusters of influence, political mobilization and financial backing. George Wallace is building a mass movement as Joseph McCarthy never did.

The right wing and the more apathetic conservatives, despite what might divide them in the realm of fiscal policy, tend to react similarly to the widespread and not wholly unrealistic feeling that there is no one in charge in America—that the country faces dissolution and anarchy. Of course, they are not aware how much they contribute to this anarchy themselves, seeing only the blacks and the militants on the left as the source of dissension.

As I have stated, the majority of conservative Americans are not repressive or fanatical. But they want to feel that the country is manageable and can be governed; they will accept progress if it does not cost too much, either in taxes or in altered symbolic values. Some of this majority were prepared to rally to Senator Eugene McCarthy, had he been nominated, because they liked his calm and respected his individualism. Indeed, many Midwestern farmers and many people who had supported Goldwater admired Eugene McCarthy, and some who had supported him in the primaries will surely vote for George Wallace. Wallace and Nixon give many voters a sense of an ability to take charge, to recognize problems of order, even though they do not lay claim to a great deal of inventiveness, a quality which no candidate now possesses.

It is not that most Americans are themselves convinced that they have the right answers to our national problems, or indeed that there are answers. There is a great deal of fluidity, uneasiness and temporizing. In this situation, the tactical advantage is decisive. On the national scene, the liberals have had that advantage for the last decade. They profited from the growing dissatisfaction with President Eisenhower, from the great accomplishment of the test-ban treaty and the partial *detente* it symbolized, from the massive defeat of Goldwater, from the energy with which President Johnson attacked the country's domestic problems early in his Administration. The fruits of sustained prosperity, increased education and the more sophisticated national media were visible all over America. Despite the war in Vietnam, a climate of unprecedented openness prevailed. In this climate, previously submerged and apparently docile groups were able to reveal latent attitudes that shocked and offended those who once enjoyed patronizing them. This was true of Negroes, South and North, and more recently of a minority of demonstrating and extremely visible college students. As Prof. S. M. Lipset has pointed out, the tactics of civil disobedience used by black and white militants were first practiced by dissident segregationists opposing the integration of Southern schools, buses or other public facilities—usually violently rather than non-violently, and always in disobedience to Federal if not local law. (George Wallace is clearly ready to take his movement to the streets—the streets that the radicals in Chicago at the time of the Democratic Convention said belonged to the people, without realizing that other people vastly outnumbering them could make the same claim.)

Both the suppressed blacks and the previously less political students have behaved as emancipated minorities generally do, with the heightened momentum that readily leads to euphoric excess; they are defiant and exuberant and they promulgate millennial claims. Demographic changes have brought these minorities together in numbers large enough to score tactical victories over vulnerable, understaffed university and city administrations. Many adult and young radicals are provincial, living in settings in which they are exposed to the like-minded, more conscious of the supposedly more pure on their left than of the vaguely sensed differences among conservative and right-wing Americans. Furthermore, many radical students have taken comfort from a feeling of identification with student demonstrators the world over, ignoring the differences among national situations. Similarly, some of the black militants see in the colored peoples of the Third World the source of eventual leverage, even within America. Yet these international connections, tenuous as they are, have increased anxieties on the right and opened many in the middle to an upsurge of nationalistic fears. Numbers of McCarthy supporters who felt betrayed because of the defeat of the Vietnam peace plank at Chicago have failed to appreciate that much recent opposition to the Vietnam War is not based on moral-political revulsion, but rather on impatience with civilian restraints on military initiative and a feeling of being misled by the Administration. (Naturally, the conservatives who have come around to weariness with the Vietnam War are not grateful to the radical students and others who helped make opposition to the war visible and less flamboyant opposition to it increasingly respectable.)

When the extreme right behaves with very bad manners or extravagant brutality, it is apt to offend the conservative majority, as Joseph McCarthy offended many and as Southern segregationist mobs often offended local as well as national leaders. There comes a point when, for many Americans, the political process loses its entertainment value and comes to be regarded as unsettling and a drain on energies. Political acquiescence may leave invisible scars, but after a while political agitators, like screaming children, may come to be resented, no matter how well one understands their causes. It is at this point that the calls for law and order, if not themselves too strident, strike home. Along with the rhetoric of traditional American virtue and patriotism, the right wing shares with the conventional conservative majority a nostalgic sense of our past. However, this past is far more violent than most Americans recognize; in fact there is less domestic violence now than in earlier periods. Some black militants *talk* more violent games against whites than they play, for in this they can draw on a long American, and especially Southern and Negro, tradition of evangelical exhortation. But some radical students, perhaps more literal-minded in this respect, take the rhetoric seriously and seek not to be outdone in militancy; in general, there is a temptation among whites to attend to the more strident black leaders and not the more pragmatic ones (who themselves share some of the feelings the militants voice). Some extreme militants have a stake in proving that all whites are equally to be distrusted, and thus they assault the reservoirs of sympathy that exist for the Negro among conservative white Americans.

The result is that the conservative majority attributes the rising national noise level to the radical left and to the liberal, educated upper-middle class, which appears to tolerate if not to sponsor the radicals. The life of the blue-collar working class and the lower-middle white-collar class tends to be a neighborhood life, with friendships based on family and propinquity, savings based on real estate and much dependence on public facilities (like schools) and semi-public ones (like churches and taverns). These people often feel themselves caught in a pincers movement between the Negroes or Puerto Ricans pressing into their neighborhoods from below and the upper-class and upper-middle-class anti-Puritan snobs who admire the poor and defiant, not the square and inhibited. (Many of the poor are square and inhibited, too, but the tradition of Western romanticism closes its eyes to this.) Policemen, schoolteachers, social workers, factory foremen and lower-level civil servants are all men in the middle, caught between their often-unruly clients and the liberal and tolerant mandates of the national elite and its media. (These mandates sometimes suffer from a credibility gap, as when they appear to deny the everyday experience of Negro crime, picturing the oppressed as victims and rarely as victimizers.)

Among the hippies and their hangers-on, there are many splinter groups, but most of them come from the affluent strata and appear to denigrate the American insistence that in a democracy everyone must strive to get ahead; they reject the advantages desperately sought by those who have risen from the working class to the lower-middle class. Hence, although some hippies celebrate the value of toil, they cannot pose as members of the "poor but honest" class who disturb nobody; on the contrary, as played up by the mass media, they contribute their share to the politics of polarization.

Some hippies share with the radicals and with many liberals the widely prevalent assumption that the country is already post-industrial, that there is no serious problem of keeping the economy going but only of redirecting its energies. This seems far-fetched to those who do not yet feel secure in the affluence they see around them, which they define as an American prerogative. Many understandably feel helpless in the face of strikes that cripple a city's transport, hospitals, schools or telephone service. I often see our society as a series of vast traffic jams, to which each idiosyncratic individual contributes his own weight, complaining about that of the others. To unsnarl America, to keep it productive, to make it so productive that it can satisfy the claims of the disinherited without aggravating the malaise of the most recent, still-undernourished heirs, is no mean task. The many intellectuals who reject industrialism and bureaucracy are tacitly assuming that it is no trick at all to keep our society's 200 million people alive, functioning and productive, and some of their discourse suggests that they would prefer a smaller country of noble frontiersmen. At this point society depends upon the ethic of production to keep going. Someday it may be possible to reject the blessings production provides, but that day cannot come until the blessings are universal, until they are fully at hand. I was mistaken in thinking at one time that abundance was assured, even though I recognized that our measure of it has depended since 1939 on a war-preparedness economy.

As vested interests can sabotage production in the economy, so each locale, each ethnic group and ideological position has in effect had its own deterrent in national politics. The anarchic right wing seeks Federal funds for its projects, but resists Federal control. In foreign affairs, however, it is the captive of its own chauvinism, and with the decline in right-wing isolationism, there have obviously been insufficient deterrents to adventurous and expensive foreign and military policies; Federal action has had many powerful friends and, despite generally declining xenophobia, few organized opponents. And since the right wing in the United States always tacitly cooperates with the right wing and militarists elsewhere, the influence of our right wing domestically grows when, for example, the Soviet military insists on the invasion of Czecho-slovakia to secure the Warsaw Pact; such cooperation has also imperiled the nuclear nonproliferation treaty and other measures of arms control.

Nevertheless, despite the unintentional assistance given American chauvinism by nationalists elsewhere, the patriotic fer-vor of Americans has continued to decline throughout the century. America is a more open society than it has ever been. Leftist radicals point to the repression of dissent against the Vietnam War, as in the trial of Dr. Spock or in the prosecution or reclassification of draft resisters. Yet compared to the way opposition to earlier wars was treated, opposition to the somewhat tangential and pa-tiently escalated war in Vietnam has not evoked fierce community pressures. There is little censure of those who avoid the draft, even though there is opprobrium for men who express opposition to America as well as to the war. The relative coolness and equanim-ity with which the majority of Americans accepted the Soviet invasion of Czechoslovakia is an indication of maturity (and, to some degree, of indifference) inconceivable a decade earlier. Even vis-a-vis Communist China—and despite fanaticism there—there is less fanaticism now in the United States than there was when Quemoy and Matsu seemed almost fighting words.

What Communist adversaries have not succeeded in doing to strengthen the American right wing, the provocative left is accom-plishing in another tacit alliance of extremes. Some on the left regard contemporary America as basically fascist and want to develop the latent film that has already, in their view, been ex-posed. "America couldn't be worse" is a frequent refrain. Little do they know. Some indeed do not want to know, since the excitement and solidarity of the politics of confrontation tend to blind them to their own destructiveness. Others vastly overestimate the potential power of militant students, militant professionals and housewives and militant blacks. They are not even aware that the Young Americans for Freedom are at least four times as numerous as the Students for a Democratic Society. There is a penchant for the theater of confrontation in which the good guys can make the bad guys look even badder on television—and radicalize still more potential good guys from the vapid, timid middle class. In the civil rights movement, this tactic succeeded with a great many liberal students and professional people, upper-middle class housewives and clergymen. But the dramas of Selma and Birmingham that helped mobilize these minorities also set in motion efforts at school and neighborhood integration which have heightened the enthusiastic support for George Wallace among young voters, both in the South and in the North, many of whom were in school when efforts at integration began.

An absolute morality tends to be characteristic of people whose experience of life has not included the give-and-take of wide human contacts and the mutual tolerance and sense for compromise that these often, but not invariably, encourage. Idealistic young people on both the right and on the left are outraged at an America that does not live up to its ideals as their parents and other significant adults interpret—and evade—them. Both extremes are concerned with the quality of American life. Some on the right want more order (at least for others), and some on the left want more experimentalism, not only for themselves but for others as well. On neither side is there a uniform view as to the lineaments of a more desirable future. But this diversity gets lost when judged from the other side of the right-left dividing line. Thus, many Americans of the right, center and left who want more participation in decision-making for the common man may have in mind quite different forms of representation, orders of decision and national priorities. When questions about these matters are turned into issues of absolute morality, where enemies are those who do not share an identical view, tactics tend also to escalate. Sometimes the tactics escalate before the goals do, requiring more elevated and demanding goals to justify the means already employed.

Speaking now only of the left, white radicals in many academic and other settings are engaged in competition with black militants as to who is more militant, more uncompromising, more total in his rejection of an America that has fallen from grace. But on the whole, both militant and moderate black leaders remain more political: there are specific things they want, and—while their dignity and powers of territoriality cannot be quickly redeemed, their schools enlightened, their dwellings made more habitable—some accommodation can be made to their demands. In contrast, the demands of the New Left and of more moderate professionals and housewives tend to be qualitative and inchoate. They want Americans to be more open to experience, less driven, less bound by birth to a particular gender, class, color or nationality. They want institutions to consider not only the products or services they turn out, but also the people in them; by emphasizing process as well as product, they seek to subordinate traditional goals of efficiency or harmony and to promote instead more complicated goals of personal autonomy—an autonomy that, as I have suggested, can sometimes become more anarchic than responsive. When these ideals are stated as absolute demands, rather than as aims to be approximated over time, the effect is sometimes to aggravate the right without much helping the left. For example, America is condemned as being racist, thus forcing on people introspection concerning their attitudes—an introspection often confused by the fact that most Negroes are lower class, while most Americans seek democratically not to be class conscious. One consequence of calling people racists who consider themselves reasonably decent and humane may well be that they will conclude: "So be it; I am a racist and will follow leadership that respects and justifies me as I am."

Incremental gains won over a long period by careful work—and capable of being easily erased by an explosion, whether nuclear or political—seem like no gains at all to impatient young people of all chronological ages. I think that one must live simultaneously on two levels: the level on which one works for incremental gains and another on which one develops the faith and vision by which to judge those gains and to evaluate both what has been accomplished and where shortcomings remain. But a sense of moral urgency has led many people on the left to an attitude a little like that of the nineteen-thirties, when left-wing radicals found in the near target of the liberals an enemy who shared enough of their own values to be despised for not sharing them *à outrance*. Thus the radicals today make a target of Vice-President Humphrey and only rarely bother with Nixon, where their attacks would not sting or provoke dramatic response. (Black militants and their white allies do attack George Wallace, and—as he has often recognized—make votes for him; when challenged about this, they are apt to say that things couldn't be worse, when in reality things have gotten so much better that the blacks are liberated from inhibition and calculation.)*

I recall talking in 1964 with some Berkeley students active in the Free Speech Movement who were elated at the way in which they had been able to mobilize support and to gain many of their ends on the campus. I told them that they should also take into account the likelihood that they could make Ronald Reagan Gover-

---

* The radicals of the right have a similar tropism which leads them to attack with special venom conservatives who appear complacent and hypocritical—President Eisenhower, for instance, or Secretary of State John Foster Dulles.

nor—maybe President of the United States. This prospect delighted them, for they preferred Reagan to Governor Edmund Brown as more real, less hypocritical; Reagan would make clear where he stood. Many on the left seem quite as dedicated to a politics of style and mood as do those on the right.

Yet the argument for caution has itself to be used with caution. Any liberal who counsels radicals to his left against revolutionary tactics in a situation where the only revolution that seems probable will come from the right is likely to be reminded that, in the period when Joseph McCarthy flourished, many timid liberals sacrificed the left without mollifying the radical right. The question of tactics is always an arguable one, and it is possible that self-restraint in the face of the right-wing danger may provoke and encourage the right. The extreme right, as we have already seen, is often in the anomalous position of being stronger than it feels. It feels persecuted because many positions of influence in Washington, New York and Hollywood are outside its control, but Goldwater's 27 million votes represent an enormous potential base to which the right wing can appeal. Yet many on the left, both black and white, make no assessment of their potential strength or that of their adversaries before plunging into battle. Some with whom I have talked justify this by saying not only that there is little to lose but also that prudence and calculation are less attractive and human than impulse and spontaneity, so why not express themselves, even in dubious battle? One difficulty with this cavalier approach is that the victims may be others than themselves, so that indulgence in spontaneity and a lack of calculation for oneself may have long-range consequenes that limit the spontaneity of others.

In the nineteen-thirties, German refugees asked people like me whether America would go fascist, whether it could happen here. My response was generally to raise the paradox that it could not happen here because in part it had already: one could not overturn a system which was not a system, which chaotically gave representation to fascist and anti-fascist tendencies alike and which was sufficiently anarchic to make difficult the dominance of any authoritarian group. But this very disorderliness can breed its own antibodies. It can lead Americans to arm themselves individually while refusing to pay higher taxes for better and more professional police. Private weapons have not reduced crime any more than private air conditioners have reduced air pollution. Most of our domestic problems are so difficult that we do not even know how to begin to resolve them; Eugene McCarthy's unhysterical campaign appeared to recognize this, which won him followers among some conservatives and liberals while failing to attract many who believed that grave national problems needed to be attacked by charisma as well as by competence. In his best moments, McCarthy sought to liberate energies and hopes so that one could discover problems and begin to cope with them, although in the aftermath of what many mistakenly regarded as his defeat, some former followers have succumbed to desperation and vindictiveness toward the disorganized Democratic party rather than resuming work at the precinct level. George Wallace comfortably puts the blame for the malaise and fears of his followers on "pseudo-intellectuals" and "Communist traitors"—nothing that a good tank or billy club could not cure. The essence of demagogy is this notion that problems are simple and enemies easily identifiable. Nixon must hold much of his following against Wallace's simplifications, and in his probable victory is likely to sweep into office many congressmen and some senators far to his own right, limiting his flexibility to conciliate the defeated minorities on his left.

In contrast to the view of simplifiers on the left, who lump Humphrey and Nixon together as unstylish and hypocritical reactionaries, an electoral victory for Humphrey might stem the country's drift toward the right. But Vice-President Humphrey's cause seems now almost certainly lost. As we have seen, his most bitter critics on the left, justifying the mistrust of professional politicians for fanatical amateurs, want to teach him a lesson, not recognizing that at the Chicago convention there were more votes for the minority peace plank than the national support for such a plank would justify, and that there were more open discussions and prospects for further opening than the left thought possible or the right wanted. In my opinion, Humphrey's past support of the war in Vietnam reflected his own idealism, which led him to a misguided hope for an American-sponsored development program for South Vietnam. (Few now remember—or like to be reminded —that Humphrey chaired the disarmament subcommittee of the Senate and supported the Arms Control and Disarmament Agency when peace had few friends.) To elite Americans, who mobilize average ones, Humphrey does not seem to be a person who can take charge of America. And in a time of prosperity union members feel free to vote their resentments by turning to Wallace rather than expressing their gratitude for old favors by remaining in the Democratic party. It has been argued that only if Nixon wins handily in the North can he dispense with the support of such

Southern Republicans as Strom Thurmond. On the other hand, one must reckon that the greater the margin of Humphrey's defeat, the more the right will feel it has won. And to the hard right, to be a loser is to be contemptible. For a liberal, to be a loser is familiar; it should make him pause, but not shake his faith.

My own view of America is that we grow slowly more civilized, though not at a rate guaranteed to prevent catastrophe. The upper-middle, educated classes become more tolerant, less xenophobic, more willing to endure complexity. The corporate executives who in 1964 turned against Goldwater because he was too provincial, muscular and brash, may reluctantly in 1968 vote for Nixon as the only man with a chance to keep America sufficiently together so that its problems can be worked on, its production maintained, its moral poise not totally shattered. Even now, more Americans are confused than are dogmatic and fanatical; more Americans are decent than are sadistic and niggardly. It is my impression from studying public-opinion polls that, except among the most militant, firm ideological polarities of left and right have not crystallized; rather the Veitnam War and the race issue overlap and combine with different constituencies to create political constellations that may not be permanent. Undoubtedly, Wallace's national showing helps make legitimate the myriad local campaigns which the right wing continuously wages. Yet other than shooting looters and bombing Haiphong, there is no coherent national right-wing pro-gram; a new long-term right-wing hegemony—as opposed to a traditional conservative one—has not been forged.

If the war should continue, a violent push to the right is likely to ensue, both abroad and at home. But if we can somehow make peace in Vietnam and survive the present era, we may discover that America's development toward further openness has been only temporarily halted.